I0025309

Stories of Feminist Protest and Resistance

Stories of Feminist Protest and Resistance

Digital Performative Assemblies

Edited by Brianna I. Wiens,
Michelle MacArthur,
Shana MacDonald,
and Milena Radzikowska

LEXINGTON BOOKS
Lanham • Boulder • New York • London

Published by Lexington Books
An imprint of The Rowman & Littlefield Publishing Group, Inc.
4501 Forbes Boulevard, Suite 200, Lanham, Maryland 20706
www.rowman.com

86-90 Paul Street, London EC2A 4NE

Copyright © 2023 by The Rowman & Littlefield Publishing Group, Inc.

All rights reserved. No part of this book may be reproduced in any form or by any elec-tronic or mechanical means, including information storage and retrieval systems, without written permission from the publisher, except by a reviewer who may quote passages in a review.

British Library Cataloguing in Publication Information Available

Library of Congress Cataloging-in-Publication Data Available

Names: Wiens, Brianna I., editor. | MacArthur, Michelle, editor. |
    MacDonald, Shana, editor.
  Title: Stories of feminist protest and resistance : digital performative
    assemblies / edited by Brianna I. Wiens, Michelle MacArthur, Shana
    MacDonald, and Milena Radzikowska.
  Description: Lanham : Lexington Books, 2023. | Includes bibliographical
    references and index.
  Identifiers: LCCN 2022048259 (print) | LCCN 2022048260 (ebook) | ISBN
    9781666913514 (cloth) | ISBN 9781666913538 (paper) | ISBN
9781666913521 (epub)
  Subjects: LCSH: Feminism--History--21st century. | Mass media and women. |
    Social networks.
  Classification: LCC HQ1155 .S868 2023 (print) | LCC HQ1155 (ebook) | DDC
    305.4201--dc23/eng/20221006
  LC record available at https://lccn.loc.gov/2022048259
  LC ebook record available at https://lccn.loc.gov/2022048260

♾™ The paper used in this publication meets the minimum requirements of American
National Standard for Information Sciences—Permanence of Paper for Printed Library
Materials, ANSI/NISO Z39.48-1992.

Contents

List of Figures

Introduction

Assemblies of Resistance

Feminist Stories, Protest, and Dissent in the Digital Age

Brianna I. Wiens, Michelle MacArthur, and Shana MacDonald

Stories and storytelling are by no means new to feminist epistemology and methodology—neither to ontology nor axiology, for that matter. Indeed, storytelling, stories, and their politics, standpoints, and affects have been central to feminism for over five decades, with their antecedents in oral histories and traditions going back much further (see, e.g., Haraway 1988; Harding 1993; Hemmings 2011; Ilmonen 2020; Lindstrom, Baptiste, and Shade 2021; Mahuika 2012; Tomlinson 2013; Sangster 1994). The ways that stories shape our political worlds are especially important given the ways that the use of and access to technology and media for the purposes of circulating stories differs based on geographical location and political atmosphere. Equally as noteworthy is the role that these technologies, including social networking sites, play in circulating media toxicities (e.g., Benjamin 2019; D'Ignazio and Klein 2020; Nakamura and Chow-White 2012; Noble 2018) and prompting polarization, effectually operating just as they were designed to (Chun 2021). Within these spaces, though, the circulation of feminist narratives amplifies important protest and resistance work, speaking directly to Whitney Phillips and Ryan M. Milner's (2021) urgent call for new stories within the current network crisis of disinformation and online hate (6). Writing, reading, circulating, analyzing, and bearing witness to feminist stories begins the work of unpacking, as Sarah Sharma (2021) writes, the "medium-specific techno-logics of how power operates in culture" (8), transforming digital spaces into sites of feminist resistance against political and social inequities.

Indeed, mainstream stories tell us one thing, but stories of feminist protest reveal another.

To this day, stories of protest and resistance remain key elements for voicing dissent and, within this digital moment (one that is sure to last), the circulation of such stories undoubtedly helps to further feminism's project. And yet, as has become abundantly clear over the last decade of networked feminisms and digital activism, feminism's calls to action have long been co-opted by white colonial neoliberal forces that benefit from the current unjust status quo. It thus remains important to embrace intersectionality (Crenshaw 1989, 1991) as a field of study, an analytic strategy, a social theory, and a critical praxis, paying attention to intersectionality's "attentiveness to power relations and social inequalities" and its recognition of how "race, class, gender, sexuality, ethnicity, nation, ability, and age are reciprocally constructing phenomena" (Collins 2015, 3). Gail Lewis (2013) has noted, however, the genealogy of intersectionality has become "a well-rehearsed story" (871), one that we might recognize as "invit[ing]" intersectionality to "settle down within" the "established frames of knowledge production" (Collins and Bilge 2016, 87). To this point, it continues to be imperative that, as researchers, teachers, and feminists, we reject the siloing of intersectionality within the academic institution that Patricia Hill Collins warns (2015) against and, instead, embrace intersectionality as a "multifaceted broad-based knowledge project" (3). As Kimberlé Crenshaw (2012) reflects, "the need to work intersectionality and to develop methods that are both recognizable and insurgent within different disciplines is part of intersectionality's travel log" (231).

The contributors to this collection attempt to do this in various ways, outlining intersectional feminist activist practices, methodologies, and theorizations that cut across disciplines, practices, and experiences. Feminism, we recognize, is not only about women and gender, but about power more broadly—who holds and wields power and who does not and cannot within the current matrix of domination (D'Ignazio and Klein 2020, drawing on Collins 1990). Drawing on the spirit of feminist activism and of those who have contributed to the success of this and other social movements through their stories, this edited collection foregrounds the importance of storytelling practices for coalitional purposes and performative assembling, spanning Nigerian, Iranian, Mexican, Russian, Canadian, and American contexts. Storytelling has been an incredibly valuable strategy for sharing and cocreating knowledges, addressing and surviving power imbalances, encouraging participation, passing on traditions and histories, and finding one's individual and community voice. Sharing stories also speaks to why certain people are drawn to certain other people, stories, and movements.

As such, this book approaches the concept of stories broadly, understanding them as "the non-linear lived, and living, histories that have led to moments of personal or other disclosure, whether those disclosures are textual, visual, verbal, or all of the above, and the possible futures that may come to be through such disclosures. Importantly, experiences and possibilities always precede and follow textual and uttered assertions, no matter how brief those assertions may be" (Wiens 2021, 10). This collection first aims to survey, analyze, and suggest tools for how a range of feminists share stories of resistance. Second, it seeks to center intersectional digital activisms and transgressions that mobilize lived experiences, personal stories, and individual craft as tactical tools of assembly for collective justice. And third, this book considers how feminist protest and resistance use conventions of assembly, performativity, and theatricality to counter the paradox of increasingly individualized and problematic approaches to activism that also draw on performance and spectacle.

CONTEXTUALIZING *STORIES OF FEMINIST PROTEST AND RESISTANCE: DIGITAL PERFORMATIVE ASSEMBLIES*

Throughout this book, we collectively frame digital feminisms as forms of public assembly that are performative and theatrical; that is, performative in that they can offer "a process, a praxis, an episteme, a mode of transmission, an accomplishment, and a means of intervening in the world" (Taylor 2003, 15), and theatrical in that they are events that may include characters, plot, the invocation of an audience, and the collective labor of multiple collaborators. As editors, we bring this framing to our previous definition of networked activisms, "the various activist forms that take place through online networks and that have material and affective impacts in both mediated and unmediated arenas, from hashtag activism to social media campaigns to hacktivism" (Wiens, MacDonald, MacArthur, and Radzikowska 2022, 4), in order to both strengthen and thicken how we approach stories of digital feminist protest and resistance. We locate feminist online activist movements as fostering counterpublics, or communities that enable "exchanges . . . distinct from authority" that "have a critical relation to power" (Warner 2002, 56). Through various forms of feminist media mobilizations, from hashtags like #MeToo, #NiUnaMenos, and #SayHerNameNigeria, online social media communities, personal blogs, and meme accounts, this book argues that digital feminists use the long-standing feminist tactics of storytelling to counter the dominant narratives of white supremacy, colonialism, heteropatriarchy, and the variety of oppressions that accompany such structures, both online and offline.

In *Hashtag Activism: Networks of Race and Gender Justice*, Jackson, Bailey, and Foucault Welles (2020) remind readers that "as technologies change, so do the methods those at the margins use to make claims of belonging and for justice" (200). Through bringing together the essays in this collection, we extend Jackson, Bailey, and Foucault-Welles's (2020) claim to focus on the stories that various networked feminist communities use to not only raise their own voices, but to find their own sense of belonging, justice, and operation through methods of public assembly (Butler 2015). In *Notes Towards a Theory of Performative Assembly* (2015), Butler advances the importance of bodies assembling in space as a form of protest that performatively asserts both "the right to appear" and demands "a more livable set of lives" for those in varying positions of precarity (25). For Butler, these assertions counter dominant institutional power insofar as they produce an "alliance among groups of people who do not otherwise find much in common" (27). Butler situates performativity as a tool of resistance that names the "power language has to bring about a new situation or to set into motion a set of effects" (28), linking this framework to protest movements such as the Arab Spring and Occupy Wall Street. While Butler looks specifically at protests in the streets, both the Arab Spring and Occupy employed digital platforms in their organization and mobilization strategies. This suggests the value of considering how performative assemblies are enacted in online spaces, and specifically, how they offer "an insistent form of appearing precisely when and where we are effaced" so that "the sphere of appearance break[s] and open[s] in new ways" (37).

Take for instance, the hashtag #SolidarityIsForWhiteWomen, started by blogger Mikki Kendall in 2013, which has, for many years now, opened a necessary public dialogue on the ways in which white feminists have failed to support Black and other racialized feminists. The hashtag and the debates that surround it performatively insist on greater recognition for Black feminist perspectives and their undeniable right to appear, take up space, and be supported within social media, physical spaces of protest, and beyond. As Tara Conley (2022) writes, "Black feminists have a long tradition of rejecting white feminism as a liberatory strategy for a select few and for its one-size-fits-all vision for the colonized subject. Black feminists continue this tradition across digital spaces to bring attention to white feminism's ineffectiveness as an organizing strategy as an ethos" (40). Within this context, the hashtag, alongside many others originating on Black Twitter over the last decade, have taken on new urgency within the last few years. Certainly, this is apparent in how popular feminism has failed to challenge the "political economic conditions that allow that inequality be profitable," ensuring the "political and material advancement of some privileged white cisgender women who are conscripted into the successful navigation of both capitalism and the sex/gender system" over and above differently situated feminists (Banet-Weiser and Portwood-Stacer 2017, 886). The reality of online spaces as sites of constraints and erasures of Black, Indigenous, and racialized people, queer, trans, and nonbinary people, and disabled communities within popular feminism speaks directly to questions of who has the right to appear in online spaces of assembly, which are already constrained by misogynist and white supremacist technologies, histories of representation, and dominant media structures. Considering these limitations, this book is guided by the overarching question of how online feminist assemblies function as vital counter-practices to these other exclusionary enactments.

While feminist visibility in the broader public eye has produced important dialogues, this politics of assembly simultaneously begs the question: "What about those who prefer not to appear, who engage in their democratic activism in another way?" (Butler 2015, 55). There are many valid reasons why feminist activists may not want, or may not be able, to appear, given the dangerous social and political climate of online spaces, rife with the violent misogyny and racism of trolling culture. "Sometimes," Butler suggests, "political action is more effective when launched from the shadows" (55). Here, we might consider the ways that feminist activism, while sometimes loud, meant to grab and hold attention, also moves consciously in the shadows—perhaps what Halberstam (2011) in *The Queer Art of Failure* alludes to as "shadow feminism": a feminism that operates out of refusal or a disavowal of certain forms of external frames of identification. For Halberstam, shadow feminism is resistance by failing to perform in ways that are self-affirming, socially acceptable, or even gender conforming. This is counterintuitive because it considers the possibility of resistance to patriarchal power through forms that appear to offer no resistance at all but are, in fact, radically passive. One area where we might locate such an aesthetic of refusal as feminist dissent is in the spaces of our secret virtual feminist communities—in online spaces closed to the public that provide a necessary space for feminists to work through issues of misogyny, white supremacy, and other responses to everyday life contexts and cultural phenomena more broadly, within a safe and supportive community space and without the prying eyes of the rather large digital public.

Given the risk of working through struggles with sexism, racism, ableism, and other intersecting oppressions in the public spaces of social media, where the potential for virulent forms of harassment and doxing is high, the option not to appear, or to not always appear in those highly visible spaces, is a necessary one. As just one example, secret virtual groups offer a mediating space that is both public and private, a space that lends opportunity for support as feminists negotiate both their public and private lives. We might, then, seek out such feminist shadow networks—those that operate under the radar—that do not seem, at first, to resist or that seem radically passive. Feminist shadow networks can be these secret or closed virtual groups, or they may be the whisper networks that exist in almost every institution and on every platform to warn people who not to go to meetings alone with or who to block and report. They might also be those that whisper to you to use the policy of the platform against itself for feminist ends. Feminist shadow networks queer the "master's tools," to use Audre Lorde's (1984) infamous phrase, to think differently about these tools—to find queer uses for them, as Sara Ahmed (2019) might say. In reworking these tools, in finding new and queer uses for them, we may, indeed, come upon a "revealing of things," where new uses can "involve heightening our awareness of things" (Ahmed 2019, 21), or realizing how the normative use of a platform is, perhaps, no longer useful. Feminist shadow networks help us to do this by offering spaces of support and information—they uncover the hidden curriculum, so to speak, and make it overt. These kinds of publicities, erasures, and ways of being in the shadows deserve consideration within current reflections on emergent feminist practices online.

This book thus gathers analyses, creative explorations, personal stories, and case studies of digital feminist activism that speak to the many ways and reasons that feminist communities assemble from a range of disciplinary perspectives, including media studies, film studies, critical cultural studies, communication studies, gender and sexuality studies, performance studies, and Indigenous studies. By critically examining a range of digital feminist activist examples of protest and resistance from various disciplines and perspectives, we encourage other scholars and activists to share their stories, research, and experiences and support them to move in new and lively ways. As scholars and activists in positions of power, we believe that it is incumbent upon us to create the kinds of spaces that center people who have been marginalized without pathologizing their everyday discrimination so that their stories that have been erased can gain momentum and flourish. These stories need to be validated and affirmed, reclaimed from the hegemonic frames that confine them, so that these experiences contribute to not only imagining but crafting and bringing to fruition more equitable and sustainable futures. By sharing stories of intersectional feminist assembly, we assert that current structures do not afford safety to all; by bringing together stories we instigate larger conversations that can begin to establish different ways of seeing and being in the world and invite others to assemble with us.

SITUATING *STORIES OF FEMINIST PROTEST AND RESISTANCE:* CHAPTER PREVIEWS

Against this backdrop, core themes of this collection reflect contemporary feminist digital coalitional methods, theories, and practices, revolving around feminist protest, resistance, persistence, and transgression—focusing on matters of intersectional feminism, anti-colonialism, Indigenous feminisms, storytelling, networked social movements, feminist activism, transgender inclusion, and queer feminism—in the face of white supremacy, heteropatriarchy, colonialism, and neoliberalism. Media studies scholars have argued for the last two decades that there is no "real" separation between "online" and "offline" spheres, and as harassment against marginalized groups amplifies, proliferates, and intensifies in coordinated ways it becomes clearer how hierarchical gendered and racialized power relations shape all digitally mediated spaces (Hine 2000; Sills et al. 2016). As such, the themes of this collection stand to not only speak to internet spaces, but also to other "offline" spaces. Ultimately, through the stories shared in this collection, we seek to push back against the neoliberal individualism that advance particular tellings of history, present, and future over others, and we seek community among other an ever-growing collective of feminists.

To address these themes, the essays in this collection, in their own unique ways, consider the following questions: for those who are marginalized based on, for example, ability, racialization, gender identity, and sexual orientation, what are their concerns about their presence (or lack thereof), experience, and perceptions in digital culture? How do feminists create, use, and circulate digital artifacts that contribute to the formation of their own communities and digital assemblies? How do these digital artifacts circulate among a variety of digital platforms, and to what ends? What examples of feminist digital culture exist online and to what effect? How are feminists performing protest and resistance online, and in what ways are they fostering collective action and coalitional affinities? And, what kinds of stories are feminists telling online, what modes are feminists telling stories through, and how are these stories working for the purposes of assembling people together?

In the opening chapter of this collection, Francesca Dennstedt challenges the presumed "global reach" of the #MeToo movement and its eclipsing of the long history of activism around gender and sexual violence undertaken in Latin America. Using as her case study #NiUnaMenos, she argues that the popular movement "urges us to reimagine the global histories of feminist solidarity by challenging the current flows of feminist movements and urging us to rethink feminist epistemologies from g-local positionalities." Dennestedt applies a cultural and area studies perspective to examine the roles of art and culture in shaping the flow of knowledge and building feminist solidarities. Rather than relying on empirical methodologies, this newer approach proposed by Dennestedt allows her to track a "recurrent triangulation" between hashtags circulated on social media, cultural production such as music, and the uses of public spaces within Ni una menos in Mexico. Dennestedt elucidates practices of feminist disappropriation and communality, showing how they create affective networks through these three triangulated factors.

She argues, "*Ni una menos* proposes a radical form of feminist praxis and decolonial solidarity by creating affective networks that challenge the flows of capital."

Like Dennstedt, Gabrielle E. Lindstrom, Sierra Shade, and Sofia Baptiste intervene in colonial framings of feminist digital activism and solidarities. In "Storying Blackfoot Resilience in the Digital Age," the authors examine the ways in which digital technologies can be used for Indigenous self-determination. The authors begin their chapter by asserting that "The default national narrative of Canada tells a story of Indigenous peoples from a deficit perspective that reinforces imagined stereotypes, often preventing Indigenous women from being anything more than problems to be solved." Drawing on autoethnography, the authors explore their own interactions with social media to create spaces to share their personal stories of settler colonial violence; counter narratives of Indigenous women rooted in the deficit model; transmit Indigenous knowledges, cultural traditions, and languages; and inspire Indigenous girls and young women by presenting images of strength. A key focus is resilience, and how, contrary to popular understandings, it is not something developed in reaction to oppression but rather something with which Blackfoot women are born. Reframing resilience online pushes back against settler understandings of Indigenous women and empowers the next generation.

Ololade Faniyi, Angel Nduka-Nwosa, and Radhika Gajjala's chapter traces the transnational feminist networks connected to #SayHerNameNigeria and #AbujaPoliceRaidOnWomen, which emerged in response to a 2019 nightclub raid in Abuja that resulted in the arrests and violent assaults of seventy women. While the authors are careful to underline the need for further action and progress in regard to gendered violence in Nigeria, they stress the importance of these hashtag movements as sites "of listening, believing, trusting, naming, and making visible the women who became victims and survivors of violence and a heritage site of young Nigerian feminist resistance against the police and the state on their own terms." Further, they write that their mixed methods approach, bringing together Twitter network analytics and textual analysis with interviews, "signals our approach to not just amplify activists' storytelling and rhetorical agency but also to see them as legitimate researchers in their own right, whose labor must not be exploited or undermined." We see resonances of this feminist approach in later chapters, including the citation practices in Lesinski, Matthews, and Drumright's chapter about birth-focused blogs and podcasts and Zaiontz and Cochrane's chapter on feminist memes, both of which center activist voices as important sources of knowledge.

Mina Momeni's chapter revisits the Green Movement in Iran through the lens of the theory of affordances, which tracks the potential actions emerging from the interaction between a user's intentions and a technology's capabilities. Focusing on the affordance of identifiability on Facebook and Twitter, Momeni examines how activists inside and outside Iran exploited this affordance to share information, build networks, and evade government surveillance. Green Movement social media activists drew attention to the authoritarian regime's myriad injustices, including its many gender-based injustices, by adopting anonymous identities and/or assuming a group identity through their social media profiles and changing their location to Tehran to confuse authorities seeking to track and punish dissidents. Pushing back against Western assumptions about the inability of social media to affect political change, Momeni compellingly argues that "it is essential to explore more intently how users in varying locales and political situations are using and interacting with these platforms and employing their communicative features in practice—especially in societies where media and communications are severely under authorities' control."

Like Momeni, Kristin Comefero examines how Facebook users are uncovering the platform's political potential despite its capitalist aims. Focusing on the emergence of "butch feminism" within butch and butch/femme Facebook groups, Comeforo shows how the social media platform can be used to achieve similar aims to consciousness-raising groups in the analog second wave. Sharing knowledge and experience through memes, posts, photos, and comments, the butch-identified users in Comeforo's chapter expressed an increased sense of self-confidence in occupying their identities in public spaces. This points to the transformative power of these Facebook groups, which provide a platform for community members to develop and express their butch identities. Though the butch-identified users in Comeforo's study do not explicitly use the f-word, as the author notes, "their activity is marked with feminist tenets and ideals," beginning with the "embodied politics" of their "transgressive gender presentation." Bringing together grounded theory with textual analysis and applying them to groups to which they belong, Comeforo models an approach to feminist autoethnography that runs through this book in chapters by contributors, including Lindstrom, Baptiste, and Shade in chapter 2 and Zaiontz and Cochrane in chapter 8.

Julie Ravary-Pilon revisits Pussy Riot and the global activism incited by the high-profile arrest of five of its members in 2012. Through an analysis of Canadian multidisciplinary artist Peaches' *Free Pussy Riot,* cowritten with Simmone Jones (2012), Ravary-Pilon elucidates what she calls the Digital Assembly Video or DAV. Ravary-Pilon traces the emergence of this genre through the fourth wave of feminism and its intersection with Web 2.0 while connecting its formal traits to earlier feminist movements and tactics.

Characterized by its DIY aesthetics and use of digital signs and conversational images, DAV "allows people to overcome a range of restrictions associated with street assembly and to find forms of public gathering spaces in which more bodies can appear." In the case of *Free Pussy Riot*, Peaches' call to action issued on her Facebook page gathered participants across borders both online and in person in a show of solidarity. The resulting video, posted on Peaches' YouTube account, features a fast-paced montage of user-submitted videos and footage of a demonstration staged in Berlin in response to the artist's call. Extending Butler's concept of performative assemblies to develop her definition of DAV, Ravary-Pilon argues, "The collective-participative process used in *Free Pussy Riot* speaks loudly to the potentials of the web as a space that can offer multiple creative possibilities for bodies to stage themselves, as well as major opportunities for people prevented from appearing in flesh in street rallies. The Digital Assembly Video thus unveils an important extension of a cultural form of resistance developed specifically within the potential of the online social networks and the bodies that need, and deserve, to appear."

In her chapter, Morgan Bimm takes a nuanced look at the invocation of pop music in digital and in-person feminist activism, tracing the "closed loop of digital mediation": "the content, memes, and music that inform protest signs are gathered via various digital networks and, similarly, are reproduced and performed in the political space of the protest with the knowledge that further sharing and mediation is inevitable." Using protest signs from the 2019 Women's March featuring Cardi B and Ariana Grande's lyrics, Bimm analyzes how the affects underpinning the politics of the march are circulated within activist remix practices that create networks and extend the event beyond its temporal and geographical bounds. She advances theory on celebrity feminism by showing how Cardi B and Grande are invoked at the march despite their physical absence and examining their role in recirculating the protest signs through their social media presence. Comparing the two artists also allows Bimm to make some important observations about their differences, particularly around the double standards applied to Black celebrity feminists and white ones. Bimm importantly refuses to dismiss the pop protest signs because of their connection to celebrity feminism, and instead highlights their potential to increase the accessibility of the march and amplify its message. She argues, "Accounting for continuously newer, queerer, and messier modes of protest opens up space for imagining how the digital might undermine the spatial, temporal, and racial logics that narrow the possibilities of more corporeal modes of protest (like the sit-in, the walkout, or the march) that remain confined to the literal street."

Keren Zaiontz and Kristen Cochrane look at digital feminist remixing of a different kind as they examine the practices of feminist meme-makers including Cochrane herself. They begin their chapter with the provocative reminder that, "Digital feminism in all variations was never born free and unlike the coterie of largely male abstract expressionists who negated the barbarism of war and capitalist markets by focusing on the formal power of brushstrokes, the feminists we discuss here must claim autonomy over their craft (i.e., memes, blogs, podcasts) by other means." The digital feminisms in their study, they remind us, are not "a mechanism for political action" but rather "a means of economic survival and the strengthening of affective bonds between creatives and their followers and/or subscribers." Nevertheless, as Zaiontz and Cochrane show, feminist meme-makers generate powerful political critique through their playful subversion of material drawn from pop culture. Through their use of social media tools such as geotagging, avatars, and the Instagram close friends list, as well as their strategic deployment of irony, the digital creators featured in this chapter test (gendered) assumptions about intimacy and labor in online spaces. Theorizing microcelebrity meme-makers by weaving critical theory with examples of memes themselves and Cochrane's own experience, the authors illustrate a collaborative approach to writing between analyst and participant that resonates with Faniyi, Nduka-Nwosa, and Gajjala's chapter earlier in the book.

Micki Burdick's chapter on the Art+Feminism Wikipedia edit-a-thon examines how this form of collective knowledge production can be used to create community through its emphasis on embodiment. Burdick argues, "The Art+Feminism campaign works inside rather than outside of the masculine-dominated canon of Wikipedia to transform digital activisms and their gendered baggage. These practices of editing craft new stories and ways of living in the world outside of gendered binaries—revealing new constructions of identity and embodiment within feminist activisms." As participants gather in person to create entries for Wikipedia focused on women and other equity-seeking groups, there is a queering of the digital space by emphasizing the visibility of cis and trans women and nonbinary folks (in this case as editors of Wikipedia, where only 10 percent of contributors are nonmen) and a queering of the shared physical space where the edit-a-thon takes place. Like Ravary-Pilon, Burdick historicizes their study within the context of DIY feminist activism, showing how digital activisms draw on more analog forms of feminist resistance from the past, from independent feminist publishing to consciousness-raising circles. Rooting their argument in the theory of collective rhetoric, Burdick demonstrates how edit-a-thons can push back against postfeminist, neoliberal conceptions of activism by focusing on the collective rather than the individual.

Shaylynn Lynch Lesinski, Tammy Rae Matthews, and Kelly J. Drumright's chapter on birth-focused blogs and podcasts underlines the importance of knowledge sharing in challenging dominant epistemologies rooted in colonialism, white supremacy, and cis-sexism. In their focus on embodied experience, the authors join other contributors, including Comeforo and Burdick, in examining how users can exploit popular online platforms to produce counter discourse and community. They argue that "sharing birth stories online privileges the experiential knowledge of birthing bodies themselves, thereby disrupting the hierarchy of knowledge in so-called Western medicine that positions birthing bodies' lived experience last." Pushing back against reductive and harmful depictions of birth circulated by the mainstream media and medical discourse, the blogs and podcasts at the center of this chapter educate and empower birthing bodies, particularly those belonging to marginalized individuals. As birthing bloggers and podcasters share their stories, they expose how biopower and biopolitics operate within Western medicalized systems and provide readers and listeners with the tools needed to advocate for themselves and their desired (and safe and healthy) birthing experience.

Like Bimm and Zaiontz and Cochrane, in their chapter Minna Aslama Horowitz and Neil Feinstein examine the intersections between popular feminism, digital activism, the economy of visibility, and celebrity. Using as their case study Susan Fowler's public sharing of her experience of harassment at Uber and the response it precipitated on social media, Horowitz and Feinstein compellingly ask what makes a collective activist movement. In so doing, the authors unsettle some of the assumptions underlying feminist activism in the digital age, in particular the idea that individuals sharing political hashtags are automatically engaged in collective activist work. Arguing for the necessity of a "multidimensional approach" to understanding digital activism in today's media landscape, the authors propose an analytical framework with which to understand actions like Fowler's, which was bolstered by the #DeleteUber and #MeToo movements. They conclude, "Not everyone is or seeks to be an activist or advocate, but we must learn how to use and connect powerful stories such as Fowler's to form more coherent, more diverse, more collaborative, and sustainable conversations, networks, alliances, actions, and even movements." The authors' warning that this may force us to rethink some of the assumptions underlying activism in the digital age and instead consider networks "as neoliberal, market-driven, data-hungry, and attention-seeking," reflects the difficulty, expressed throughout this book, of disentangling feminist activism from the broader sociopolitical and economic contexts in which it occurs online.

In "'I Want Us to Own the Goddamned Servers': The Feminist Principles of Archive of Our Own," Sid Heeg traces the history of the fan-run site Archive of Our Own (AO3) and its emergence in response to the censorship of several fan fiction sites in the mid-2000s. Heeg contrasts fan communities' frequent centering of women's and queer voices with the corporate and often heterosexual male interests intervening with content on sites like FFN, LiveJournal, and FanLib. Heeg frames these interventions as attempts to control female and queer desires, self-expression, and labor. AO3, Heeg argues, "not only provides a functional space for a wide variety of fan fiction, but it provides functional space in a way that other fan fiction websites do not through the ways that the foundation values the privacy and safety of fans first, ensuring their content and their communities are protected." It is fitting that Heeg's chapter concludes the book given its focus on fandom cultures. Fans, as Heeg shows, operate from a place of love, reworking popular stories across media to generate new meanings. Similarly, many of the chapters in this collection reflect on how feminist activists take mainstream platforms and materials from the dominant culture and transform them in an effort to create community and incite change—online and off.

ONWARD: STORIES, SOLIDARITIES, AND FEMINIST SURVIVAL

Assembling an edited collection is a hugely collaborative—and intensely rewarding—effort, which informs a key takeaway of both this and our last collection, *Networked Feminisms: Digital Practices and Activist Assemblies* (Lexington, 2021), and that is the importance of intersectional solidarity. Solidarity can be a method for anti-racism and for fighting white supremacy and imperialism; solidarity is a tactic for opposing misogyny and trans and queerphobia. Solidarity is also what drives feminist shadow networks. It is what enables us as feminists to highlight that which resists—because we've fostered solidarity, mutual support, and care. But that solidarity has to be grounded in intersectional feminism to resist its tokenization and the over-reliance on white feminism that hinges on a binary focus on gender to the neglect of other intersecting systems of oppression. As Sara Ahmed (2017) writes in *Living a Feminist Life*, "to be committed to a feminist life means we cannot not do this work; we cannot not fight for this cause. . . . Survival thus becomes a shared feminist project" (235–36). If we think about solidarity as a shared feminist project—as, together, finding new ways forward—then we can, even in small ways, find modes of pushing back. These small moments of solidarity matter as they begin to unravel what solidarity looks like at the everyday micro level, giving us insights into larger scale protests and movements as we push onward for more just, more intersectional, futures. We can't wait for those stories to unfold.

REFERENCES

Ahmed, Sara. 2017. *Living a Feminist Life*. Duke University Press.
———. 2019. *What's the Use? On the Uses of Use*. Duke University Press.
Banet-Weiser, Sarah, and Laura Portwood-Stacer. 2017. "The Traffic in Feminism: An Introduction to the Commentary and Criticism on Popular Feminism." *Feminist Media Studies* 17 (5): 884–88.
Benjamin, Ruha. 2019. *Race After Technology: Abolitionist Tools for the New Jim Code*. Polity Press.
Butler, Judith. 2015. *Notes Toward a Performative Theory of Assembly*. Harvard University Press.
Chun, Wendy. 2021. *Discriminating Data: Correlation, Neighborhoods, and the New Politics of Recognition*. MIT Press.
Collins, Patricia Hill. 2015. "Intersectionality's Definitional Dilemmas." *Annual Review of Sociology* 41 (1): 1–20.
Collins, Patricia Hill, and Sirma Bilge. 2016. *Intersectionality*. Polity.
Conley, Tara L. 2022. "A Sign of the Times: Hashtag Feminism as a Conceptual Framework." In *Networked Feminisms: Activist Assemblies and Digital Practices*, edited by Shana MacDonald, Milena Radzikowska, Michelle MacArthur, and Brianna I. Wiens. Lexington Books, 21–48.
Crenshaw, Kimberlé Williams. 1989. "Demarginalizing the Intersection of Race and Sex: A Black Feminist Critique of Antidiscrimination Doctrine, Feminist Theory and Antiracist Politics." *University of Chicago Legal Forum*, 139–67.
———. 1991. "Mapping the Margins: Intersectionality, Identity Politics, and Violence Against Women of Color." *Stanford Law Review* 43 (6): 1241–1300.
———. 2012. "Postscript." In *Framing Intersectionality: Debates on a Multi-Faceted Concept in Gender Studies*, edited by Helma Lutz, Maria Teresa Herrera Vivar, and Linda Supik. Ashgate, 221–33.
D'Ignazio, Catherine, and Lauren F. Klein. 2020. *Data Feminism*. MIT Press.
Halberstam, J. J. 2011. *The Queer Art of Failure*. Duke University Press.
Haraway, Donna J. 1988. "Situated Knowledges: The Science Question in Feminism and the Privilege of Partial Perspective." *Feminist Studies* 14 (3): 575–99.
Harding, Sandra. 1993. "Rethinking Standpoint Epistemology: What Is Strong Objectivity?" In *Feminist Epistemologies*. Routledge, 49–82.
Hemmings, Clare. 2011. *Why Stories Matter: The Political Grammar of Feminist Theory*. Duke University Press.
Hine, Christine. 2000. *Virtual Ethnography*. Sage Publications.
Ilmonen, Karisa. 2020. "Feminist Storytelling and Narratives of Intersectionality." *Signs: Journal of Women in Culture and Society* 45 (2): 347–71.
Jackson, Sarah J., Moya Bailey, Brooke Foucault Welles. 2020. *#HashtagActivism: Networks of Race and Gender Justice*. MIT Press.
Kendall, Mikki. 2020. *Hood Feminism: Notes From the Women That a Movement Forgot*. Bloomsbury.
Lindstrom, Gabrielle, Sofia Baptiste, and Sierra Shade. 2021. "'Mokakit Iyikakimaat': Autoethnographic Reflections as Movement towards a Pedagogy of Resilience." In

Brave Work in Indigenous Education, edited by Jennifer Markides and Jennifer MacDonald, 1–17.

Lorde, Audre. 1984. *Sister Outsider: Essays and Speeches*. Crossing Press.

Mahuika, Nēpia. 2012. "'Kōrero Tuku Iho': Reconfiguring Oral History and Oral Tradition." Doctoral Thesis, University of Waikato.

Nakamura, Lisa, and Peter A. Chow-White. 2012. "Race and Digital Technology: Code, the Color Line, and the Information Society." In *Race After the Internet*, edited by Lisa Nakamura and Peter A. Chow-White. Routledge, 1–18.

Noble, Safia. 2018. *Algorithms of Oppression: How Search Engines Reinforce Racism*. New York University Press.

Phillips, Whitney, and Ryan M. Milner. 2021. *You Are Here: A Field Guide for Navigating Polarized Speech, Conspiracy Theories, and Our Polluted Media Landscape*. MIT Press.

Taylor, Diana. 2003. *The Archive and the Repertoire: Performing Cultural Memory in the Americas*. Duke University Press.

Tomlinson, Barbara. 2013. "To Tell the Truth and Not Get Trapped: Desire, Distance, and Intersectionality at the Scene of Argument." *Signs* 38 (4): 993–1017.

Sangster, Joan. 1994. "Telling Our Stories: Feminist Debates and the Use of Oral History." *Women's History Review* 3 (1): 5–28.

Sharma, Sarah. 2021. "Introduction: A Feminist Medium Is the Message." In *Re-Understanding Media: Feminist Extensions of Marshall McLuhan*, edited by Sharma, Sarah, and Rianka Singh. Duke University Press, 1–22.

Sills, Sophie, Chelsea Pickens, Karishma Beach, Lloyd Jones, Octavia Calder-Dawe, Paulette Benton-Greig, and Nicola Gavey. 2016. "Rape Culture and Social Media: Young Critics and a Feminist Counterpublic." *Feminist Media Studies* 16 (6): 935–51.

Warner, Michael. 2002. "Publics and Counterpublics." *Quarterly Journal of Speech* 88: 413–25.

Wiens, Brianna I. 2022. "Moving with Stories of 'Me too.': Towards a Theory and Praxis of Intersectional Entanglements." PhD Dissertation. York University, York Space Institutional Repository.

Wiens, Brianna I., Shana MacDonald, Michelle MacArthur, and Milena Radzikowska. 2021. "Introduction: Feminist Takes on Networking Justice." In *Networked Feminisms: Activist Assemblies and Digital Practices*, edited by Shana MacDonald, Milena Radzikowska, Michelle MacArthur, and Brianna I. Wiens. Lexington Books, 1–20.

Chapter 1

Tactics of Feminist Disappropriation and Cultural Directions in Our Global Digital Era

A Case for #NiUnaMenos in Times of #MeToo

Francesca Dennstedt

In October 2018, Tarana Burke gave a speech in a chapel full of undergraduate students in their early twenties at Washington University in St. Louis, where I was pursuing my graduate education. By the time I got to listen to her speech, I had been following from afar #MeToo and everything it uncovered in the United States: sexual harassment and violence, structural racism, and the issues with white neoliberal feminism, to mention a few. But like the Argentine-Brazilian scholar Rita Laura Segato had stated in several interviews by this time, I too felt—as a woman who has lived mainly in Mexico—that #MeToo was not my movement nor debate.[1] Being in a chapel full of people saying "me too" is indeed very powerful. And yet I felt uncomfortable. That day, Burke explained that the hashtag initiated a conversation about sexual violence at the national level and then expanded to reach an international community of survivors, creating a global movement of solidarity as a reparative strategy and as a form of feminist politics. However, by the time #MeToo went viral in 2017, feminist activists in Latin America had been fighting to raise awareness on sexual and gender violence for years through different viral hashtag movements, such as #NiUnaMás, #VivasLasQueremos, #SiMeMatan, #MiPrimerAcoso, and #NiUnaMenos being the latter, the one that has gained more strength since then.[2] Thus my discomfort with the alleged "global reach" of #MeToo that was reproduced both in social media and in the mainstream US media, and that Burke was echoing in her powerful speech. This "global reach" feels at best like a decontextualized translation of other international hashtags and, at worst, like another form of reproducing old colonial practices. Even if #MeToo was not part of the Latin American conversation around gender violence, thinking critically about the colonial flows between feminist discourses from the so-called global north and south has always been at the core of Latin American feminism.[3]

What Burke's speech reminded me of that day is that in relation to global and transnational feminisms, creating networks of feminist solidarity is always (and should remain) an uncomfortable task. My discomfort with Burke's talk comes from the ease with which the cultural and sociohistorical specificities of local spaces are erased to favor global narratives. Even as just a figure of speech, the epistemic flows between spaces marked by the imprint of colonial power are very complex and should not be lost in translation. That, perhaps, feminist solidarity in the global digital era is less about building bridges, as Gloria Anzaldúa and Cherríe Moraga imagined in the 1980s, and more about exploring the unofficial paths that surround the bridge (and maybe the forested trail next to it?). As Sara Ahmed (2006) reminds us, the hope of changing directions is "that we don't always know where some paths may take us" (21)—that changing directions might bring us new possibilities.

In the context of global, transnational feminism, many theorists have criticized identity as a ground for feminist solidarity, either rejecting it altogether in favor of coalitions (Chandra Mohanty) or have redrawn identity politics to incorporate both relations of identification and the recognition of relations of power (Sirma Bilge, Maria Lugones, and Allison Weir). Through this chapter, I take different routes to get to these known points for feminist studies—identification as a ground for solidarity is messy, decolonial approaches to feminist solidarity recognize relations of power, and solidarity plays a role in constituting our own positionalities—in the hope that such lines of deviation might take us to a rough terrain, forcing us to grasp things that we would hardly grapple with if we had taken the bridges that lift us off the ground. The deviating line that I propose here is to look at feminist theoretical claims from a cultural and area studies perspective—that is, from a particular geographical, national, or cultural region. I am a literary scholar who specializes in Mexican cultural studies with an interest in how culture and art shape the flows of feminist epistemologies. In this case, I propose that Ni una menos urges us to reimagine the global histories of feminist solidarity by challenging the current flows of feminist movements and urging us to rethink feminist epistemologies from g-local positionalities. In the following pages, I demonstrate how Ni una menos presents other models and languages to create, maintain, and mobilize collective action and decolonial feminist solidarity in this digital world.

ROUTES OF DEVIATION OR NI UNA
MENOS IN TIMES OF ME TOO

What Me Too and Ni una menos unequivocally share is the uses of social media and other Internet-based applications as platforms for activism and tools for raising social awareness. As I will show in the following pages, however, the type of solidarity that these movements are creating and performing is very different, as are the ways they use social media to achieve it. Judith Butler has already pointed out the main differences between these similar movements in an interview for the *New York Times*.[4] As she explains, Ni una menos is a movement that "has distinguished itself from individualist modes of feminism that are based on personal liberty and the right of the individual subject" (Butler in Yancy 2019). This does not mean that "individual histories and stories do not matter," Butler warns us, later clarifying, "but forms of feminism that do not engage a critique of capitalism tend to reproduce individualism as a matter of course" (in Yancy 2019). The critique of capitalism should be accompanied by a critique of the coloniality of power that emerged in the modern era, as Maria Lugones and Aníbal Quijano explain, to bring attention to the oppressive capital structures that Butler is referring to.[5]

A counterpoint to individualist modes of feminism is raised by Verónica Gago, who notices that an ambiguity has marked current Latin American movements—an ambiguity that comes from the popular nature of these movements (Gago and Sztulwark 2016, 611) and from the lessons of feminismos comunitarios, a type of feminism that links the violence of gender with forms of labor exploitation, police and state violence, and corporate offensives against common resources; and its focus is building sustainable communities (2019). In the case of Ni una menos, collective action is formed through the creation of a solidarity that recognizes that what is happening with feminicidios[6] is also happening to other people, whether it is "violence, debt or subjection to patriarchal authority" (Butler in Yancy 2019)—hence the ambiguous character signaled by Gago. The ambiguity comes from the combination of social struggles that remake social conflict beyond identity markers. The pattern that connects everything into a complex assemblage is colonial structures, contained in the new necropolitical regimes that Sayak Valencia (2016) calls gore capitalism (25), where women's bodies are seen as disposable.

Let me illustrate this shift in feminist solidarities with an example. In the beginning of September 2020, a group of relatives of the desaparecidos[7] arrived in Mexico City to demand justice from the current government of Andrés Manuel López Obrador. After being treated inhumanely by the national human rights commission (Comisión Nacional de Derechos Humanos-CNDH), the mother of one of the survivors of sexual violence decided to not leave the building. With the help of feminist collectives, the CNDH was taken and renamed "Ocupa Casa de Refugio Ni Una Menos México. Bloque Negro" (Animal Político 2020). This name exemplifies very precisely the complexity of the social assemblage that unites these women. On the one hand, it references the ocupa movement that resists neoliberal politics and the dispossession of land to satisfy the demands of global capital in Mexico City. By establishing itself as a refuge that welcomes any victim of systemic violence, this group of feminists clearly (and spatially) establishes a bond of solidarity with other victims of the Mexican necropolitical state: immigrants, the struggle of Indigenous people and the lower class, unions, abortion rights, etc.

With Ni Una Menos México, on the one hand they nod to g-local strategies—Ni una menos is a Latin American movement that works from local spaces to create transnational agencies—and on the other, they point to the urgent fight against patriarchal structures because in the current moment, the quantity and the conditions in which feminicidios occur indicate that gender violence is an extremely urgent matter. Lastly, rather than positioning a feminist collective as responsible for squatting in the now refuge, the reference to Bloque Negro qualifies the type of feminism behind this act. Dressed in black and hooded, these feminists are the ones taking the streets, doing graffiti on walls, burning buildings, and smashing windows. These are the women who are making the system tremble.

What motivates these women to create and maintain solidarity is rage and (the "violent") desire to knock down the system that marks gendered bodies as disposable—that is, an affective solidarity. As Natália Maria Félix de Souza (2019) explains for the case of Ni una menos in Argentina: "feminists are seen not only as identity groups representing a minority position within a larger and more important movement against capital and oppression, but as occupying the forefront of the political arena—which has been harnessing renewed waves of anger and sympathy" (90). By occupying the forefront of the political arena, they point to feminism as the central discourse for sociopolitical change, but also shift to a feminism that builds "inter-movement" solidarity also directed to "non-feminist movements and collectives" (Félix de Souza 2019, 90). What moves Ni una menos into collective action is not the sum of individual stories nor the possible reparative strategies contained in feminist solidarity, but exhaustion and a desire to burn it all down. That is why in recent years the hashtag #NiUnaMenos is commonly followed by the phrase "Quémalo todo" (Burn it all) and the hashtag #SeVaCaer ([the patriarchy] is going to fall), phrases that vindicate the supposed feminist violence—burning buildings, wearing hoodies, taking public spaces, smashing windows, and other types of practices linked to anarcho-feminism—as the main force of political mobilization. Thus, the phrase "Ni una menos" highlights a double meaning: due to neither feminicidio nor the violent consequences of gore capitalism, not one more woman will be lost to violence. This is one of the key differences between the mainstream, white, (neo)liberal version of feminism tied to #MeToo and Ni una menos, and the type of feminist solidarity that they are trying to perform.[8] But how is this collective political force created, maintained, and mobilized?

This question takes me to my methods. In Latin America, social movements and their relation to social media as means for unification have been studied from the social sciences using quantitative and ethnographic methods, but research from a cultural and area studies perspective is still a very new approach.[9] One example of the latter is the work of Marcela A. Fuentes, one of the few scholars who analyzes the intricate connections between social media and culture in Argentina. Fuentes (2019) discusses aesthetic tactics to mobilize support for #NiUnaMenos Argentina and claims that by "using hashtags and physically situated performance as both ephemeral and enduring cultural practice, NUM'S activists lay out the building blocks for radical change, linking memory and emergence: that is, learned and improvised tactics" (173). Following her lead, I noticed a recurrent triangulation between social media (specifically hashtags and memes), the uses of public spaces, and cultural production for the case of Ni una menos in Mexico. This affective assemblage serves to produce a form of counter knowledge and to generate strategies to cope with the difficulty of resisting a system sustained by the systematic annihilation of women. The political force of Ni una menos lies in its ability to mock the system while at the same time grieving losses and demanding a feminist future where human lives are not disposable. Thus, instead of drowning in a state of political despair, social media is used to animate a conversation where art and politics are equally worthwhile. Art becomes a tactic in social media not only as a means—for some, naive—to bear all the deaths while taking the streets, but also as a democratic way of disseminating knowledge and practicing cultural change. The choreography of exhaustion and laughter generated by the feminists' killjoy[10] moments performed by Ni una menos holds and produces in the present the promise of a revolutionary feminist future.

TACTICS OF FEMINIST DISAPPROPRIATION: HASHTAGS, "CANCIÓN SIN MIEDO," AND THE CULTURAL DIRECTIONS OF THE ANTI-GRITA

Cristina Rivera Garza: "Digámoslo así: un tuit no produce sentido sino presente." Women's collectives and feminist activists in Mexico have been using what I call tactics of feminist disappropriation to transmit counter knowledge, belonging, and dissent. The idea comes from Mexican intellectual Cristina Rivera Garza, who has analyzed what it means to write in a necropolitical context traversed by the rise and uses of digital technologies. Here I use the concept of necropolitics as defined by Sayak Valencia (2016), who understands it as a countervalue that is inscribed in the same register as biopolitics, but its focus is on death—that is, a form of politics that desecrates and commodifies the processes of dying (156). As a writer herself, Rivera Garza is preoccupied by the ethical implications of writing literature when surrounded by dead bodies. In a powerful act of self-reflection, in *Los muertos indóciles*, Rivera Garza (2013) asks if it is possible to dismantle neoliberal power and its war machine with and from writing. Echoing Indigenous epistemologies, she identifies writing processes that are communal and constantly question the concept and practice of ownership; writings that happen in conditions of extreme mortality, using digital tools, and where the political and the aesthetic are equally valuable. The strategies identified by Rivera Garza are very similar to the ones being performed by Ni una menos: what matters is less the production of logical individual trains of thought, and more the production of the present, provoking emotions, and ideas of disappropriation through activist techniques that highlight communality, such as pastiche, collage, or ready-made techniques.

Disappropriation is a form of poetics, Rivera Garza (2020) explains, that constantly challenges the concept and practice of property and propriety to issue a warning about what is at stake in the here and now: the construction of a communal horizon to collectively distribute wealth. "This poetics of disappropriation forms *communalities* of writing. In unveiling work created by many people in communality (as the Mixe anthropological root-word implies), communalities of writing address survival strategies based on mutual care and the protection of the common good, challenging the ease and apparent immanence that marks the languages of globalized capitalism" (5). Rivera Garza writes, "Unlike the paternalistic 'giving voice to the voiceless' promoted by certain imperial subjectivities, and unlike naive putting-of-oneself into another's shoes, these writing practices incorporate those shoes and those others into the materiality of a text" (5). In other words, the construction of an active collectivity that can redirect the neoliberal state

that has embraced maximum profit as a guiding principle to more ethical
practices of relationality. Needless to say, Rivera Garza is thinking about
the role of literature and the writer in the digital era in a necropolitical state.
Given that I am thinking about the role of art and feminist solidarity under
the same conditions, I borrow her ideas to define tactics of feminist disappropriation as instances where the production of meaning shifts from the radical
tide of the uniqueness of feminist collectives or from identity politics toward
the function of a problematized "all," who instead of appropriating the material of the world that is the other, disavow it (Rivera Garza 2013, 22). These
tactics of feminist disappropriation are at the core of the shift that I identify
in the type of feminist solidarity that Ni una menos is performing.

Let me elaborate with an example. During the first weekend of March 2020
and as part of the commemoration of International Women's Day, Mexican
feminist collectives called once more to take the streets to demand *ni una
menos* and abortion rights. What is significant about this revolutionary act of
defiance is the number of women who took their demands to the streets—one
of the largest contingents ever seen and right when the rest of the world was
going into quarantine due to the COVID-19 global pandemic. The central
propeller for this networked protest was the use of hashtags (#NiUnaMenos
and #UnDíaSinNosotras), the promise of pintas, and "The Festival Tiempo de
Mujeres," a music festival in Mexico City's zocalo the eve before protesters
marched down the streets. Thus, this well-organized feminist revolutionary
act was divided into three main events: a night of singing to gather strength,
a day to march and intervene in public spaces with graffiti, and lastly, on
Monday, a strike asking women to disappear from the public and private
spheres. This tripartite event had never been coordinated before and women
knew they were practicing in the present a form of political activism for a
feminist future. The sense of this feminist future is being felt, envisioned, and
enacted at the moment of the protest. As an example, one of the most popular
chants is a utopic impulse that promises a feminist future in the present: "se
va a caer,"—the participants shout—because "lo vamos a tumbar" ("is going
to fall" / "we are going to knock it down"), followed by various actions that
make patriarchal structures tremble such as the ones I study here. I want to
focus on the uses of hashtags and music, during and after this event, as tactics
of feminists disappropriation to later tie them to the uses of public space and
the artistic interventions that happened during the aforementioned episode of
the Casa Refugio Ni Una Menos.

As hyperlinked labels or metadata tags, hashtags organize information
around shared interests and transform an individual issue into an act of participation. For example, by interlinking a personal story with #MeToo, the
individual participates in a broader conversation around sexual harassment.
For Fuentes (2019), hashtags are also performative—that is, they "do things

in the world rather than merely describe what exists" (180). That is to say that hashtags are citational practices with worldmaking effects. It is a form of writing that potentially challenges the question of property, which is central for Rivera Garza's disappropriation techniques, to create new worlds.

#NiUnaMenos was first used in Argentina in 2015 after a case of feminicidio. Since then, the hashtag is an active slogan that through repetition, accumulation, recombination, and other recycling techniques of generation and degeneration maintains the momentum and holds everyone together. In Mexico, #NiUnaMenos replaces #NiUnaMás, the most publicly visible campaign of awareness during the history of violence in Mexico (Finnegan 2019, 24). This displacement is significant. While #NiUnaMás was centered in denouncing the impunity around the increasing cases of feminicidio, as a feminist tactic of disappropriation #NiUnaMenos shifted the conversation in two significant ways. Disappropriation here is a form of undoing in which the same process of undoing can be traced and felt as a conscious form of practicing feminist politics. First, it moves the attention from numbers to the subjectivities of the victims. The word "menos" (or "less" in English) disappropriates the act of counting bodies as a feminist praxis of signification to incorporate the materiality of the bodies of the victims—a materiality that returns them their denied subjectivity.[11] Secondly, in Mexico, #NiUnaMenos was mobilized as a critique of the fact that some bodies were worth more than others after the feminicidio of an Indigenous woman in Puebla that did not receive the same attention as others. Thus, #NiUnaMenos practices a decolonial way of solidarity from the communal performativity of this hashtag.

Another tactic of feminist disappropriation comes with #UnDíaSinNosotras. A feminist collective from Veracruz, Las brujas del mar, called for a national strike on the Monday after International Women's Day. The idea was that for twenty-four hours women would disappear without a trace from the public and private spheres: no work, no family, no consumption, no ecological footprint. It was an invitation to reflect about our own role in neoliberal economies while simultaneously creating affective reactions. The effect of disappearing would hopefully cause questions among friends and family to spark a conversation about the political happenings of the weekend, creating once more a communal experience of learning beyond the knowledge produced by feminist collectives. Lastly, this hashtag is a form of disappropriation because of the type of citational practice that it performs. As a hyperlink, it can be indexed with other types of feminist strikes such as "A day without women" in the United States or "Black Monday" in Poland. But it remains a g-local form of activism—that is, a practice that maintains the local specificities of the movements without disconnecting them from global narratives.

But hashtags alone do not mobilize the type of feminist solidarity that we saw that March 2020 weekend. As an act of mutual care, Chilean singer

Mon Laferte participated in the aforementioned music festival, sharing the stage with various artists such as Vivir Quintana and Ana Tijoux, breaking the boundaries and geographies of nation-state politics. Tijoux and to a lesser extent, Laferte, have developed a musical tradition that seeks other routes for organizing global politics.[12] Between lettered and popular spheres, and connected to social movements, for these women music constitutes an effective, affective, and lyrical means of communication and representation of feminist insurgency. Sheltered by this tradition, Mexican singer Vivir Quintana debuted her song "Canción sin miedo," which has since become a collective scream. That day Quintana sang alongside Laferte and the collective El palomar, a group of Latin American women singers that seeks to change the role of women in the music industry. Once more, the song is an act of feminist disappropriation.

Wearing the pañoleta verde, symbol of support for the decriminalization of abortion, a choir of powerful voices simultaneously sings without fear:

> Ya nada me calla, ya todo me sobra
> Si tocan a una, respondemos todas.[13]

The song ends with a powerful reference to the Mexican national anthem: "y retiemble en sus centros la tierra / al sororo rugir del amor." Instead of the earth trembling to the sound of war and cannons, as the original anthem says, the tremble here comes from feminist solidarity. By citing hashtags and incorporating practices of communality in her writing, Quintana's song performs exactly the type of solidarity that it claims. By the time she debuted this song, the lyrics had already been shared through WhatsApp, and the voices of the artists were joined by all the other feminists standing there that night. To this day, there are several versions of this song that respond to the local context, retaining a sense of translocal solidarity through affect—in this case, through the physical response of our bodies that unequivocally scream together ni una menos. "Canción sin miedo" is a tactic of disappropriation because it challenges the question of music rights—Quintana has declared several times that this is not her song but a communal act—and displaces the production of meaning from the composer to the listener, who instead of giving meaning, practices a form of communal trembling to produce a feminist future, here and now.

The last point that I want to address with this song is the challenge to propriety as a fundamental aspect of disappropriation. The feminist politics that the song seeks to express are not hidden behind any type of aesthetic language. Instead, Quintana uses feminist slogans and hashtags to express feminist methods of insurrection: burn and break everything if one day some woman is not walking next to you. This invitation to violently intervene in public spaces comes from the outrage of knowing that a wall, as the alleged heritage of humanity, has more legal rights than women's bodies in Mexico. The accepted standards of behavior and morals demand that feminist activists behave "properly," without violence. The concept of violence is quite fluctuating within this context as it can mean the painting of a wall, protesting with pink glitter, the pro-abortion movement, the burning of buildings, or any other act that the current sense of propriety qualifies as such. So, it is not surprising that Quintana joined the performative acts of resistance of the Casa Refugio Ni Una Menos during the commemoration of Mexican independence as the ultimate challenge to propriety. Once more, feminist activists gathered outside the refugio to perform an anti-grita, a communal performance of discontent with the patriarchal discourses of nation-state politics, where "Canción sin miedo" was sung as an anti-anthem. But the central piece of this performance, in my opinion, was the exhibition of the feminist interventions of the painted portraits of the national heroes (all men) that decorate the walls of the former CNDH building.

Days before the commemoration of Mexican independence, the feminist collectives spread the images of the intervened paintings through social media. The "serious" portrait of Francisco I. Madero, painted by José Manuel Nuñez A, now has a ribbon and purple hair. The acronym ACAB is written on his forehead and the hashtag #Aliade in the background. His masculine suit is now covered in purple flowers. The feminist collectives organized a fake auction on the streets to raise funds for their ocupa act. That's how the portraits went viral. I specifically mention the portrait of Madero because the "original" artist issued a complaint on his social media. Damaging the art of the state does not solve gender violence, but rather is a setback in Mexican values, according to Nuñez: "eres grande rayando *mi* obra . . . " to later declare that destroying history is not the way (El universal 2020). I stress the possessive "my" because of the irony of highlighting authorship and state property in a necropolitical context that urges us to understand art in more critical ways. A lot can be said about Nuñez's infantile and masculinist visions of art, but my aim here is not to give more space to the never-ending tale of the phallus. Instead, I suggest that what matters in this story is the irritated laughter that this auction caused. Once more, feminist collectives used hashtags, communal forms of art, and public space to gain momentum and to keep screaming "ni una menos" in a new reality (COVID-19) that is forcing us back into individual forms of living. The cultural directions and tactics of feminist disappropriation materially and symbolically bring together different forms of social agencies. Placed in contiguity, hashtags, the uses of public space, and art drawn on connections among different forms of violence, connecting national discourses to economic systems to feminicidios to ocupa movements. Pairing #NiUnaMenos with #UnDíaSinNosotras, "Canción sin miedo" and the anti-grita, shows us how decolonial solidarities emerge in contexts of extreme violence through practices of communality and disappropriation that create affective assemblages through the triangulation of social media, cultural production, and space. Decolonial solidarities suspend a sense of political identity and organize their collectivity not through identity categories but through affective spaces that produce in the present a sense of togetherness against larger systems of oppression. Ni una menos proposes a radical form of feminist praxis and decolonial solidarity by creating affective networks that challenge the flows of capital.

Several activists and scholars have questioned the role of social media in social movements and have ironically asked if the revolution can be tweeted. For example, Paolo Gerbaudo (2012) argues that the power of social media lies in collective action, but problems arise when social media is turned into a "fetish" of collective action. In other words, the problem is when social media obscures the work of groups and organizers to become a neoliberal ideology incapable of understanding collective action except as a result of a technological miracle. With examples from around the world, Gerbaudo shows that the crucial element in understanding social media in contemporary social movements is their interaction with and mediation of public gatherings. What Ni una menos shows is another crucial element: the way they produce counter-knowledge and practice communal agencies through cultural production. By creating affective assemblages in this triangulated process, Ni una menos is trying to find other routes for organizing politics, outside the "binary choice between capitalism and communism, or between individualism and no future" (Gómez-Barris 2018, 44). Going against conventional forms of cultural production, by misusing public space and social media, Ni una menos shows us how to undo coloniality and bolster another type of solidarity. In times of me too, let us scream "ni una menos."

THE DISCOMFORT OF WRITING (IN) THE PRESENT: SOME NOTES OF SELF-REFLECTION

Any attempt to produce knowledge about feminicidio makes me uncomfortable. Writing about feminicidio bothers me. While writing this chapter, I juggle the anxiety that manifests itself physically and emotionally in my body: what does it mean to write about feminicidios when we are surrounded by dead bodies? What does it mean to write about feminist solidarity in a necropolitics whose primary activity is to remove any hint of our humanity? I do not have sharp insights such as Rivera Garza's to these questions. (Perhaps, I lack these insights because I doubt the ethics of representation in academic writing—after all, my research does not change the material conditions of any woman in Mexico.) I still do not know if it is ethical to write about Ni una menos regardless of whether I recognize my privilege, whether I have taken the streets with Ni una menos, and if I too have someone that is not here; or if I have ever been a potential victim of feminicidio. However, the prevailing of feminicidios succinctly disarms any further argument that I could have advanced here.

My initial interest was to draw on forms of solidarity that differ from neo-liberal or identity models in the hope of tracing new histories and flows of transnational feminist solidarity. To look in different directions—geographical and cultural flows—in the hope of finding new answers to old feminist questions. Instead of producing knowledge, my desire lines—a term used in landscape architecture that describes the "marks left on the ground that show everyday comings and goings, where people deviate from the paths they are supposed to follow" (Ahmed 2006, 20)—took me in a different direction (perhaps another type of disappropriation?). In the end, more than producing knowledge or addressing counter-ways of thinking about solidarity, I ended up writing about the present. Could creating a sense of the present instead of knowledge be a kind of feminist disappropriation tactic? I do not know. But I do hope it makes my reader uncomfortable.

REFERENCES

Ahmed, Sara. 2006. *Queer Phenomenology. Orientations, Objects, Others.* Duke University Press.
———. 2010. *The Promise of Happiness*. Duke University Press.
Animal politico. 2020. "En fotos: La toma feminista y contra la impunidad del edificio de CNDH." *Animal politico*. September 6, 2020.
Annaunziata, Rocío and Tomás Gold. 2018. "El ciclo de *Cacerolazos* (2012–2013) y la movilización #NIUNAMENOS (2015) en Argentina."*Desarrollo económico* 57 (223): 461–85.
Domínguez, Edmé R. 2020. "Mexico and Latin America. From #MeToo to #NiUnaMenos." In *The Routledge Handbook of the Politics of the #MeToo*, edited by Giti Chandra and Irma Erlingsdóttir, 423–38. Routledge.
Eubanks, Virginia. 2018. *Automating Inequality. How High-Tech Tools Profile, Police, and Punish the Poor.* Picador.
Félix de Souza, Natália Maria. 2019. "When the Body Speaks (to) the Political: Feminist Activism in Latin America and the Quest for Alternative Democratic Futures." *Contexto Internacional* 41 (1): 89–112.
Ferreyra, Marta. 2018. "Crecer después de la tormenta." *La razón*, February 2, 2018.
Finnegan, Nuala. 2019. *Cultural representations of Feminicidio at the US-Mexico Border*. Routledge.

Fuentes, Marecla A. 2019. "#NiUnaMenos (#NotOneWomanLess): Hashtag Performativity, Memory, and Direct Action against Gender Violence in Argentina." *Women Mobilizing Memory.* Ayşe Gül Altýnay, María José Contreras, Marianne Hirsch, Jean Howard, Banu Karaca, and Alisa Solomon, eds. Columbia University Press.

Gago, Verónica 2019. *La potencia feminista. O el deseo de cambairlo todo.* Tinta Limón y Traficantes de sueños.

Gargallo, Francesca. 2006. *Ideas feministas latinoamericanas.* Universidad Autónoma de la Ciudad de Mexico.

Gerbaudo, Paolo. 2012. *Tweets and the Streets. Social Media and Contemporary Activism.* Pluto Press.

Gómez-Barris, Macarena. 2018. "Sounds Radical: Ana Tijoux, Student Protest, and Palestinian Solidarity." In *Beyond the Pink Tide: Art and Political Undercurrents in the Americas,* 22–46. University of California Press.

Lamas, Marta. 2018. *Acoso ¿Denuncia legítima o victimización?* Mexico: Fondo de cultura económica.

Laudano, Claudia N. 2019. "Acerca del uso estratégico de TIC en movilizaciones feministas." *Tecnologías digitales. Miradas de la apropiación en América Latina.* Ana Laura Rivoir and María Julia Morales, eds. CLACSO.

Lugones, Maria. 2016. "The Coloniality of Gender." *The Palgrave Handbook of Gender and Development.* Palgrave Macmillan.

Petersen, Amanda L. 2019. "Breaking Silences and Revealing Ghosts: Spectral Moments of Gender Violence in Mexico." *iMex. México Interdisciplinari / Interdisciplinary Mexico.* 8 (16): 22–40.

Quijano, Aníbal. 2000. "Colonialidad del poder y clasificacisión social." *Journal of World Systems Research* 6 (2): 342–86.

Rivera Garza, Cristina. 2013. *Los muertos indóciles: Necroescrituras y desapropiación.* TusQuets editores.

———. 2020. *The Restless Dead: Necrowriting and Disappropriation.* Trans. Robin Myers. Vanderbilt University Press.

Tufekci, Zeynep. 2017. *Twitter and Tear Gas: The Power and Fragility of Networked Protest.* Yale University Press.

El universal. 2020. "Autor del retrato de Madero en la CNDH se queja por intervención feminista." *El universal,* September 8, 2020.

Vacarezza, Nayla Luz. 2017. "Judith Butler en Argentina. Recepción y polémicas en torno a la teoría de la performatividad del género." *Estudos feministas* 25 (3): 1257–76.

Valencia, Sayak. 2016. *Capitalismo gore: Control económico, violencia y narcopoder.* Mexico: Paidós.

Yancy, George. 2019. "Judith Butler: When Killing Women Isn't a Crime." *New York Times,* July 10, 2019.

NOTES

1. "[Metoo] no es nuestro debate. No perdamos tiempo en esto" (Segato in Ferreyra 2018).

2. Amanda Petersen (2019) argues that the spring of 2016 was particularly impactful in Latin America in relation to the uses of hashtags as tools for mobilization: "it became known as the 'purple spring' in Latin America, full of well publicized massive protest accompanied by an explosion of hashtag movements that create spectral moments as they break the silence of gender violence throughout Mexico (and Latin America)" (26).

3. This chapter was submitted for publication prior to the publication of *El invencible verano de Liliana* (2021) by Cristina Rivera Garza.

4. I quote Judith Butler not without being aware of the messiness of referencing specifically this US feminist philosopher. I recognize that Butler's ideas on gender performativity have not been well received in Latin America due to the question of materiality and the body (Natália Maria Félix de Souza, Nayla Luz Vacarezza, and Verónica Gago), and that it is important to question the genealogies of feminist epistemologies and to value Latin American thought (see more in Francesca Gargallo's *Ideas feministas latinoamericanas*), which is in part what I later propose in this chapter with Cristina Rivera Garza's ideas on disappropriation. This interview is merely an instrument that sums up very well the differences of the movements. It is also interesting to note that, at least in the case of Mexico, #MeToo was discussed not so much in relation to #NiUnaMenos, in part because feminist scholars and activists are very aware of the differences. But it was discussed in terms of the cultural differences about sexual behavior—mainly a critique of US sexual negativity and puritanism—a critique that in turn led Mexican feminism to a generational divide. While older feminists focus the discussion of sexual harassment in terms of legitimate accusations versus victimization (Marta Lamas), younger feminists highlight that thinking through this division is feminism at the service of patriarchal structures. This is another deviation line, which unfortunately I will not follow in this chapter, that promises new insights into the discussion about sexual harassment, cultural politics, and situated feminism.

5. Aníbal Quijano (2000) explains that modernity is born with the fusing of experiences of colonialism and coloniality with the necessities of capitalism, which creates intersubjective relations of domination under a Eurocentric hegemony (343). Later, in "The Coloniality of Gender," Lugones (2016) criticizes the indifference that men like Quijano exhibit to the systematic violence of gender, claiming that gender is a central category in these intersubjective relations of domination.

6. The word feminicidio is not equivalent to femicide nor feminicide. The Spanish version allows for a more expanded definition to include "its systematic nature on the one hand and the involvement of the state on the other" (Finnegan 2019, 3). For a cultural representation of what this systematic nature and the involvement of the state entails, see the Netflix documentary *Las tres muertes de Marisela Escobedo* (2020) directed by Carlos Pérez Osorio.

7. Throughout this article, I refuse to translate several terms, phrases, and hashtags. Sometimes my refusal has to do with the fact that the English word does not grasp the same nuances as the one in Spanish, in which case I will explain the definition, such as the aforementioned case for feminicidio. Nevertheless, in most cases, my refusal is a decolonial move. My reader needs to do the work, pause the reading, and do the research. My hope is that by recognizing translation as an uncomfortable process—pausing the reading, opening Google Translate, typing the word only to get frustrated by the fact that Google still cannot translate cultural nuances—we can affectively start thinking about the political power of being uncomfortable to create global networks of collaboration. Hint: Google Translate translates the word desaparecidos into "missing," which erases the history of oppressive political regimes that in Latin America have disappeared people as a torture mechanism to maintain power, among other things.

8. Doing a comparative analysis of Burke's Me Too as a project of Black feminisms in relation to Ni Una Menos, and the type of solidarity these movements perform, is beyond the scope of this chapter. Since my interest lies in the flows of feminist knowledge, I focus my analysis on the problematic mainstream use of #MeToo, which is the version that traveled to Mexico. See more about the #MeToo hashtag in relation to Mexico in "Mexico and Latin America. From #MeToo to #NiUnaMenos" by Edmé Domínguez R.

9. For Latin America, I am thinking in the work of Claudia N. Laudano on the strategic use of ICT in feminists' movements and the article "El ciclo de *Cacerolazos* (2012–2013) y la movilización #NIUNAMENOS (2015) en Argentina" by Rocío Annuzziata y Tomás Gold. But also, on the work of Virgina Eubanks (2018) in *Automating Inequality, Twitter and Tear Gas* by Zeynep Tufekci (2017), and *Tweets and the Streets* by Paolo Gerbaudo (2012).

10. For Sara Ahmed (2010), the feminist is an affected alien, a killjoy: "Does the feminist kill other people's joy by pointing out moments of sexism? Or does she expose the bad feelings that get hidden, displaced, or negated under public signs of joy? . . . she might even kill joy because she refuses to share an orientation toward certain things as being good because she does not find the objects that promise happiness to be quite promising" (39).

11. Another example of this is the interactive map created by María Salguero "Yo te nombro: el mapa de los feminicidios en México." This map gives name to the victims of feminicidio and tries to provide all the data about their femnicidios with the intention of given context and with it, a sense of humanity. Put simply, the map is a way of using numbers beyond frivolous statistics. See the map at https://feminicidiosmx .crowdmap.com.

12. For more about the global politics of Ana Tijoux, see "Sounds Radical: Ana Tijoux, Student Protest, and Palestinian Solidarity" in *Beyond the Pink Tide* by Macarena Gómez-Barris (2018).

13. "Nothing silences me anymore/It's all gone too far/If they touch one, we answer all" (Quintana 2020, my translation).

Chapter 2

Storying Blackfoot Resilience in the Digital Age

Gabrielle E. Lindstrom, Sierra Shade, and Sofia Baptiste

In this chapter, we embark upon a critical conceptual journey aimed at illuminating the challenges and triumphs that contextualize the ways that we, as Blackfoot women, animate our perseverance in today's digital age. Within the national state context of Canada, Indigenous peoples have endured a historical and contemporary pattern of colonial violence that has been manifested through government policies of forced assimilation. The default national narrative of Canada tells a story of Indigenous peoples from a deficit perspective that reinforces imagined stereotypes, often preventing Indigenous women from being anything more than problems to be solved. However, the narrative of Indigenous women has always been one that holds the heartbeat of communities and, with the release of the National Inquiry into missing and murdered Indigenous women and girls final report (2020), increased attention is finally being given to the devastating violence and continued oppression that has been a consistent theme in their personal stories.

As Blackfoot women, one an emerging scholar and two student research assistants, our classroom experiences as both professor and students have led us to challenge the deficit paradigm that continues to be held by far too many non-Indigenous Canadians by reframing common definitions that have been applied to Indigenous peoples. The current research that informs this chapter focuses on Indigenous conceptualizations of resilience and is aimed at counteracting deficit understandings of Indigenous peoples that emerge when the sorrow-stories, barriers, and challenges to advancement in society become the defining features of Indigenous experiences in Canada. Strength-based discourses in the fields of education, health, and social service may offer an understanding of these deficit narratives using resilience as the base for analysis. However, these discourses are continuously constructed through a Western, Euro-centered paradigm and therefore insufficient for authentically capturing the meaning of resilience from a distinct Indigenous perspective. Moreover, mobilizing our current study's research findings in ways that ensure it reaches Indigenous communities presents distinct challenges in terms of dissemination given that many Indigenous peoples do not access academic journals or utilize scholarly research findings. Hence, counternarratives presented through a variety of digital methods can effectively bridge these challenges because they not only offer a new platform for conceptualizing and mobilizing ancient traditional knowledges but are easily accessed by a diverse range of audiences as opposed to simply catering to the academic elite through traditional avenues for academic dissemination. Counternarratives not only align with an Indigenous oral tradition but are also key to advancing Indigenous women's voices both in academia and beyond. Settler colonialism and its expressions of heteropatriarchy have not only silenced Indigenous women's voices through systemic gendered discrimination that is evident in colonial policy such as the Indian Act, but as Dhillon (2020) argues, have violated Indigenous womanhood via pervasive and persistent acts of sexual and physical violence. Counternarratives provide a venue for Indigenous women to push back against these colonial forces by sharing their stories of resistance and regaining a sense of agency. However, given the objectification of Indigenous women's bodies, digital technologies, particularly social media, come with risks that must be acknowledged and illuminated.

Informed by our autoethnographic study that aims to redefine resilience from a distinct Blackfoot paradigm, this chapter invites readers to reflect on the ways that traditional Indigenous knowledge, protocols, and processes intersect with technology in order to advance Blackfoot resilience as digital pedagogy. Employing autoethnography and grounded in the literature surrounding Indigenous resilience and Indigenous digital practices, we offer an overview of the current research and connect it to our own journey toward conceptualizing a Blackfoot woman's digital culture. In keeping with autoethnographic writing (Wall 2008), this chapter is deliberately structured around our voices and the stories and personal reflections that have emerged from our experiences within a virtual landscape. The reader can assume that, aside from self-positioning and personal reflections, the primary standpoint emerges from the principal investigator, Dr. Gabrielle Lindstrom. This chapter is organized into four interconnected topic areas. In the first section we outline the purpose and methodology of our research study and position it within the broader context of Indigenous studies and Indigenous research. Secondly, we discuss how Indigenous knowledge translation has evolved through the use of digital platforms such as social media and highlight some risks that technologies pose to the well-being of Indigenous women as these issues emerged in the literature. We then outline how our experiences in the digital world have enabled us, as Blackfoot women, to nurture self-agency and cultural continuity. We conclude the chapter by briefly outlining how digital technologies can provide another pedagogical access point for Indigenous nations to advance their own distinct definitions via the synthesis of our experiences as Blackfoot women interacting with digital technologies.

RESEARCHER SELF-LOCATION

In keeping with Indigenous research protocols (Absolon 2012), we first position ourselves to establish how our identities as Indigenous women are interwoven into the cultural fabric of this research. We begin with Gabrielle's introduction, principal investigator and assistant professor of Indigenous Studies, then move on to Sierra, and finally, conclude with Sofia, both student research assistants on this project.

Oki. Niisto nitanikkoo Tsapinaki. Nimok'tooto Kainaiwa. Greetings. My name is Gabrielle Lindstrom (nee Weasel Head) and I am from Kainaiwa which is widely known as the Blood Indian Reserve. More specifically, I am from the Blackfoot-speaking tribes and a member of the Niitsitapi, Blackfoot Confederacy. My parents are Eagleribs, Peter Weasel Head, and American Horse Woman, Wanda Weasel Head. My paternal grandparents are Mokakin, Pat Weasel Head Sr., and Poonah, Paula Weasel Head. My maternal grandparents are Alan and Beulah Standing Alone. I am from the Mamoyiksi, the Fish Eaters clan. I am mother to Maria, Rachel, and Nora and wife to PiitaNinna, Eagleman, Desi Lindstrom who is Bear Clan from the Anishnaabe nation in the area now known as Thunder Bay, Ontario. By declaring my cultural positioning, I center my identity within a Blackfoot worldview and illuminate the cultural frame of reference from which this research is conceptualized. My experiences as a Blackfoot woman are brought to bear in my research and directly inform the research design and application of the findings.

Oki niisto nitanikkoo Pookakiwun nimok'tooto Kainaiawa and am a part of the Mamoyiksi (fish eater) clan and aah kaa poo kahks. Ninna aanistawa Chad Bare Shin Bone and Niksissta aanistawa Kimmy Shade Naahsiksi anistayawa Hank and Deanna Shade (maternal) and Jordan and Susan Bareshinbone (paternal). Hello, my name is Sierra Shade. I am from Kainaiwa and am part of the Fish Eaters and Many Children's clan. My father is Chad Bare Shin Bone and my Mother is Kimmy Shade. My grandparents are Hank and Deanna Shade (maternal) and Jordan and Susan Bare Shin Bone (paternal). It is significant for me to introduce myself in this way and acknowledge my community, clans, parents, grandparents, and those who have come before me. I believe we as Niitsitapi, or any Indigenous group for this matter, are always guided by our relations—whether that be spiritually when those who came before us are walking with us and supporting us to survive in these academic institutions which were not made for us, or physically, when we are all crammed in a house eating and laughing. We would oftentimes mark out a spot in a public event with a blanket and some masking tape. This is what grounds me in who I am, where I come from, who I come from, and offers a foundation that orients me throughout this chapter.

Oki, my name is Sofia Baptiste. I am Blackfoot, Dene (Tsuut'ina), and Cree. I was born in Mohkinstis, (Blackfoot for Calgary) located on Treaty 7 territory. I am registered as Ermineskin Cree. Ermineskin band is a part of the four-band reserve in Maskwacis. I did not grow up here. My home is on Pigeon Lake reserve. Pigeon Lake is a satellite reserve of Maskwacis. I spent my life traveling back and forth between Treaty 6 and Treaty 7. My dad is Cree. My mom is Blackfoot and Tsuut'ina. I may be registered as Cree, but through my mom I have a deep connection to my Blackfoot and Dene side. I also spent a large amount of my life living in Tsuut'ina as it is a reserve that borders Calgary. Growing up in rural Alberta had a huge impact on my own self-esteem and self-worth. I felt the effects of colonial violence as well as intergenerational trauma. I felt like I did not belong anywhere. As I started my own journey into learning the truth about the history of Canada, I began to learn more about my family history and how deep my roots are in these lands. This is why I am so detailed in acknowledging all the areas my ancestors come from.

INDIGENOUS STUDIES AND INDIGENOUS RESEARCH DESIGN: TOWARD A BLACKFOOT PEDAGOGY OF RESILIENCE

Since its inception within Western academia in the late 1960s (Taner 1999), Indigenous studies has developed into a burgeoning field of study attracting emerging high-quality scholars as well as maintaining a pool of well-established academics who have contributed seminal works (Bastien 2004; Battiste 2002; Littlebear 2000; Smith 1999) to this growing discipline. With an interdisciplinary focus, Indigenous studies offers diverse and multifaceted entry points to exploring and relating to knowledge in order to better understand real-world problems and strategize toward practical solutions based on a combination of tradition, theory, and direct experience with multiple ways of knowing (Battiste 2002). An enduring and salient theme central to Indigenous studies is related to the histories of colonial oppression and the continued marginalization, misinterpretation, and decontextualization of Indigenous ways of knowing. Direct experiences with colonial violence, systemic discrimination, and structural racism influence the research designs, knowledge dissemination platforms (Dei 2012), and pedagogies (Stewart-Harawira 2018) of Indigenous studies scholars. Yet, many are just as influenced by the strengths of tribal paradigms to inform innovative scholarship as they envision a more just and equitable society for all our relations. Mobilizing tribal philosophies and relational wisdom offers an array of imaginative and original research methodologies that not only act as a vehicle for tribal self-determination but also help to build our society's relational capacity to provide equitable and brave solutions to existing problems that benefit Indigenous communities and challenge the foundations of colonial ideologies. Advancing tribal paradigms within academia and other educational contexts, however, is fraught with conceptual and practical barriers in terms of the epistemic divide between non-Indigenous peoples' ability to meaningfully engage with Indigenous ways of knowing, particularly members of Settler society. Yet, as our research demonstrates, these tribal paradigms hold promise for both reframing how Western systems of thought perceive Indigenous knowledges as well as transforming how we build intercultural relationships.

Lindstrom's doctoral research (2018) provided the inspiration for this current study. In it, she recommended future explorations of how Western and Indigenous theory and philosophy intersect through an examination of the ways resilience lives in classrooms of higher education in order to contribute to the success of Indigenous adult learners (Lindstrom 2018). This chapter is designed to challenge the social and systemic discourses that represent Indigenous peoples within a deficit perspective and to offer a starting point for educational and social systems' collaboration around the creation of an Indigenous resilience framework. The research questions are: 1) What are the theoretical intersections between transformative learning theory within an Adult learning context and Blackfoot perspectives on resilience? 2) What pedagogical approaches and teaching methods foster learning resilience in both Indigenous and non-Indigenous postsecondary adult learners? The research takes a blended methodological approach through the use of autoethnography, emerging from Western research traditions, in combination with Indigenous research methods, the incorporation of an Indigenous philosophical paradigm and data gathering through use of talking circles with student participants, and informal, conversational interviews with four Blackfoot Elders.

The theoretical framework of this chapter is informed by two primary stances: 1) transformative learning theory; and 2) Indigenous philosophical perspectives on learning. Developed by Mezirow (1978) and employed within an adult learning context, transformative learning theory has been used to conceptualize how adults make meaning of experience through a process of critical self-reflection that offers profound shifts in understanding, thus leading to new insights and interpretations of the world around us (Taylor 2008). From an Indigenous perspective, the study draws on the work of Bastien (2003, 2004) and Ermine (2007, 1995) to inform the creation of ethical classroom spaces and validate the spirit held within Indigenous pedagogy. Indigenous epistemology posits that individual growth is premised within a pursuit of personal self-development, wherein individuals aim to reach their full potential in life through acts of inward reflection (Bastien 2003; Ermine 1995). Notably, a disorienting dilemma—which can either be a cumulative series of stressful events or a single event such as a natural disaster, car crash, or other major trauma—serves as the impetus for learners to critically reevaluate their existing frame of reference in order to interrogate deficiencies in their previous understandings and integrate new insights based on a transformed perspective. An emphasis on critical reflection offers a parallel path to envisioning Indigenous epistemological perspectives. Data collection methods included the use of talking circles and conversational-style interviews provided "a connection to Indigenous knowledge, a location within an Indigenous paradigm, a relational nature, [and] a purpose (which is often decolonizing)" (Drawson, Toombs, and Mysquah 2017, 4). Autoethnography is well-suited for this research, because it is oriented from the personal perspective of the researcher's experiences, which can be applied in an Indigenous research context in an effort toward self-determination. Further, its use originates from research in "which the dominance of traditional science and research is questioned and many ways of knowing and inquiring are legitimated" (Wall 2008, 39).

This chapter draws on the voices of Blackfoot Elders as a central guiding force. The perspectives of the students, both Indigenous and non-Indigenous, who attended Indigenous studies classes provide deepened insights into how Indigenous knowledges and pedagogies can potentiate transformative learning within the university classroom. At the time of writing, our research was stalled due to the COVID-19 pandemic. Given that Indigenous research is relational (Wilson 2008), it has been difficult to maintain regular face-to-face visits with Elders, a communication method that they prefer. However, we have begun the data analysis process, which is interpreted through the theoretical lens outlined above and informed by our experiences as Blackfoot women. The early findings of this research reveal a distinct conceptualization of resilience that is temporally and philosophically positioned within a Blackfoot paradigm. Resilience here is understood as a quality that Blackfoot peoples are born with, as opposed to something that has been defined for them. Implications for classroom pedagogy include fostering deeper self-explorations of learner identities using dialogical teaching strategies, honoring the spiritual aspect of knowledge through the cocreation of new knowledge, and teaching through kimmapiiyipitssini, a Blackfoot term that translates to kindness and compassion. One of the most interesting aspects of this research project has been the contexts within which resilience is both understood and experienced by Blackfoot peoples. The dialogical interplay between the conversations with Elders and student voices, when taken together, highlight how our journey through anguish or suffering, whether that journey has been in an Indian Residential School or in a university classroom, inspires others to persevere through their own hardships. Blackfoot resilience is empowering because it enables us to adapt to our changing circumstances in ways that generate new knowledge and form the basis of enduring stories and new communication practices that are appropriate for our current times.

OLD KNOWLEDGE IN NEW FORMS

In attempting to conceptualize how digital and media technologies are transforming how Indigenous women are mobilizing their power, one must first recognize that Indigenous cultures are not static, and, like any other culture, we evolve in response to the changes surrounding us. This has always been true. Before contact with European colonial settlers, Indigenous peoples in what is now North America were connected through extensive trade routes that enabled exchanges of cultural artifacts, protocols, practices, and ideas on a mass level (Dickason and Calder 2006). Communication was not considered a major barrier as many Indigenous nations were either linguistically fluent in regional dialects and other Indigenous languages or had developed sign-language communication that was sufficient for trading (Dickason and Newbigging 2015). Our relationships with each other and the natural world reflected the constant flux, an Indigenous philosophical paradigm that guides our values, beliefs, and interactions with the world around us (Littlebear 2000). How we communicated and the responsibilities we had in these relationships were defined in the context of constant flux. Indigenous knowledges are a reflection of our spiritual and physical interactions within the flux of our relational milieus—meaning the relationships we have with our land, other living energies, and with self. Conflict was managed by entering into peace treaties that were grounded in notions of self-determination and respecting the autonomy of other nations (Simpson 2008).

The transmission of Indigenous knowledges was impacted through colonial assimilation policies that were aimed at eradicating Indigenous cultures. Indigenous knowledges are complex, and many Indigenous peoples understand they cannot be accessed or analyzed solely through a Eurocentric paradigm (Bastien 2016; Battiste 2002). Although there is no single definition (Hart 2010), Indigenous knowledges are relational and experiential epistemological understandings of place that shape the languages, practices, and worldviews of Indigenous nations. Because of this complexity, Indigenous knowledges represent sites of confusion and misunderstandings (Semali and Kincheloe 1999) particularly with regard to authority and the appropriate contexts of knowledge transmission and generation. For example, sacred knowledge is not the kind that is accessible to everyone but instead is transferred through a series of highly structured and specific series of ceremonies (Bastien 2004; Hungry Wolf 1982). Other knowledges, such as those passed on through teachings contained in creation stories and trickster tales, are widely accessible and can be thought of as equivalent to secular knowledge. Amid the complicated conceptual landscape of Indigenous knowledges, debates ensue as to the place of Indigenous knowledges within the academy (Dei 2000). Despite these complexities, or perhaps because of them, digital technologies are being increasingly recognized by critical Indigenous scholars (Poitras-Pratt 2020; Wemigwans 2016) as sites that are well-suited for the transmission of Indigenous knowledge. In the context of Indigenous knowledges, Wemigwans (2016) conceptualized "indigenous media practices as a kind of shield against the unethical use, erasure or exploitation of their knowledge—and, as a way to ensure that some way of introducing and bridging to the real sources of indigenous knowledge—on the land and steeped in living languages, communities and cultures—exists for those who might otherwise have no opportunity to even begin to approach such knowledge" (4). The evolving nature of digital technologies presents new and exciting ways for Indigenous peoples to communicate, access, and share cultural knowledge (Steeves 2015). Digital technologies also represent a vast collection of communication practices and outlets for creative expressions of Indigenous identities. Our autoethnographic narratives and personal reflections provide significant insight into the ways Indigenous women are potentiating the empowering quality of digital technologies, particularly social media.

STORIES AND REFLECTIONS OF
RESILIENCE IN THE DIGITAL WORLD

Stories are the knowledge containers that hold the histories and knowledges of Indigenous peoples and also highlight the role of Indigenous women in traditional society. Since the onset of colonization, Indigenous women have had their stories told for them. Today, many of us are telling our own stories in creative ways that spotlight our perseverance by harnessing the power of digital technologies to both challenge oppression and ongoing colonial violence and educate a broad audience about our strengths as Indigenous women. Below, we offer our individual stories and personal reflections that speak to a deliberate attempt to express our voices as Blackfoot women engulfed in a world that seeks to consume us. We first begin with Gabrielle's story, then move into Sierra's reflections and conclude with Sofia's experiences.

A STORY OF RESISTANCE

The purpose of this short narrative is not to give a personal historical recount of my life or trace my pathway of healing, although both go hand in hand. Instead, I will share how I've come to use digital technologies, specifically social media, as a platform to assert my self-determination as a Blackfoot aaki (woman) in challenging systemic racism within the academy. I position my use of social media within the conceptual framework of my current research study on Blackfoot resilience.

When I finished my first degree, I was thirty-four years old. Today, I'm not quite sure how I pulled that off given the late-night parties and normalized chaos that characterized my life during that time. I remember how many White people around me would comment on how "resilient" I was that I had made it through university and had risen above all the challenges that I was born into. Many would comment that if I could do it, then so could the other "Indians." When I completed my master's degree at age thirty-eight, being labeled as resilient by other White people around me was a regular occurrence, yet it always made me uneasy. Indeed, being called resilient felt both patronizing and condescending, as if the hundreds of years of oppression, racism, and cultural destruction were being erased by that term. It angered me because it simplified my people's struggles and minimized the many hurdles I had leapt over in order to stay alive. I felt that being educated made me no more resilient than the other Blackfoot women and, if anything, my education set me apart from my community members. The research that I conducted for my doctoral degree revealed an alternative conceptualization of resilience, one that was more consistent with my cultural orientation and experiences as a Blackfoot woman. My research findings demonstrated how definitions such as resilience and trauma are continuously imposed on Indigenous peoples (Lindstrom 2018; Lindstrom, Baptiste, and Shade 2021) in ways that either simplify our perseverance or pathologize our suffering.

As I write this chapter, it is late fall, and Old Man Winter is at my doorstep. The warmth of the past summer is now only a memory and as I look back to those recent times, I realize that Creator had guided my journey in ways that have enabled me to better understand my strength and purpose, to know myself just a little bit more. I've never been a big user of digital media, and aside from Facebook, my use of them had been limited. However, that changed recently. In 2017, I accepted a tenure-track appointment as an assistant professor in Indigenous Studies at a small undergraduate university in western Canada, an institution located on the ancestral territories of the Blackfoot Confederacy, my ancestral homelands. When I attended the first faculty council meeting, one tenured faculty member's voice stood out loud and clear as this person challenged the validity of Indigenous knowledges, questioned the relevancy of Indigenization initiatives on campus, and championed the benefits of genocidal policies such as the Indian Residential Schools, all of which were framed within the context of academic freedom. I sat stunned as those around me either ignored this professor or passively rolled their eyes. Very rarely would anyone deliberately challenge the clearly racist and violent viewpoints espoused by the faculty member. I realized that the faculty member's views were tolerated, and although most other faculty disagreed with her, there were also those that shared her views. Indeed, this faculty member not only expressed disdain for Indigenous people on campus but also consistently showed up at external academic events to advance racist and discriminatory opinions guised as academic debate. Students would regularly come to me during office hours to share their concerns when taking this person's classes. Indeed, racism was not new to me, so I pushed my pedagogy and research aims forward and did my best to also ignore the voices of hate and engaged in my fair share of eye-rolling. That all changed because of two catalyzing moments on Twitter: supporting students as they stood up to this tenured professor's abuse of power and realizing this same person put out tweets that mocked Indigenous Elders and evoked the benefits of the Indian Residential Schools. Admittedly, I became angered knowing how my parents suffered in these schools and endured unimaginable abuse simply for being born Indigenous. Previously, my Twitter account was pretty boring and usually consisted of retweeting others' posts. However, I was determined to challenge racism using the same technologies that were platforms to also spread hate and apathy.

The students, encouraged by the Black Lives Matter movement, recognized the support that I was offering by showcasing their tweets and Instagram posts and began to feel empowered by the pushback against systemic racism. Other faculty stood in solidarity with the students and also supported me as the attacks from the faculty member directed at myself, the students, and others who supported us escalated. All the while, leadership at the university were unresponsive to the demands by students to address both the overt racism being advanced by the faculty member as well as the university's long-standing complicity in systemic racism. Indeed, my own pleas for support were met with silence—not surprising given that it reinforced my belief that the institution protected itself as a moniker of White/Western knowledge that Cree scholar Willie Ermine (2007) referred to as a universal, God's-eye view of human reality.

The events of the summer culminated in a student-led demonstration that gained media attention and served to elevate the voices of non-White students, including young Indigenous women, in ways that ultimately created critical awareness around the institution as a protector of systemic racism. During that time, I decided to resign from my position as assistant professor and take another position at a larger university wherein my capacities as an Indigenous academic might be better supported. At least, this is my hope. My engagement with social media is not over, though, and I have since learned that social media can be a platform to assert an Indigenous stance on equity, challenge power imbalances, and inspire others toward changing circumstances and regaining a sense of agency. I have also learned that despite my previous efforts to always be kind and treat others with compassion, there are people who deliberately choose to spread hate and intolerance. I used to believe that anyone could transform their frame of reference toward a more equitable and caring perspective if they were treated with kindness and provided with opportunities to connect with the suffering of others in ways that not only caused them to recognize their own suffering and work toward healing it, but also empowered human relationships and catalyzed a vision toward a more just future. I have since learned that my energies are best directed toward mutual relationships that nurture relational connections in ways that allow us all to feel empowered because of our personal agency—not someone else's—in working toward a vision of a shared humanity as opposed to responding to people's hate and racism.

I don't consider my resignation from my assistant professor appointment as a failure. My ordeal in confronting and challenging systemic racism within Twitter's virtual environment revealed a novel and empowering experience within which my voice helped to uplift others as other voices uplifted my own. The road before me does not seem so daunting, and I realize that Twitter helped to illuminate another pathway along my learning journey that will help me to find new opportunities for fostering resilience.

LEARNING THROUGH DIGITAL TECHNOLOGIES: SIERRA'S REFLECTIONS

Indigenous self-determination within a digital landscape helps us to recount our stories of resilience using our own voices and deciding how these stories are told. For some, the wide-spread availability of digital technologies means telling stories that would have never been shared before due to lack of access to a listening audience, which includes members who provide advocacy and support to the storyteller. At this moment in time, through digital technologies, I am seeing our own Indigenous women being educated through dance, Indigenous language revitalization, beadwork, and sewing. Narratives are being digitally spun and showcased via TikTok, Instagram, Facebook, Snapchat, Twitter, and YouTube.

Regardless of how we are sharing stories, Indigenous peoples are establishing space that highlights where we come from and where we are going. Holding this virtual space is a powerful act because it is also accessible to non-Indigenous people who can begin to conceptualize Indigenous women in a positive light in ways that our society does not always allow for. This is just as important for young Indigenous girls because they can easily access the stories of strong Indigenous women—women who look like them, come from the same places, and have similar upbringings and experiences as them. Young Indigenous girls can also see how Indigenous women persevered in Western institutions such as universities. In this way, digital technologies are platforms for inspiration.

Personally, I grow tired of hearing stories of non-Indigenous people who successfully learn and work in academic institutions—institutions that were designed specifically for them—because these stories hold little relevance for me. As a young Blackfoot woman, I cannot see my story reflected in their narratives. I need to hear about how successful Blackfoot women overcame addictions, how they made it through university with a baby on their hip and little to no support. I need to learn more about the Blackfoot women who survived the Indian Residential Schools and are now matriarchs in my community. Today, a global pandemic has forced us to rely on digital technologies as our primary source of communication, which presents both potentials and risks for Indigenous women.

The dark side of digital technology includes the clash of two distinct worldviews—Indigenous and Western—each with their own distinct values and perspectives, as well as the different protocols that are involved in transferring and "owning" knowledge. Despite technology being a powerful tool throughout "Indian Country," its use can more easily spread animosity across Indigenous communities. In my experiences on social media, I have witnessed increasing lateral violence in Indigenous communities and, rather than attribute it to the impacts of colonial oppression, the fingers of blame are too easily pointed at fellow community members.

As a Kainaikii (Blood woman), I utilize social media as a means to stay connected with my relations and my community while I live away from home in order to complete my Bachelor of Education degree. I often deactivate my social media accounts because of the demand of attention that my education requires. But what I enjoy most when I am active on social media is being able to appreciate our humour through memes and TikTok, as well as the inspiring Indigenous women whose stories I have heard through digital storytelling mediums. As I expressed earlier, access to remarkable stories from our Indigenous women from all over Turtle Island (North America) is increasingly made possible through digital technologies. It has been my honour to learn from these stories and this learning has encouraged me to assert my roles and responsibilities as a Kainaikii in university. Part of these responsibilities include living well in our modern digital age all the while staying grounded to where I come from and where I am going.

FINDING A VOICE THROUGH DIGITAL TECHNOLOGIES: SOFIA'S REFLECTIONS

As asserted throughout this chapter, digital technologies can reach a large audience and connect Indigenous peoples in a variety of contexts. There is a level of accessibility and comfort in which people seem more willing to share their knowledge as well as preserve aspects of Indigenous identity. I see work around digitizing Indigenous languages in hopes of preserving them. There are language applications for smartphones that are available for Indigenous peoples who want to begin learning their language. Sometimes, through isolation, dislocation, and now the challenges brought with the global pandemic, it may be difficult to access Indigenous cultural teachings and practices in person, but digital technologies make it possible to remain connected to Indigenous knowledges. However, as Sierra mentions above, I too feel that Indigenous women can be put at risk for violence and other abuses through digital technologies. We can become overexposed and thus vulnerable to online bullying or harassment. In fact, I am aware of a land protector who has been exposed to Settler violence due to her activism. Lateral violence within and across Indigenous communities tends to spread more easily through online interactions, and as such I am wary of sharing my location online because of the risks.

And yet, digital technologies can also be a tool for teaching non-Indigenous peoples of Indigenous worldviews, making it easier for allies to learn and share information. In an urban environment where Indigeneity is so easily erased, digital technologies and social media platforms have the power to connect Indigenous peoples to cultural traditions and practices in ways they may not otherwise be able to access. I have seen Indigenous peoples teach Indigenous languages through online language classes. I have accessed social media posts through which Indigenous peoples are educating others about the lived experience of what it means to be Indigenous in an age of ongoing colonization. For example, the Idle No More social movement, which brings attention to missing and murdered Indigenous women, gained a lot of momentum through social media and was able to spread globally. These movements, which involved public awareness events through a variety of platforms, were followed by teach-ins to inform people about the political atmosphere that contributed to the continued assaults on our natural water sources.

In terms of my own cultural learning, I have accessed YouTube to learn powwow dance steps and viewed various instructional videos around beading and sewing ribbon skirts. I also access social media that highlight the use of memes to bring awareness and inspiration regarding Indigenous worldviews. It seems the latest trend is to post informative videos on TikTok that are focused on cultural teachings and locates where Indigenous people are in their cultural learning journey. I particularly enjoy following pages that speak to Indigenous cultural truths gleaned from direct lived experience. Up until recently, I've been much more of a "sharer" of information by reposting impactful content in order to elevate other people's voices because I am inspired by their stories.

Recently, I created a post on Instagram of my experience of being racially profiled in a popular cosmetics store. I felt this post was important, because it sheds light on my lived experiences as an Indigenous woman in Settler society. Within the post, I shared my encounter with systemic racism beginning from the moment I entered the store. There were approximately six interactions between the store's employees and me. In all honesty, I am used to being racially profiled any time I enter any type of store. I have had security follow me. I have had employees suddenly start stocking their shelves beside me. However, I have never before felt as if the entire store was aggressively watching me. As I was shopping for the items on my list, I noticed how every time I looked in any direction there was someone looking directly back toward me. I understand that to those who have not experienced these types of microaggressions, this may not seem that terrible but, for me, it was traumatic. I was upset. After sharing my experience with some friends, they encouraged me to speak out. I did through my Instagram account. The feedback I received was a mixture of support from non-Indigenous peoples and from others who could relate to my experience. Many of my close friends were incredibly upset at how I was treated. They were angered by what happened to me. I felt hopeless when I experienced this behavior because it is so common. Utilizing social media to share my experience and the feedback from my connections leads me to believe that it is important not to silence myself and that my voice matters. Sharing my lived experience with racism empowered me and fostered a sense of agency and resilience.

CONCLUSION

Our autoethnographic narratives and reflections offer an example of how Indigenous women are employing digital technologies to intentionally assert a knowledge transmission agenda that is grounded in Indigenous self-determination. As Blackfoot women, we are reframing Western definitions that have been used to label our unique experiences. This is critical because as distinct nations, the notion of self-determination has always been part of the Indigenous worldview (Alfred 2016; Ermine 2007). Digital technologies provide a pathway for Indigenous peoples to be self-determining (Alcantara 2017), and, just as social media has transformed how the world communicates and engages in economic enterprises (Edosomwan 2011), it has changed the ways that Indigenous nations, communities, and individuals interact within Western-Settler societies. Despite the empowering nature of digital medias and other technologies, Indigenous scholars such as Wemigwans (2016) caution that "it is important to recognize that no mere tool, no matter how well designed or used, can ever replace—or even come close to—oral, person-to-person transmission of traditional cultural knowledge" (10). This statement resonates with us as we continue along our research pathway and seek to reconcile our dissatisfaction with having to replace our in-person conversations with Blackfoot elders with virtual interviewing methods made necessary due to the pandemic. Moreover, we also recognize that disseminating the emergent knowledge must be consistent with Indigenous research, which is ultimately community-engaged research. Despite some of the risks and limitations presented by digital technologies, we know that disseminating our research via technology can increase accessibility. Given that Indigenous knowledge is local knowledge, it is important that our research reaches the tribal communities located on reserves, many of whom do not have access to, or any interest in, academic publications.

Through this chapter, we have offered a brief glimpse into who we are as Blackfoot women by deliberately positioning our identities within the context of our research and through reframing our experiences with ongoing colonial oppression into sources of ongoing strength and perseverance. We outlined and connected our research study on Blackfoot resilience to the current discourses surrounding Indigenous knowledges and the use of digital technologies as a pathway to Indigenous self-determination and empowerment. The voices of Indigenous women have always been the backbone of Indigenous nations, and, despite the many challenges we continue to face, we will always find ways to make use of tools, conceptual or otherwise, for the betterment of communities and for our children yet to be born.

REFERENCES

Alcantara, Christopher, and Caroline Dick. 2017. "Decolonization in a Digital Age: Cryptocurrencies and Indigenous Self-Determination in Canada." *Canadian*

Journal of Law and Society/Revue Canadienne Droit et Société 32 (1): 19–35. doi:10.1017/cls.2017.1.

Alfred, Taiaiake. 2011. "Colonial Stains on Our Existence." In *Racism, Colonialism, and Indigeneity in Canada*, edited by Martin J. Cannon and Lina Sunseri, 2nd ed., Oxford University Press, 11–18.

Bastien, Betty. 2017. "Indigenous Pedagogy: A Way Out of Dependency." In *Racism, Colonialism, and Indigeneity in Canada*, edited by Martin J. Cannon and Lina Sunseri, 2nd ed., Oxford University Press, 3–11.

———. 2004. *Blackfoot Ways of Knowing: The Worldview of the Siksikaitsitapi.* Edited by Jürgen W. Kremer. University of Calgary Press. doi:10.2307/j.ctv6gqrdz.

———. 2003. "The Cultural Practice of Participatory Transpersonal Visions: An Indigenous Perspective." *ReVision* 26 (2): 41–48.

Battiste, Marie. 2002. "Indigenous Knowledge and Pedagogy in First Nations Education: A Literature Review with Recommendations.' Indian and Northern Affairs Canada.

Dei, George Sefa. 2012. "Indigenous Anti-Colonial Knowledge as 'Heritage Knowledge' for Promoting Black/African Education in Diasporic Contexts." *Decolonization: Indigeneity, Education & Society* 1 (1): 101–19.

———. 2000. "Rethinking the Role of Indigenous Knowledges in the Academy." *International Journal of Inclusive Education* 4 (2): 111–32. doi:10.1080/136031100284849.

Dhillon, Carla M. 2020. "Indigenous Feminisms: Disturbing Colonialism in Environmental Science Partnerships." *Sociology of Race and Ethnicity* 6 (4): 483–500. doi:10.1177/2332649220908608.

Dickason, Olive Patricia, and Moira Jean Calder. 2006. *A Concise History of Canada's First Nations*. 4th ed. Oxford University Press.

Dickason, Olive Patricia, and William Newbigging. 2015. *Concise History of Canada's First Nations.* Oxford University Press.

Drawson, Alexandra S., Elaine Toombs, and Christopher J. Mushquash. 2017. "Indigenous Research Methods: A Systematic Review." *The International Indigenous Policy Journal* 8 (2). doi:10.18584/iipj.2017.8.2.5.

Edosomwan, Simeon, Sitalaskshmi Kalangot Prakasan, Doriane Kouame, Jonelle Watson, and Tom Seymour. 2011. "The History of Social Media and Its Impact on Business." *The Journal of Applied Management and Entrepreneurship* 16 (3): 79–91.

Ermine, Willie. 1995. "Aboriginal Epistemology." In *First Nation Education in Canada: The Circle Unfolds*, edited by Marie Battiste and Jean Barman. UBC Press.

———. 2007. "Ethical Space of Engagement." *Indigenous Law Journal* 6 (1): 193–203.

Hart, Michael A. 2010. "Indigenous Worldviews, Knowledge, and Research: The Development of an Indigenous Research Paradigm." *Journal of Indigenous Voices in Social Work* 6 (1): 1–16.

Hungry Wolf, Beverly. 1982. *The Ways of My Grandmothers*. 1st ed. Quill.

Lindstrom, Gabrielle. 2018. "Trauma and Resilience in Aboriginal Adult Learners' Post-Secondary Experience." Unpublished doctoral dissertation, University of Calgary.

Lindstrom, Gabrielle, Sofia Baptiste, and Sierra Shade. 2021. "'Mokakit Iyikakimaat': Autoethnographic Reflections as Movement towards a Pedagogy of Resilience." In *Brave Work in Indigenous Education*, edited by Jennifer Markides and Jennifer MacDonald, 1–17.

Littlebear, Leroy. 2000. "Jagged Worldviews Colliding." In *Reclaiming Indigenous Voice and Vision*, edited by Marie Battiste, 77–85. UBC Press.

Mezirow, Jack. 1978. Education for Perspective Transformation: Women's Re-Entry Programs in Community Colleges. Columbia University Press.

Poitras Pratt, Yvonne. 2020. *Digital Storytelling in Indigenous Education: A Decolonizing Journey for a Métis Community*. Routledge.

"Reclaiming Power and Place: The Final Report of the National Inquiry into Missing and Murdered Indigenous Women and Girls." 2020. National Inquiry into Missing and Murdered Indigenous Women and Girls. www.mmiwg-ffada.ca/wp-content/uploads/2019/06/Final_Report_Vol_1a-1.pdf.

Semali, Ladislaus, and Joe L. Kincheloe, eds. 1999. *What Is Indigenous Knowledge? Voices from the Academy*. Falmer Press.

Simpson, Leanne. 2008. "Looking after Gdoo-Naaganinaa: Precolonial Nishnaabeg Diplomatic and Treaty Relationships." *Wicazo Sa Review* 23 (2): 29–42. doi:10.1353/wic.0.0001.

Smith, Linda Tuhiwai. 1999. *Decolonizing Methodologies*. Zed Books.

Steeves, Catherine. 2015. "Digital Technologies and Indigenous Knowledge." blogs.ubc.ca/steevesc/files/2015/06/Digital-Technology-and-Indigenous-Knowledge.pdf.

Stewart-Harawira, Makere. 2018. "Indigenous Resilience and Pedagogies of Resistance: Responding to the Crisis of Our Age." *SSRN Electronic Journal*. doi:10.2139/ssrn.3185625.

Taylor, Edward W. 2008. "Transformative Learning Theory." In *Third Update on Adult Learning Theory*, edited by Sharan B. Merriam, Jossey-Bass, 5–15.

Wall, Sarah. 2008. "Easier Said than Done: Writing an Autoethnography." *International Journal of Qualitative Methods* 7 (1): 38–51.

Wemigwans, Jennifer. 2016. "A Digital Bundle: Exploring the Impact of Indigenous Knowledge Online Through FourDirectionsTeachings.Com." University of Toronto. ProQuest Dissertations Publishing.

Whitinui, Paul. 2014. "Indigenous Autoethnography: Exploring, Engaging, and Experiencing 'Self' as a Native Method of Inquiry." *Journal of Contemporary Ethnography* 43 (4): 456–87.

Wilson, Shawn. 2008. *Research Is Ceremony: Indigenous Research Methods*. Fernwood.

Chapter 3

#SayHerNameNigeria

Nigerian Feminists Resist Police Sexual Violence on Women's Bodies

Ololade Faniyi, Angel Nduka-Nwosu, and Radhika Gajjala

The 2010s presented a significant increase in feminist agitations, organizing, and protest groundwork against the state in Nigeria, just as women capitalized on the affective structures of social media to move their grievances from the margins to the middle of the internet. From #BringBackOurGirls to several #JusticeFor protests decrying rape, sexual assault, and violence against women, the discursive political and ideological function of Twitter hashtags has been centered as women engage with the rhetorical agency of hashtags to highlight their experiences and challenge violence against women's bodies. Within this context, we point to April 27, 2019, when members of the Abuja police force division and officials of the Abuja Environmental Protection Board (AEPB) raided nightclubs in the Nigerian capital, arresting up to seventy women and detaining, beating, and forcibly demanding sex for bail. #SayHerNameNigeria, alongside #AbujaPoliceRaidOnWomen, emerged as hashtags, drawing attention to narratives of how police brutality impacts women on the margins in Nigeria and growing concerns of extreme policing and impunity in the country. Across emergent digital protests in Nigeria, women have been at the forefront, dedicating their efforts as amplifiers, advocates, organizers, and funders of ensuing on-site protests. Rooting these efforts in feminist rage, collective action, radical care, and transnational feminist crossings (see Cooper 2020; Chemaly 2020; Faniyi and Omotoso 2022; Mohanty 2013), young feminists and human rights defenders in Nigeria have especially framed the current wave of contemporary feminist activism in Nigeria within the last decade.

Given this background, in this chapter, we examine the creation and spread of #SayHerNameNigeria, which produced online visibility for ground protests across some Nigerian and Ghanian cities, Lagos, Abuja, Ibadan, and Accra, and London, UK, denouncing the rape and harassment of women in police custody in Nigeria's capital. As feminist researchers, we consider the transnational feminist links of this hashtag movement to the United States' #SayHerName movement by examining its intersectional coverage. Likewise, as this hashtag movement was precipitated by feminized violence perpetrated by male state actors, we examine the sociopolitical conditions that made this hashtag movement pivotal for young Nigerian feminist activism in a period markedly defined by the visibility of hashtag activism. In particular, we look at Twitter as our focal data medium because it was the primary site of the #SayHerNameNigeria movement.

Therefore, in this article, we map how the mediated visibility of protests against police brutality targeted at female bodies in Nigeria are produced through Twitter publics, especially how and what these tell us about Nigerian feminist organizing and transnational crossings. We demonstrate our methodological strengths of bridging digital quantitative data and humanities theorizing in ways that map these tweets into networks while highlighting the labor undertaken by activists. Relying on the availability of Twitter Developer Access and Python script for collecting historical data, we show how social network analyzing and visualization tools like Gephi allow us to scrape and work through thousands of tweets to reveal actors and the connections between them as they narrate both online and offline events. Our mixed methods include a close feminist reading of Twitter network analytics and tweet texts and an in-depth interview with the creator of the hashtag #SayHerNameNigeria, feminist activist and journalist Angel Nduka-Nwosu. Beyond the interview, we asked Angel to speak to this network in which she appeared as a node (people involved in the networked activity) to tell us about her motivations, the success or otherwise of the hashtag movement, and her reflections years after this hashtag movement. Our inclusion of Angel's voice in this paper, as well as the examples of tweets we included in our analysis, signals our approach to not just amplify activists' storytelling and rhetorical agency but also to see them as legitimate researchers in their own right whose labor must not be exploited or undermined.

As feminist digital humanities researchers, our interest is to shed light on hashtag networks emerging from subaltern locations that enact affective circulations, crossings, and coalitions through social media. To do this, our research seeks to establish a balance that authentically represents hashtag creators/activists and establishes our own positionalities. We build on observations by Jackson, Bailey, and Foucault-Welles (2020) and Sobande (2020) in the context of Black women and other women of color using digital tools (the power of the hashtag) to amplify often sidelined experiences, as well as the former's precedent in examining networked and visualized Twitter data. Our theoretical model draws on intersectional approaches underpinned by the African feminist framework of Stiwanism in exploring the interstices of gender, age, culture, location, ability, class, and digital capital as it informs women's resistance to police violence in Nigeria. Our definition of digital capital relies on Anderson and Grace (2015), who explore the work of feminists whose social capital is defined by digital and critical fluencies, that is, their ability to engage academically and policy-rooted feminist concerns such as #SayHerName, as well as their ability to use digital media to frontier the struggles for women's rights.

NIGERIAN FEMINISM MOVES ONLINE: RAGE, ONLINE COMMUNITY MANAGEMENT, AND COUNTERPUBLICS

In the last decade, feminist activism in Nigeria has taken the form of more unapologetic social movements; hashtag activism; and protests against rape and assault, police brutality, LGBT+ discrimination, school shootings, kidnappings, misogynist and oligarchical governance, and more. Hashtags such as #BringBackOurGirls, #MarketMarch, #SayHerNameNigeria, and several #JusticeFor campaigns have emerged from feminist counterpublics, and these series of protests mentioned above indicate how women across generations, especially young African women utilizing their digital capital, are moving from whisper networks to the streets and the middle of the internet and refusing disrespect and oppression. As the American feminist activist of Nigerian descent, Ijeoma Oluo (2018) maintains, "If you wanted to avoid our rage, maybe you shouldn't have left us with so little to lose" (para. 11). Rage and the unrelenting efforts to get the mainstream publics to listen to, believe, and stand with women have defined the phenomenon of contemporary Nigerian feminist activism. As Brittany Cooper (2018) argues, in the context of the United States, too many Black men have ignored the fight for Black women's lives, "citing lack of interest, lack of urgency, or dogma" (65). Thus, the lack of politics that centers Nigerian women has resulted in an existential reality of women being victims of police violence, kidnappings, terror, ethnoreligious violence, and more.

The kidnapping of over 250 girls by the terrorist group Boko Haram on April 14, 2013, sparked the movement #BringBackOurGirls, cofounded by the former Nigerian Minister of Education Oby Ezekwesili and Nigerian

Muslim activist Aisha Yesufu, and established the first wave of transnational feminist crossings with hashtags emerging from Nigeria. However, this first wave resulted in a series of posture solidarities and feminist appropriations (Maxfield 2015) with Western women, including First Lady Michelle Obama, holding cardboard signs upon which the hashtag was written, and other women rocking a gele (traditional Nigerian hair tie) for our girls. At the same time, it established the beginnings of Nigerian feminists using hashtags to insist on retrieving these girls and prevent the erasure of Northern Nigerian schoolgirls who were victims of terrorist kidnappings. Eight years after, many of these girls are still at large, with several raped, impregnated, and forced into servitude. The cross-connections of groundwork offline and online have led to not just protest actions but also other reactionary forms of resistance. For instance, over a hundred women joined the formerly all-male Civilian Joint Taskforce (C-JTF) to patrol the Sambisa Forest, notoriously known as the den of the terrorists, even with threats of death and societal mockery. Others choose to operate solo, like Aisha Bakari Gombi, dubbed the Boko Haram Huntress, to thwart the actions of these terrorists, reappropriating the outfits and weapons the terrorists have used to strike fear in civilians (see AlJazeera.com and Documentwomen.com).

As a feminist activist who has done groundwork in Nigeria, the first author has been implicated in the workings of Twitter hashtags, just as she has been watching how they promote young feminist storytelling and labor involved in the series of protests against rape and sexual assault in Nigeria from 2018 to the present, including #WWNBS (We Will Not Be Silent), #SayHerNameNigeria, #StateOfEmergencyGBV (Gender-Based Violence), #ChurchToo, #MarketMarch, and #WARN (War Against Rape Nigeria). These hashtags attest to the work of Nigeria's feminist counterpublic doing feminist labor online and producing visibility for their offline organizing. As Axel Burns and Jean Burgess (2015) argue, Twitter hashtags have been means of coordinating publics, that is, discursive networks "being formed, re-formed, and coordinated via dynamic networks of communication and social connectivity organized primarily around issues or events rather than pre-existing social groups" (13). The complexities of the hashtag have especially influenced calculated "performative" publics, drawing particular attention to the contours around the usage of different hashtags, the immediacy or other-wise of the consensus that led to its emergence, the debates around its usage, as well as the emergence of competing publics with different hashtags (14).

Lisa Nakamura's (2015) article, "The Unwanted Labour of Social Media: Women of Colour Call Out Culture as Venture Community Management," compels us to look closely at the creation of these calculated performative publics to identify feminist labor within the digital economy of social media as a significant engine that powers the internet. With their unpaid, often unappreciated, labor, feminist activists have assumed the roles of online community managers who must moderate sexist discrimination online and offline (106). Despite the consistent push against this feminist labor in Nigeria, there is an inherent "desire for debate and willingness to affront" (Brock 2020, 220). To that end, feminist networked activity and online community management have established active and interacting counterpublics online as spaces of counter-discourses that almost eventually leak to the middle of the internet, especially when amplified by the discursive logic of the hashtag.

In exploring hashtag movements, Jackson, Bailey, and Foucault-Welles (2020) address how hashtags amplify the digital labor of feminist, racial, trans, and allied counterpublics from the margins to the middle of the internet. With often overwhelming narratives that exclude Black people, women, trans and queer people, and everyone between, and which threaten to present cis-heteropatriarchy as the dominant internet identity, these othered identities repurpose Twitter as a space for counternarratives and culturally mediated discourses on issues affecting them that are otherwise absent in elite media spaces. Hashtags thus become the lingua franca of networked activities from these counterpublics, from #MeToo to #BlackLivesMatter, #SayHerName, #YesAllMen, and several others across interacting feminist publics online. Across contexts, these hashtags have introduced otherwise complex concepts of intersectionality into accessible conversations online, expanding the utility, scope, and visibility of feminist discourse.

INTERSECTIONALITY AND FEMINISM IN NIGERIA

Since 1989, Kimberlé Crenshaw's intersectionality has been a foundational Black feminist and legal text that draws on early arguments of Black women activists, including Sojourner Truth, Anna Julia Cooper, and the women of the Combahee River Collective. In *Mapping the Margins: Intersectionality, Identity Politics, and Violence against Women of Color*, Crenshaw (1990) argues that the experiences of Black women were not limited to "traditional boundaries of race or gender discrimination" and thus addressing gender or race as factors determining a Black woman's fate in isolated and individual ways could not wholly capture their experiences. Intersectionality as a critical theory thus becomes central to studying the multifaceted nature of inequalities, power, and difference, as it affects the "almost routine violence" that shapes Black women's lives (Crenshaw 1990; Collins 2015; Yuval-Davis 2015). At its core, this pivotal theory investigates the intersecting forces of race, class, gender, sexuality, ethnicity, nation, ability, and age (Crenshaw 1990; Collins 2002). However, as Yuval-Davis (2015) argues, intersectionality is more appropriately defined as a range of theoretical and conceptual tools rather than a unified theory, as intersectional standpoint manifests in non-linear ways. For the young Nigerian feminist, for instance, intersectionality must consider not only the factors above but also colonialism and neocolonialism, colorism, self-repression, cultural and traditional subjugation, and underdevelopment (Ogundipe 1994). With intersectionality's strength lying in its "attentiveness to power relations and social inequalities" (Collins 2015), it illuminates these reciprocally constructing phenomena that shape violence targeted at female bodies by mapping its overt and covert manifestations.

As the hashtag creator of #SayHerNameNigeria, Angel Nduka-Nwosu, confirms during our in-depth interview, there were some reservations from some other feminist collaborators regarding the use of "SayHerName" as a prefix for the Nigerian protests against police brutality on women's bodies. Hence, the sister descriptive hashtag #AbujaPoliceRaidOnWomen was used alongside #SayHerNameNigeria, confirming patterns we had noticed as we worked through the datasets we collected. However, Angel, who had encountered a TED Talk by Kimberlé Crenshaw on #SayHerName as a core vision of Black feminist resistance (see Angel's reflections in Table 1), was insistent on amplifying #SayHerNameNigeria as a focal hashtag to connect with the transnational legibility of feminized police violence and the feminist solidarity it motivated.

Our analysis is thus informed by internationally legible feminist arguments and a critical Nigerian feminist standpoint, and our model of intersectionality draws on Crenshaw, Collins, and Molara Ogundipe's Stiwanism (Social Transformation in Africa Including Women), which maintains that Nigerian women's experiences are shaped by interacting metaphorical mountains of "Oppression from outside; traditional structures; her backwardness; man; her colour and race; and herself" (228). Molara Ogundipe, writing in 1994 when African feminist submissions were embattled by claims of imitation from Western frameworks, argued: "I have since advocated the word 'Stiwanism,' instead of feminism, to bypass the combative discourses that ensue whenever one raises the issue of feminism in Africa" (229). However, this chapter is unabashed in its use of intersectionality and feminist claims as it describes its theoretical stance and the politics of young feminist activism in Nigeria. Feminist lenses turned toward the creation and labor that defined #SayHerNameNigeria must consider multiple inequalities affecting feminist work even as activists resist attempts to make the labor of young feminist activists invisible.

METHODS

The methods guiding our work are interdisciplinary, following the precedent set by scholars such as Jackson, Bailey, and Foucault-Welles (2020), who maintain their arguments on the significance of capturing online publics into networked data to identify how hashtags (otherwise machine-to-machine talk) produce and distribute affective flows (Papacharissi 2015) and amplify the digital labor of feminist activists. Our methods include an in-depth interview with the hashtag's creator, Angel Nduka-Nwosu, and a close feminist reading of Twitter data. Since this data is "historical"—that is, we did not collect it live but collected it after the active period of offline events surrounding #SayHernameNigeria in April and May of 2019—we used a Python script along with academic Twitter developer Application Programming Interface (API) permissions. The script we used came to us from Bryan Tarpley at the Center of Digital Humanities Research at Texas A&M University, and we got the data into formats as a .json file, which we converted for reading convenience to .csv using https://data.page. We also networked the users' hashtags by using the data converted to Gephi nodes (the people in the network) and edges (the connections between them) files and uploading them to Gephi for analysis while locating their original tweet texts from the .json files for a closer look.

Although our work would have benefited further from interviews with other activists via snowballing sampling, we encountered complaints of fatigue, burnout, and trauma from those we reached out to. Following the events of Nigeria's 2018–2020 series of feminist protests and the #EndSARS movement, driven in good part by rage and feminist physical, online, and financial labor, we were quick to acknowledge their request to withdraw their consent. We also recognize that radical care manifests in many forms (Faniyi and Omotoso 2020), including taking some time away from hypervisibility provoked by feminist labor and storytelling. Our approach further identified Angel Nduka-Nwosu as a legitimate collaborator and second author in this article. Our work principles regarding informed consent, anonymity, and confidentiality rely on the third author's Bowling Green State University's Institutional Review Board's digital activism permission, under which the first author has also been trained.

We started by scraping from what we knew to be periods of significance based on the first and second authors' involvement as activists between April and June 2019. In this article, the third author's role was mainly to work with the online data and with the first author in connecting themes with offline activity and with the larger body of scholarly work around issues of feminist hashtag activism. In working with Twitter data, that is, using the Twitter developer account access to the API, we focused on the hashtag dataset of #SayHerNameNigeria, before moving on to #AbujaPoliceRaidOnWomen. We, therefore, started by scraping #SayHerNameNigeria between the dates April 1, 2019, and June 30, 2019. We then broke up the data into smaller sections in order to import it to Gephi and observe the networks visually between April 1 to April 15, 2019, and then April 30 to May 15, 2019. After that, we scraped #SayHerName to see how the transnational linking to #SayHerNameNigeria may have played out on Twitter. Again, we did this in smaller batches to see how the feminist connection of the hashtag may have played out between April 2019 and the highlight of the #EndSARS movement, Nigeria's mass struggle against police brutality, in October 2020. We scraped hourly from April 17–18, 2022 and found that #SayHerNameNigeria had been used 74,059 times between April 2019 and December 2020. This identification of patterns thus formed the beginning of our analysis as we interpreted the meanings that the nodes and clusters offered us using an intersectional lens.

#SAYHERNAMENIGERIA: CHALLENGING POLICE SEXUAL VIOLENCE

On April 28, 2019, Nigerian policemen and officials of the Abuja Environmental Protection Board (AEPB) arrested seventy women, beating and raping them with plastic sachet water bags. These women were assaulted on the grounds of prostitution, and the job of the AEPB, who had police cover to embark on their duty, was illegitimately expanded beyond being a "service-oriented organization saddled with the responsibility of evacuation of waste, maintenance of sewer lines, preservation of biological diversity, fumigation and vector control services" within the Nigerian capital (BPE. GOV.NG). This detestable act by Nigerian policemen reinforced arguments on how women in Nigeria are viewed and treated as second-tier citizens. The policemen who performed the horrendous hate crime of corrective rape in punishing these women wear the faces of double enemies—as men and as state-constituted actors—oppressing and selfishly sustaining an existential inferiority of women. The Nigerian woman's society, nation, continent, and location thus work reciprocally to oppress and police her body and choices (Ogundipe 1994).

With the news of this extreme discrimination against these women breaking in the next couple of days, online outcries emerged from feminist publics. Their outcries highlighted the distinctly gendered ways in which women in Nigeria have been targeted by the police, especially as conversations starting in late 2017 primarily centered the social profiling and brutal policing of young men by the police division Special Anti-Robbery Squad (SARS), in what constituted police brutality in Nigeria. In response, Angel Nduka-Nwosu tweeted on her organization's page @AsEqualsAfrica on April 29, 2019: "Since it has become obvious that #EndSARS and other anti–police brutality movements in Nigeria do not care about women victims, we at As Equals Africa are demanding justice for Nigerian women victims of police brutality by ourselves. That is why we should #SayHerNameNigeria."

In the days that followed, feminists from the collectives Stand to End Rape Nigeria, We Will Not Be Silent Nigeria, Through the Eyes of an African Woman, As Equals Africa, and Market March formed a coalition centered on #SayHerNameNigeria, using a WhatsApp group, which we learned from an interview with Angel on April 23, 2022, to organize the online production of visibility for the hashtag and offline protests in Accra, Ghana, London, and the Nigerian cities of Abuja, Lagos, and Ibadan. On May 2, 2019, @marketmarch shared a tweet establishing the visibility of this coalition in networked archives: "In light of the recent raids in Abuja, we're working with @StandtoEndRape @WWNBSNigeria @TeawAfrica @AsEqualsAfrica to organize protests against police violence specifically against women. Join us this Saturday in Abuja or Lagos & next Saturday in Accra! #SayHerNameNigeria."

Confirming this activity, we noticed a considerable amplification of the hashtag beginning on May 4, 2019, the first day of the protests. The hashtag with the second-highest frequency in our datasets was #AbujaPoliceRaidOnWomen, which began a sister hashtag to #SayHerNameNigeria based on some users' reluctance to co-opt the Black feminist naming strategy of the latter. However, several users used both hashtags in their tweet texts. In this dataset, user @ mizzaina, who describes herself as a defender of womanhood and whose bio reads "feminism| corporate communications| reluctantly adulting| sdg5|," had the highest frequency. Her most retweeted tweet contained both hashtags and shared a video recording of Nigerian Muslim activist and cofounder of #BringBackOurGirls, Aisha Yesufu, on-site at the Abuja protests on May 4, 2019. In the video, Aisha Yesufu holds a cardboard sign on which was written #SayHerName, as she vehemently spoke to a hailing crowd: "I have a choice to wear whatever, I have the right to wear a hijab, another has the right to wear mini, and another has the right not to wear anything at all. It is a fundamental human right. You do not have the right to label a woman prostitute because of what she wears. The fact that we are women does not make us subhuman."

On April 24, 2022, the third author began building an "Angel Nduka-Nwosu" network from a Twitter data search for Angel from May 2019 to show the network of tweet texts and who cross-referenced whom. In the image below, we show that Angel Nduka-Nwosu, username @asangelwassayin, was the

REFLECTIONS ON CREATING
#SAYHERNAMENIGERIA

Angel Nduka-Nwosu

The first time I vividly recall feeling a sense of solidarity over the experiences of Black women at the hands of the police came from YouTube.
It was a video of African American feminist Kimberlé Crenshaw offering a TED Talk on the ways in which Black women in America often
had their stories of brutality with the police ignored, especially during
the use of hashtags to raise awareness on social media.

It was not the first time I was hearing of #SayHerName, intersectionality, and BlackLivesMatter. America's cultural power makes it
almost impossible to ignore trends used in its social justice movements
even as a Nigerian woman living in Nigeria. I was moved deeply by
a slideshow of murdered Black women which Ms. Crenshaw gave at
the end of the talk. In a strange way, her words hit a nerve for me and
reminded me of how women the world over are unsafe from the very
structures sworn to protect us.

This realization became stronger in April 2019 when reports came
in that policemen from the Abuja Environmental Protection Board had
arrested seventy women in a lounge using the excuse that they were
"prostitutes." These men told the women to either pay five thousand
naira or accept rape. It was also said that the police went ahead to rape
some women using sachet water nylons as makeshift condoms.

Now, compared to the stories of men harassed by another branch of
the Nigerian police called SARS, I noticed that there wasn't as much
outrage online for the women who had been raped by the Nigerian
Police and AEPB officials. In thinking of a hashtag that could totally
capture this realization of online double standards, my mind kept going
back to Kimberlé Crenshaw's TED Talk.

I decided then that I would name the hashtag #SayHerNameNigeria.
It was to draw solidarity from the already existing framework of
#SayHerName while still asserting our place as Nigerian women in the
conversation of global gendered police brutality. We ended up protesting in four Nigerian cities and in Ghana and England.

During the October 2020 protests against SARS, one question that
kept popping in my mind was: "Why didn't #SayHerNameNigeria
cause a nationwide and global revolution even from women?" I got

immensely attacked for stating my discomfort with feminist participation in a cause whose victories would have done nothing for women structurally. This is because SARS attacks mostly young men due to the prevailing belief that young men are more likely to engage in cybercriminal fraud.

Although SARS does attack women in minute numbers, their rapes and deaths are barely enough to cause the global revolution that was October 2020. Most times, even female victims of SARS brutality face slut shaming from the very men who protest online against SARS.

I have mentioned the #EndSARS protests in this detail, because it is impossible to talk about the gendered dynamics of #SayHerNameNigeria without mentioning #EndSARS, especially as it taught women to not ignore gender. In the months following the #EndSARS protests, feminist groups like Feminist Coalition and other notable women who offered legal aid have been insulted and called thieves and liars, even by the men who praised them for spearheading the protests.

I like to think that in the Nigerian context, #EndSARS is the equivalent of #BlackLives Matter. It is the hashtag that taught Nigerian women never to imagine that fighting side by side with men will guarantee that their own rights will be attended to.

During the #EndSARS protests, when I was being attacked online for stating my discomfort, I held on to the words of leading feminist writer Mona Eltahawy. She said and, I shall quote to conclude this essay, "Who is the revolution for? Who is your fight as a woman in service of?"

In all things in and out of police brutality, my fight remains in service of the needs of Nigerian women and girls first.

most networked user with the highest node frequency of 12, and @asangelwassayin has a strong connection to the hashtag "SayHerNameNigeria" that appeared in this particular dataset nine times.

Looking at the data we collected around #SayHerNameNigeria between April 30, 2019, and May 15, 2019, in collaboration with our focal interview with Angel, we confirmed the deliberate attempt to co-opt the strategy, publicness, and intersectional coverage of #SayHerName to draw attention to women's experiences of police sexual violence and how it defines what constitutes police violence in Nigeria. As Angel shares, the extension of offline protest coverage to Accra and London was primarily motivated by a commitment to feminist sisterhood and solidarity, as members of the affiliated groups come from all over the continent, and some lived, schooled, or

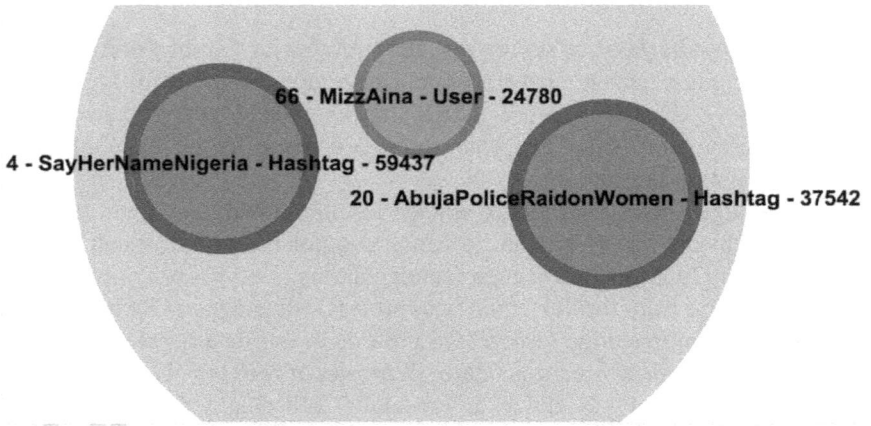

Figure 3.1. Image showing the top frequency in users and hashtags on the first day of the protests, May 4, 2019. *#SayHerNameNigeria project. Created by Ololade Faniyi and Radhika Gajjala.*

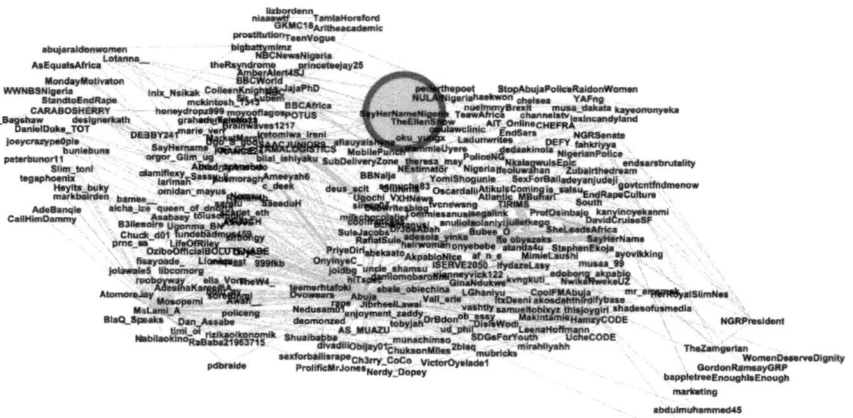

Figure 3.2. Data scraped between May 1 and May 15, 2019 to locate the day when #SayHerNameNigeria began being amplified (#SayHerNameNigeria has the largest node ranking in this image). *#SayHerNameNigeria project. Created by Ololade Faniyi and Radhika Gajjala.*

worked in London. After we scraped #SayHerNameNigeria to see how the transnational/global linking may have played out on Twitter, we found that, beyond the simultaneous series of protests in Accra and London, there were no transnational actors in the dataset collected between April 30 and May 15, 2019, who made explicit solidarity crossings between #SayHerName

monaeltahawy - 1
theslumflower - 1
kehinde_bb - 1
CynnerR - 1   your_stepdad - 1
kikimordi - 1   Chivie___ - 2 SayHerNameNigeria - 9
lazzarinrita - 1
connybush - 1   asangelwassayin - 12
ElegantSavant - 1   Bubee_O - 2
MurderGeeWrote - 1 Chigozielsu - 1
Nigeria - 11 ZuWilliams_ - 1
thebukunmi - 1
womyn_witch - 1

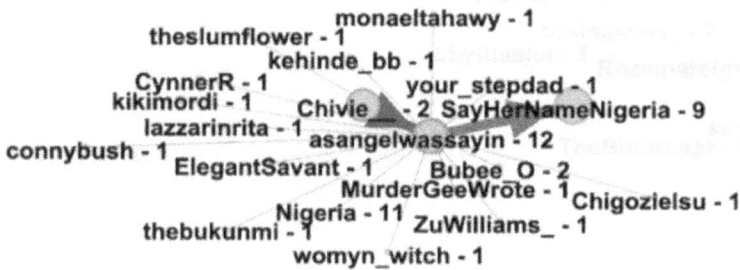

Figure 3.3. Image showing Angel's node frequency and connection to other nodes and #SayHerNameNigeria between April 30 and May 15, 2019. *#SayHerNameNigeria project. Created by Ololade Faniyi and Radhika Gajjala.*

and #SayHerNameNigeria in ways similar to the global #MeToo wave, for instance. This was unlike #EndSARS, the Nigerian hashtag movement protesting police brutality mainly targeted at young men, which drew multiple transnational solidarities in October 2020 from actors like former Twitter CEO Jack Dorsey and Congressmen Al Green and Joaquin Castro. User @ lanaire_aderemi, a Nigerian feminist residing in London, shared a tweet that pointed to this crossing: "love how transnational feminist movements are. Interesting that Crenshaw's #sayhername is deployed in Nigeria via #sayhernamenigeria. We know naming is important, it is not new, but it gives me so much joy knowing that our feminism(s) have gone beyond borders, and we are resisting."

A relatively academically rooted hashtag created by critical race theorist Kimberlé Crenshaw, #SayHerName focused on Black women and girls' experiences of police brutality and other state and communal violence. It became a memorial site for female victims of police officers like Rekia Boyd (Jackson, Bailey, and Foucault-Welles 2020). #SayHerName also evolved to amplify the stories of women of color, including LGBTQIA+ and nonbinary Black people. Amid the Black Lives Matter Movement, #SayHerName's ideological connection with the movement drew attention to the ambiguity surrounding the death of Black women like Sandra Bland, with a series of tweets resulting in what Jackson, Bailey, and Foucault-Welles (2020) referred to as the "hashtagified" name. In this way, #SayHerName reflected a radical politics of intersectionality connecting with #BLM, #MeToo, and #BlackTransLivesMatter. #SayHerName, by eulogizing and demanding visibility for Black women and girls, also embodied integration of offline and online activism, driving rhetoric of academic thought, politics, protest events, and more.

Like the US phenomenon, women in Nigeria experience police violence in particularly gendered ways, with their bodies and resources exploited while being subjected to sex for bail, forced undressing, rape, beatings, verbal abuse, slut shaming, and corruption. Even while connecting their outrage to an internationally legible intersectional movement, Nigerian feminists did not achieve the international visibility that came with #EndSARS. Thus, the question remains: "Why is the rape and harassment of women by the police not addressed in wider publics as constituting police brutality in Nigeria?" We argue that this is reflective of concerted patriarchal attempts to make invisible the labor of women in activist movements and a refusal to amplify movements that do not center Nigerian men. #EndSARS was an inevitable mass response to years of police violence and impunity that, because of its uniqueness, size, and organizing, drew transnational attention, social media rubber stamp hierarchies, and celebrity interventions. However, the affective exclusion of women's concerns problematizes the movement, especially the narcissism of male actors who insist on being viewed solely as the most vulnerable entities within the movement.

As Angel relates, Nigerian feminist activists used the hashtag #SayHerNameNigeria to center and legitimize their experiences and grievances, challenging unequal traditions underpinned by patriarchy that has long normalized this violence on women's bodies and sidelined their quest for justice. We must therefore emphasize in our archives that #SayHerNameNigeria marked Nigeria's unprecedented groundwork and first young feminist coalition against police brutality. #SayHerNameNigeria laid the models for a reflective politics of intersectionality in calling out police brutality, which spilled over into the October 2020 #EndSARS movement. However, the latter's primary attention to the experiences of Nigerian men resisted this refocusing of public attention and outrage.

SEEKING JUSTICE WITH #SAYHERNAMENIGERIA

It would not be until over two years after that some semblance of justice would be attained for the victims of the police and Abuja Environmental Protection Board's assault. In August 2021, the Federal High Court in Abuja held that the arrests and assaults violated women's rights and ordered the payment of 2–4 million naira ($4,819–$9,629) to six survivors. The court further ruled that the actions of the Abuja Environmental Protection Board exceeded its scope and issued an injunction restraining the police and other state-constituted bodies from arresting women in gender-discriminatory ways. While this was a welcome and necessary enactment of justice, little to no significant political and cultural changes have molded a broader picture of police violence.

Angel recounts that her concerns for a necessary refocusing of attention to the impacts of police brutality on women and queer folks were met with online vitriol and accusations of "distracting people from the main issue," that is, police violence on cis-het male bodies. The goals of #EndSARS as Nigeria's mass movement against police brutality, she says, have done nothing in the grand scheme for women and queer people. As we worked through our data, it was also clear that the push for this affective inclusion in the 74,059 times #SayHerNameNigeria had been used between April 2019 and December 2020 resided primarily in feminist counterpublics and was enacted by users who made up core feminist and queer networked assemblies, especially users and groups from the affiliated #SayHerNameNigeria coalition who had strong connections to the hashtag.

In addition, the culturally sanctioned approval given to Nigerian men to label women as prostitutes remains an issue yet to be rectified. Just as women are at risk of corrective rape, beatings, and other forms of humiliating punishments from state and non-state male actors in Nigeria on the grounds of contextually answerable inappropriate dressing and nightclubbing, women who dare to speak against gender discrimination and affirm their feminist dissent are liberally labeled prostitutes. This phenomenon played out in the vitriol against Nigerian feminists, particularly women of the collective Feminist Coalition, during #EndSARS in October 2020, when they remixed the affective flows of the hashtag movement to include police violence against women and queer bodies. In reaction to this derisive naming, conjured to undermine the power and force of raging, vocal, and visible women, Nigerian feminists have reclaimed the word "prostitute" or, in Nigerian parlance, "Ashawo or Olosho (Hoelosho)" as terms signaling their embodiments of power and freedom. This act is reminiscent of Kristin Sollee's (2017) argument about how the naming act of the "witch-slut-feminist trifecta" reveals the terror of the patriarchy as women affirm their choices and rights. Aisha Yesufu, activist and cofounder of #BringBackOurGirls, summarily addressed this at the #SayHerNameNigeria protest site in Abuja on May 4, 2019, "We are called prostitutes, our mothers, our grandmothers. The moment you have a voice, you are called prostitute. If having a voice means I am a prostitute, then that is what I am."

While #SayHerNameNigeria reminds us of the yet-to-be-filled gaps in the attention given to women's experiences of police brutality amid other forms of violence in Nigeria, it nonetheless became the site of listening, believing, trusting, naming, and making visible the women who became victims and survivors of violence and a heritage site of young Nigerian feminist resistance against the police and the state on their own terms. By making accessible and visible naming with intersectional intent in Nigerian Twitter publics, the hashtag movement and offline activism amplified the storytelling agency of Nigerian women, as it insistently drove attention to the often-taken-for-granted violent events reciprocally shaping their lives.

REFERENCES

Anderson, Wendy K. Z., and Kittie E. Grace. 2015. "'Taking Mama Steps' Toward Authority, Alternatives, and Advocacy: Feminist Consciousness-Raising Within a Digital Motherhood Community." *Feminist Media Studies* 15 (6): 942–59.

Brock, André. 2020. *Distributed Blackness*. New York University Press.

Burns, Axel, and Jean Burgess. 2015. "Twitter Hashtags from AdHoc to Calculated Publics" *Hashtag Publics: The Power and Politics of Discursive Networks*, edited by Nathan Rambukkana. Peter Lang, pp. 13–27.

Chemaly, Soraya. 2018. *Rage Becomes Her*. Simon & Schuster.

Collins, Patricia Hill. 2002. *Black Feminist Thought: Knowledge, Consciousness, and the Politics of Empowerment*. Routledge.

———. 2015. "Intersectionality's Definitional Dilemmas." *Annual Review of Sociology* 41 (1): 1–20.

Cooper, Brittney. 2018. *Eloquent Rage: A Black Feminist Discovers Her Superpower*. St. Martin's Press.

Crenshaw, Kimberlé. 1990. "Mapping the Margins: Intersectionality, Identity Politics, and Violence against Women of Color." *Stan. L. Rev.* 43 (6): 1241–99.

Faniyi, Ololade, and Sharon Omotoso. 2022. "Young Feminists Redefining Principles of Care in Nigeria." *WSQ: Women's Studies Quarterly* 50 (1): 49–67.

Jackson, Sarah J., Moya Bailey, and Brooke Foucault Welles. 2020. *#HashtagActivism: Networks of Race and Gender Justice*. MIT Press.

Maxfield, Mary. 2016. "History Retweeting Itself: Imperial Feminist Appropriations of 'Bring Back Our Girls.'" *Feminist Media Studies* 16 (5): 886–900.

Mohanty, Chandra Talpade. 2013. "Transnational Feminist Crossings: On Neoliberalism and Radical Critique." *Signs: Journal of Women in Culture and Society* 38 (4): 967–91.

Nakamura, Lisa. 2015. "The Unwanted Labour of Social Media: Women of Colour Call Out Culture as Venture Community Management." *New Formations* 86 (86): 106–12.

Ogundipe-Leslie, Molara. 1994. *Re-creating Ourselves: African Women & Critical Transformations*. Africa World Press.

Oluo, Ijeoma. 2018. "Does This Year Make Me Look Angry?" *ELLE Magazine*. January 11, 2018. www.elle.com/culture/career-politics/a15063942/women-and-rage-2018/.

Papacharissi, Zizi. 2015. *Affective Publics: Sentiment, Technology, and Politics*. Oxford University Press.

Sollée, Krister J. 2017. *Witches, Sluts, Feminists: Conjuring the Sex Positive*. Stone Bridge Press, Inc.

Yuval-Davis, Nira. 2015. "Situated Intersectionality: A Reflection on Ange-Marie Hancock's Forthcoming Book: *Intersectionality—An Intellectual History*." *New Political Science* 37 (4): 637–42.

Chapter 4

Interfering with State Surveillance and Data Collection

Hacking the Affordance of "Identifiability" as Resistance on Social Media

Mina Momeni

During the past decade, grassroots movements have grown significantly, from the Occupy Wall Street (Castañeda 2012; Gleason 2013) and Black Lives Matter (Carney 2016; Mundt et al. 2018) movements in the United States, to the Arab Spring (Eltantawy & Wiest 2011; Wolfsfeld, Segev, and Sheafer 2013), and the Iranian Green Movement (Elson et al., 2012; Gaffney, 2010; Milani, 2010) in the Middle East. Crucially, what differentiates these newer movements from their precursors is the shift from traditional organization-led mobilizing to unofficial grassroots-led organizing (Bennett and Segerberg 2012). Digital technologies have been used by individuals during recent movements to make their voices heard, mobilize their actions, and connect them with broader communities. Particularly, Facebook (now Meta) and Twitter have been popular platforms for political activism and civic engagement. For instance, in different movements such as the Arab Spring, the Iranian Green Movement, and the Tunisian Revolution, Facebook, and Twitter allowed individuals to connect, share ideas, and mobilize on a large scale against their autocratic regimes. Individuals' use of social media has gone beyond casual socializing on these platforms. Despite all the privacy concerns and scandals, Facebook now operates with 2.37 billion monthly active users (Hutchinson 2019), with over 270 million users in India alone and the United States and Indonesia housing 190 million and 130 million users respectively (Statista 2019). Twitter has similarly grown, becoming one of the most popular microblogging platforms to date to serve over 126 million daily users (Shaban 2019), finding particular popularity in the United States with 48.65 million active users, Japan (36.7 million), and the United Kingdom (41.1 million) (Statista 2019).

There has been an ongoing debate among scholars about the role digital media technologies play in political engagement of citizens and the potential of these platforms to democratize online communication. The relationship between social networking sites and political involvement has been examined by digital and social media scholars for the last decade (e.g., Halpern and Gibbs 2013; Gleason 2013; Lawrence et al. 2014; Hayes et al. 2016). While some studies have indicated a potent and positive relationship between social media use and political engagement (Bode 2012; Carty 2015; Valenzuela, Park, and Kee 2009; Zhang, Seltzer, and Bichard 2013), others have demonstrated a weak connection, arguing that not many people rely on social media for political activities and that these platforms do not increase users' political involvement in remarkable ways (e.g., Baumgartner & Morris 2009; Dimitrova & Bystrom, 2013). Moreover, some argue that social networking sites aggravate political polarization, and the potential of the Internet and social media to democratize and empower is being overstated (Iosifidis 2011; Stroud 2010; Sunstein 2001). Within the context of digital activism, others argue that although social networks enable the circulation of activist work, they simultaneously preserve classism, misogyny, and white supremacy that must be addressed if we seek intersectional feminist activism (Wiens and MacDonald 2020).

Despite these considerations of social media and political movements in scholarly literature, there remains an important gap in our understanding about how the affordances of these platforms are being used to enhance civic involvement within different political contexts.

It is thus imperative to explore more closely and compare how users in dissimilar political contexts are employing the various potentials of social media platforms in their political activism. In this chapter, I argue that it is essential to explore more intently how users in varying locales and political situations are using and interacting with these platforms and employing their communicative features in practice—especially in societies where media and communications are severely under authorities' control. I suggest that it is undeniable that social networking sites wield the potential to affect political and societal change and that, without exaggerating the power of these platforms, it is imperative to explore their abilities to better comprehend the role that social media play in empowering or disempowering users in their political activism.

As such, this chapter considers the theory of affordances, a notion that has become well received in technology studies, to make sense of human communication with various technologies and can be used to explain how affordances make some activities achievable while constraining others. The theory of affordances was originally developed in the field of ecological psychology (Gibson 1979) and has since been adopted in the field of media and communication studies where it is commonly used to explain what objects and artifacts, such as media technologies, allow users to do (Halpern and Gibbs 2013; Gleason 2013; Lawrence, et al. 2014; Hayes et al. 2016; boyd 2010; Literat and Kligler-Vilenchik 2019). An affordance refers to the "mutuality of actor intentions and technology capabilities that provide the potential for a particular action" (Majchrzak et al. 2013, 39). To this definition, as danah boyd (2010) asserts, "the affordances and dynamics of networked publics can shed light on why people engage the way they do" (15). Because platforms utilize different affordances for a variety of ends, the field requires further study to conceptualize the affordances of social media platforms, particularly the affordances that can facilitate political activism of users and share their stories. Bringing these ideas together, this chapter suggests that affordances are a valuable framework for examining technologies that are user-centered in order to better understand the capabilities and limitations that social media has to offer to users in making their voices heard.

By focusing on the affordance of identifiability on Facebook and Twitter, this chapter explores how identifiability has been employed during the Green Movement in Iran. I look specifically toward the Green Movement because of the noteworthy role that Facebook and Twitter played in mobilizing and promoting this movement, as well as the momentous and empowering role that Iranian women took on in the movement. To explore identifiability in the Green Movement, I first offer an overview of the movement to illustrate the motivation behind the Green Movement and address certain controversies raised by scholars about the use of social media and its power during the movement. I then conceptualize the affordance of identifiability to clarify how this affordance plays a critical role in users' political activism on social media, before exploring how the affordance of identifiability has been employed by Iranian users, especially Iranian women, during the Green Movement. To support my analysis, I draw examples from the Facebook profiles of Iranian users, as well as tweets related to the discourse during the movement.

EXPLAINING THE GREEN MOVEMENT

The Green Movement was a political movement that occurred after the 2009 Iranian presidential election. Social media was employed by Iranian citizens, and especially by Iranian women, to bring attention to the Iranian regime's injustices. At that time, such a prolific use of social media astonished elites and drew the attention of scholars to the power of social networking sites. During the movement, protesters demanded the removal of President Mahmoud Ahmadinejad from office, since the leaders of the opposition, Mir Hossein Mousavi[1] and Mehdi Karroubi,[2] claimed that the election was fraudulent. Hundreds of the opposition's defenders demonstrated to express their discontentment about the election results. While the color green was primarily used as the symbol of Mir Hossein Mousavi's campaign, it became a universal symbol of unity and faith after the election.

Since the Iranian Revolution of 1978, the Iranian regime has been violating and disregarding women's rights. Nevertheless, women have resisted, and their participation has played an undeniably significant role in the Green Movement. According to Islamic rules, it is forbidden for a man to touch a woman if they are not close relatives. Therefore, during the demonstrations, women were marching in the front row to decrease the regime's guards' ability to arrest the protestors (Dabashi 2011). As Victoria Tahmasebi-Birgani (2010) notes, "Watching images and videos from these demonstrations, there was no doubt in anyone's mind that Iran's body politic was invaded by feminine power" (70). The Iranian regime was afraid of ideas that were against their rules and, thus, the government applied severe public restrictions and controlled all public spaces to limit any political activities that could give voices to their opponents. In response, Iranian women's online collective actions formed public opinions about the regime's intervention in the election and its brutality in suppressing demonstrators. As Michael Warner (2002) specifies, a public exists "by virtue of being addressed"; therefore, by addressing their issues, these women made their public known. Because Iranian women made the decision to participate in protests to address their concerns, Iranian women were no longer just a crowd, a group, or spectators: they were a public. Here, rather than Warner's concept of a counterpublic (the existence of a public in relationship to a larger dominant public), I use the language of a public to reclaim the identity that many Iranian women lost because of the government's anti-feminist approaches and rules since the Iranian Revolution in 1979. Many Iranian women were against the regime; however, they were not formally known to be a part of any public in Iranian society. As such, through making themselves known and through ensuring that their issues were acknowledged, Iranian women protesters became a public once again.

The Green Movement's major protest, held on June 15, 2009, drew around three million protestors in Tehran. This demonstration is notable for being one of the largest and most momentous anti-regime protests since the Iranian Revolution of 1978. Social media was extensively used to announce, promote, and mobilize the protest. Hundreds of the opposition's supporters, especially women, gathered to demonstrate their dissatisfaction about the election results. "Where Is My Vote" was written on handmade placards carried by demonstrators, and the slogan quickly trended on social media. Protestors, especially women, used social media as an effective organizing source to enhance the movement's political opportunities and reach supporters globally (Sohrabi-Haghighat and Mansouri 2010). The Green Movement persisted for around twenty months[3] and displayed the power of unity and, ultimately, of social media communication to the Iranian government.

In response to the rise of social media during the Green Movement in Iran, Andrew Sullivan (2009), who was renowned for his tweets about the Iran demonstrations, famously stated, "The revolution will be twittered." Similarly, Clay Shirky (2011) proclaimed in an interview, "This is it—the big one!" However, some scholars were skeptical about the importance of Twitter's role in the political upheaval in Iran. For instance, Golnaz Esfandiari (2010) wrote in *Foreign Policy* magazine that Western users generated larger numbers of Twitter posts about Iran's protests, and she asserted that bloggers like Sullivan misinterpreted the situation. Furthermore, Evgeny Morozov (2009) claims that many skeptics believe "it was just a myth, dreamed up and advanced by cyber-utopian Western commentators" (11). Devin Gaffney (2010) also expressed his concerns when he stated, "it is difficult to say with any certainty what the role of Twitter was." Their concerns raise questions around the degree to which social media truly played an influential role in the Green Movement.

To shed light on controversy about the "Twitter Revolution" in Iran, it is necessary to draw our attention to the way that social media's affordances function to perform an action as a whole. All platforms have some affordances that indicate the potentials of these platforms; by employing them, users can find or share information, connect, and communicate with each other, and eventually, in the case of social movements, increase political activism. For example, different affordances of Twitter, such as shareability and searchability, were used during the Green Movement by various users from different locations, which facilitated circulation of news relevant to the movement. Individuals used Twitter to first post information about the protests, such as images, news, and videos, and their activities increased citizen journalism inside the country. The Iranian diaspora correspondingly mobilized outside to spread this content and assisted in organizing more protests in different places. The act of users both inside and outside of the country enhanced awareness, demonstrating how these affordances collectively played an imperative role in the construction of networked publics.

In this case, the affordances of social media facilitated the collective action of users in this networked world, which is an imperative aspect of political activism—by connecting and coming together to circulate information about an issue, thereby amplifying it through making it publicly visible, users make their voices heard with the potential to draw international attention and support. Thus, suggesting that social media platforms were not influential in expanding the Green Movement because other social media users from different geographical locations also got involved and, with their collective action, boosted the movement, disregards the way that these platforms actually function.

THE AFFORDANCE OF IDENTIFIABILITY

There has been an ongoing debate between those who believe that one's real identity should be used on social media accounts and those who perceive the significance of using pliable identities and remaining anonymous. This particular debate reflects the value of the affordance of identifiability, pointing toward what identification allows and disallows in online spaces. Some social networking sites underscore that their users are expected to use their real or legal name. For instance, Facebook specifically states in its user policies that "The name on your profile should be the name that your friends call you in everyday life. This name should also appear on an ID or document from our ID list" (Facebook Help Center, 2020), and users should also use their own photograph on their profile. In the past, Zuckerberg has claimed that "having two identities for yourself is an example of a lack of integrity" (Zimmer 2010). In an example of this belief at play, Facebook informed account holders who were drag queens that they should use their birth names instead of their drag names and removed the accounts of hundreds of members of the drag community, since Facebook decided that these profiles were violating Facebook policy (Buhr 2014).

In contrast, social media platforms such as Reddit allow users to choose any username and pseudonym and remain anonymous. boyd (2011) argues that there are several applicable reasons individuals prefer not to reveal their real identities on social media: "The people who most heavily rely on pseudonyms in online spaces are those who are most marginalized by systems of power. 'Real names' policies aren't empowering; they're an authoritarian assertion of power over vulnerable people" (para. 5). In online political activism, many individuals desire to share their political opinions without impacting their careers. Particularly in countries where authorities control citizens' online activism, using pseudonyms assists users in masking their real identities, fighting against government surveillance, and avoiding arrest by the authorities.

In research on youth politics, Daniel Lane (2020) explores how the affordances of social media have affected the political engagement of young Americans between eighteen and twenty-four years old. Lane indicates that participants were more confident in declaring their political opinions when their identities on social media were anonymous, as opposed to identifiable. Furthermore, Lane discovered that anonymity decreased the self-presentation anxieties that arose when users were recognizable; therefore, anonymity emboldened political expression, and "unbounded environments—where users are physically dispersed—were perceived as better places to exert political voice and influence" (3). Helms (2001) argues that we are deprived of privacy through the development of "identification technologies" and asserts that "anonymity is an essential tool in protecting free speech and action on the Internet, even if accountability is marginally diminished" (304). Therefore, the affordance of identifiability serves to both expand and limit online activism for different users of social networks.

Further studies have also proposed that the identifiability of users on social networking sites disheartens youth political activism (Ekström 2016; Thorson 2013; Weinstein 2014), where individuals, especially youth, may refrain from articulating their political views on social media if speaking up leads to their social isolation, which is compatible with the "spiral of silence" theory.[4] Furthermore, context collapse frequently happens when users express and share their opinions to large audiences that can recognize them on social media. Exposing opinions becomes very challenging when users have a variety of people in their networks, such as their colleagues, family members, and friends. Although anonymity may generate further involvement in political and ethical discussions on social media, it also creates some challenges for online communication. For instance, Haines et al. (2014) argue that while anonymity develops more discourses and liberates individuals to declare their opinions about topics that are less favorable socially, anonymous debates exert less effect on beliefs than commentaries with identifiable participants. The opinions of recognized participants thus have more influence on final decision making.

Since social networking sites afford identifiability—some by policy—and users can reveal their personal information on their accounts, communication among them can become more trustworthy, and users can attract more support in their network from users that identify with them. By using their real identities, individuals also attach themselves to their online activities and build trust. When individuals use their real identities on social media, they can make connections with people on the Web, similar to connecting in the real world. In contrast, concealing personal identity for political activists creates a shell around them to help avoid harassment that might prevent users from participating in activism. For instance, Anonymous is a decentralized hacktivist group that conceals members' identities and participates in collective political actions, such as launching cyberattacks against governments, hacking websites, and participating in political protests.

Social media platforms that require using real identities and claim that "real names" policies create a safer social media environment should consider that not all users can safely reveal their real identities, especially individuals who are less protected in countries that track and control the political activism of their citizens when they are identifiable, as in the case of the Green Movement. Although anonymity can assist political activism to allow people to freely object and express their dissatisfaction and criticize the government for their inefficiency and corruption, the affordance of identifiability can play a fundamental role in unifying individuals in political engagement. Therefore, identifiability and anonymity on social media possess their own advantages and shortcomings and play different roles in various contexts.

MASKING TO DEFEAT SOCIAL MEDIA SURVEILLANCE

The affordance of identifiability has been employed quite unconventionally during the Green Movement. As was mentioned earlier in this chapter, Facebook specifically states in its user policies that users should use their own real name in their profile, which "should also appear on an ID or document from our ID list"[5] (Facebook Help Center 2020). As per the policy, if users lose access to their account, Facebook asks for a copy of an ID to retrieve their account; this ultimately persuades individuals to use their real name when they first create their profiles. Furthermore, using one's own identity purportedly develops users' social ties, as users can share and receive information from people that they know or can identify with. As Donatella Della Porta and Mario Diani (2000) indicate, political movement identities are the "process by which social actors recognize themselves and are recognized by other actors" (85). As one of social media's affordances, identifiability increases user-to-user messages and plays an important role in online deliberation (Halpern and Gibbs 2013). Thus, with the Green Movement, recognizing that real users were supporting the cause assisted in determining the identity and verifiability of the movement and increased participants' communication on social media.

Given these dynamics of identifiability, we can begin to see how the affordance was employed creatively during the Green Movement. When the Iranian regime realized that Iranian citizens were using Facebook and Twitter to spread the news about the movement, they began monitoring the online activities of citizens, especially on social media; in many cases, they were able to identify and arrest individuals for their online political activism. However, Iranian citizens, especially women, continued to use social media to resist the authoritarian regime, increase political discourses, and to convey their own political messaging. Since the Iranian regime applied strict surveillance to identify protestors and suppress the movement, most of the Iranian users did not use their actual identities on social media; instead, they applied a technique that Finn Brunton and Helen Nissenbaum (2015) identify as "group identity: many people under one name" as "one of the simplest and most notable examples of obfuscation" (15). Many users have changed their last name on their Facebook profile and used the word Irani (which means from Iran) as their surname instead of using their own real family names to disguise their real identities in order to allow their profile to elude identification by authorities.

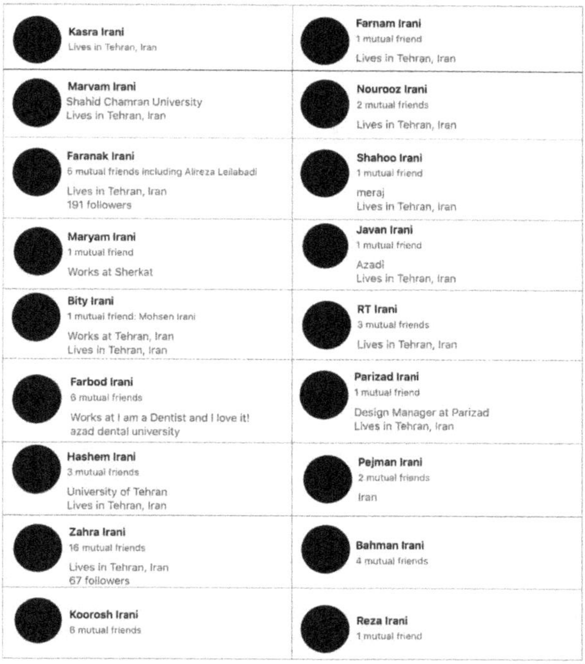

Figure 4.1. Screenshot from the author's Facebook account illustrating how users changed their last names on their Facebook profiles to be Irani, meaning from Iran, to disguise their identities. *Courtesy of Mina Momeni.*

To express solidarity, the Iranian diaspora did the same to conceal their identity, especially because the government started to search Facebook to find people and probe their activities when they entered the country. The actions of the Iranian diaspora fostered solidarity and resistance during the movement for three main reasons: Firstly, by using the word Irani as their last name in their account, the Iranian diaspora amplified the number of users with the same last name on this platform, demonstrating mutual support and resilience among Iranians who defended the movement. Secondly, members of the Iranian diaspora connected themselves to the other advocates inside the country and displayed their shared involvement in online activism. As a result, a more worldwide level of connectivity occurred during the movement. Finally, using this technique assisted users in creating a shell around themselves, allowing advocates and activists to conceal their real identities and stay active on the platform, making it much more difficult for the government to trace users.

To this third point, as Brunton and Nissenbaum (2015) explain, "Obfuscation is the deliberate addition of ambiguous, confusing, or misleading information to interfere with surveillance and data collection" (1). By using this technique, Iranian citizens could fight against government surveillance, blocking harassment by the regime. At the time of publication of this chapter, many social media users in Iran continue to avoid using their real identities on these platforms so that they may be able to continue engaging in political discourses and resistance against the government. To further prevent surveillance by the Iranian authorities, some Iranians have created two Facebook accounts. One Facebook account features a users' real identity, where posts made by this account would not be considered controversial by the Iranian government. Conversely, the other Facebook page uses a fake identity to enthusiastically antagonize the regime and its policies and to express support for, and share information about, political movements and protests to actively mobilize the Green Movement. As Esfandiari (2011) remarks, "One Facebook user says the two-page solution gives him a place to vent his anger at Iranian leaders over the poor state of the economy and lack of freedom."

In the days following the 2009 election, Twitter users—particularly those belonging to the Iranian diaspora—showed further creative uses of the affordance of identifiability, urging users to change their location to Tehran, Iran, no matter where they were globally located in an attempt to confuse authorities. This change in location made it increasingly challenging for officials to locate, inspect, and detain users who were tweeting in opposition to the establishment. The Iranian government knew how to monitor Twitter and find individuals in the country who were using this platform as a way to spread news about the protests. For example, they could determine which tweets were from Iranians by looking at which accounts were registered to users who identify as being from Iran. During the movement, the authorities banned freelance and foreign journalists from producing any information and visual content from the demonstrations because the government did not want to showcase the many ways in which the regime was brutally suppressing the movement. Nevertheless, activists and advocates were constantly posting the latest information about the location of demonstrations, statements from the leaders of the movement, and visual content, such as images and videos of the protests. Therefore, locating, monitoring, and suppressing people who were posting information about the movement was of key importance for authorities. By changing their location to Tehran, advocates overwhelmed and confused the censors with users who were tweeting about massive protests from Iran, and they could protect those living in Iran who were doing so. Consequently, many activists were not identified and could not be arrested by the authorities, thus continuing their activism. This act of defiance affected the Iranian authorities' ability to employ the affordance of searchability efficiently, thereby preventing the government from finding users effortlessly.

Against the backdrop of Iranian citizens working with and against identifiable information on social media, we can see how the affordance of identifiability can empower social media users through the ways it encourages the development of users' social ties and user-to-user messages. This affordance can also facilitate the functionality of direct communication of social media among users that recognize each other on these platforms. As Daniel Halpern and Jennifer Gibbs (2013) indicate, platforms such as Facebook that "allow for greater affordances of identifiability," are better suited for discussion than other platforms, such as YouTube, and they also can "integrate diverse sectors of the population" (1167). In contrast, in countries where authorities heavily suppress the rights to freedom of expression, being able to mask real identities enables users to avoid government surveillance to some extent and fight attempts at suppression. As seen here, despite issues of surveillance and data gathering associated with social media platforms, social networking sites have globalized communications that are key for political activism and advocacy, demonstrating how digital media have the potential to expand the role of the public in political discourses (Browning 1996; Jones 1997; Shirky 2011).

By assessing the situation and strategizing alternative possibilities that the affordances of Facebook and Twitter could provide for them, Iranian social media users employed group identity and multiple Facebook accounts and confused the government by changing their location in order to perform their political activism and mobilization efforts. Using these techniques disrupted the search function of social media for the Iranian authorities, demonstrating how one affordance can be used differently to disable another affordance to assist users to perform an action. Iranian authorities employed the affordance of searchability to identify and suppress users who distributed information related to the movement. However, by masking their real identities, users limited the effectiveness of the affordance of searchability and the actions of the government. Adopting different approaches toward the affordance of identifiability expanded citizens' choices for self-expression and facilitated discussion on these platforms within different political systems and contexts. By employing the affordance of identifiability creatively during the Green Movement, users shaped a unique and distinguishable identity to form a community on Facebook that involved Iranians from both inside and outside of the country. As a result, more discussion and information sharing about the movement occurred, and more attention was garnered.

CONCLUSION

To contribute to the ongoing discussions around social media political activism, this chapter has put forth the theory of affordances as a theoretical framework to examine how the affordance of identifiability facilitates and restricts the political activism of users on social media, and how it was used by participants during the Green Movement to share their stories. While anonymity does enable people to freely object and articulate their discontent with various political issues and criticize the government for its inefficiency, lack of identification is less effective at cultivating community and encouraging user-to-user messaging. One might assume that, given that the affordances of social media provide particular opportunities to perform a specific action, they would be utilized similarly in various political events. However, as this chapter has demonstrated, the affordance of identifiability was used in alternative and creative ways during the Iranian Green Movement, where users, especially activists and advocates, employed group identity to mask their real identities to evade government surveillance and continue their political activism on social media. Furthermore, by changing their location to Tehran, users misled the Iranian regime and prevented it from tracking, locating, and arresting activists and advocates. Social media affordances present new possibilities for action, making it possible for activists and advocates to employ them unconventionally for democratic means, such as how identifiability was used differently in this case of the Iranian Green Movement.

REFERENCES

Baumgartner, Jody C., and Jonathan S. Morris. 2010. "MyFaceTube Politics: Social Networking Web Sites and Political Engagement of Young Adults." *Social Science Computer Review* 28 (1): 24–44.

BBC. 2020. "Mark Zuckerberg: Facebook boss urges tighter regulation." BBC. February 14, 2020. www.bbc.com/news/technology-51518773.

Bennett, W. Lance, and Alexandra Segerberg. 2009. "Collective action dilemmas with individual mobilization through digital networks." Center for Communication and Civic Engagement Working Paper 2009.

Berman, Ali. 2009. "Iran's Twitter revolution." *The Nation.* June 15, 2009. www.thenation.com/article/irans-twitter-revolution/.

Bode, Leticia. 2012. "Facebooking It to the Polls: A Study in Online Social Networking and Political Behavior." *Journal of Information Technology & Politics* 9 (4): 352–69.

boyd, danah. 2010. "Social network sites as networked publics: Affordances, dynamics, and implications." In *A Networked Self,* edited By Zizi Papacharissi. Routledge, 47–66.

boyd, danah. 2011. "Real Names" Policies Are an Abuse of Power, *Apophenia.* www.zephoria.org/thoughts/archives/2011/08/04/real-names.html.

Browning, Graeme. 1996. *Electronic Democracy: Using the Internet to Transform American Politics.* Pemberton Press.

Brunton, Finn, and Helen Fay Nissenbaum. 2015. *Obfuscation: A User's Guide for Privacy and Protest.* The MIT Press.

Buhr, Sarah. 2014. "Facebook Won't Budge on Letting Drag Queens Keep Their Names." TechCrunch. September 18, 2014. https://techcrunch.com/2014/09/18/facebook-wont-budge-on-letting-drag-queens-keep-their-names/.

Carney, Nikita. 2016. "All Lives Matter, but So Does Race: Black Lives Matter and the Evolving Role of Social Media." *Humanity & Society* 40 (2): 180–99.

Carty, Victoria. 2018. *Social Movements and New Technology.* Routledge.

Castañeda, Ernesto. 2012. "The Indignados of Spain: A Precedent to Occupy Wall Street." *Social Movement Studies* 11 (3–4): 309–19.

Dabashi, Hamid. 2011. *The Green Movement in Iran.* Transaction Publishers.

Della Porta, Donatella, and Mario Diani. 2000. *Social Movements: An Introduction.* Blackwell Publishers.

Dimitrova, Daniela V., and Dianne Bystrom. 2013. "The Effects of Social Media on Political Participation and Candidate Image Evaluations in the 2012 Iowa Caucuses." *The American Behavioral Scientist* 57 (11): 1568–83.

Ekström, Mats. 2016. "Young People's Everyday Political Talk: A Social Achievement of Democratic Engagement." *Journal of Youth Studies,* 19 (1): 1–19.

Elson, Sara Beth, Douglas Yeung, Parisa Roshan, S. R. Bohandy, and Alireza Nader. 2012. "Background on Social Media use in Iran and Events Surrounding the 2009 Election." RAND Corporation.

Eltantawy, Nahed, and Julie B. Wiest. 2011. "Social Media in the Egyptian Revolution: Reconsidering Resource Mobilization Theory." *International Journal of Communication* (19328036): 5.

Esfandiari, Golnaz. 2011. "In Iran, Beware of New Facebook 'Friends,'" Radio Free Europe, Radio Liberty. June 8, 2011. www.rferl.org/a/if_youre_iranian_beware_of _new_facebook_friends/24228798.html.

———. 2010. "The Twitter Devolution: Far from Being a Tool of Revolution in Iran over the Last Year, the Internet, in Many Ways, Just Complicated the Picture." *Foreign Policy.* June 8, 2010. foreignpolicy.com/2010/06/08/the-twitter-devolution/.

Facebook. 2020. Community Standards. https://www.facebook.com/ communitystandards/.

———. 2020. Community Standards. Manipulated Media. https://www.facebook .com/communitystandards/recentupdates/manipulated_media/.

Facebook Help Center. 2020. "What names are allowed on Facebook?" www .facebook.com/help/112146705538576.

Gaffney, Devin. 2010. "#iranElection: Quantifying Online Activism." In *Proceedings of the Web Science Conference.* April 26–27, 2010.

Gibson, James J. 1979. *The Ecological Approach to Visual Perception.* Classic ed. Psychology Press.

Gleason, Benjamin. 2013."#Occupy Wall Street: Exploring Informal Learning About a Social Movement on Twitter." *American Behavioral Scientist* 57 (7): 966–82.

Haines, Russell, Jill Hough, Lan Cao, and Douglas Haines. 2014. "Anonymity in Computer-Mediated Communication: More Contrarian Ideas with Less Influence." *Group Decision and Negotiation* 23 (4): 765–86.

Halpern, Daniel, and Jennifer Gibbs. 2013. "Social media as a catalyst for online deliberation? Exploring the affordances of Facebook and YouTube for political expression." *Computers in Human Behavior* 29 (3): 1159–68.

Hayes, Rebecca A., Caleb T. Carr, and Donghee Yvette Wohn. 2016. "One Click, Many Meanings: Interpreting Paralinguistic Digital Affordances in Social Media." *Journal of Broadcasting & Electronic Media* 60 (1): 171–87.

Helms, Shawn C. 2001. "Translating privacy values with technology." *BUJ Sci. & Tech. L.* (7): 288.

Hutchinson, Andrew. 2019. "Facebook Reaches 2.38 Billion Users, Beats Revenue Estimates in Latest Update." Social Media Today. April 24, 2019. www .socialmediatoday.com/news/facebook-reaches-238-billion-users-beats-revenue -estimates-in-latest-upda/553403/.

Iosifidis, Petros. 2011. "The Public Sphere, Social Networks and Public Service Media." *Information, Communication & Society* 14 (5): 619–37.

Jones, Steve. (ed.). 1997.*Virtual Culture: Identity and Communication in Cybersociety.* Sage.

Klemm, Konstantin. 2013. "Searchability of Central Nodes in Networks." *Journal of Statistical Physics* 151 (3): 707–19.

Lane, Daniel S. 2020. "Social Media Design for Youth Political Expression: Testing the Roles of Identifiability and Geo-Boundedness." *New Media & Society* 22 (8): 1394–1413.

Lawrence, Regina G., Logan Molyneux, Mark Coddington, and Avery Holton. 2014. "Tweeting Conventions: Political Journalists' use of Twitter to Cover the 2012 Presidential Campaign." *Journalism Studies* 15 (6): 789–806.

Literat, Ioana, and Neta Kligler-Vilenchik. 2019. "Youth Collective Political Expression on Social Media: The Role of Affordances and Memetic Dimensions for Voicing Political Views." *New Media & Society* 21 (9): 1988–2009.

Ma, Xiao, Jeff Hancock, and Mor Naaman. 2016. "Anonymity, intimacy and self-disclosure in social media." *Proceedings of the 2016 CHI conference on human factors in computing systems.*

Majchrzak, Ann, Samer Faraj, Gerald C. Kane, and Bijan Azad. 2013. "The Contradictory Influence of Social Media Affordances on Online Communal Knowledge Sharing." *Journal of Computer-Mediated Communication* 19 (1): 38–55.

Malsbender, Andrea, Sara Hofmann, and Jörg Becker. 2013. "Aligning capabilities and social media affordances for open innovation in governments." In *ACIS 2013: Information Systems: Transforming the Future: Proceedings of the 24th Australasian Conference on Information Systems*, 1–11. RMIT University.

Milani, Abbas. 2010. "The Green Movement. United States Institute of Peace." The Iran Primer. October 6, 2010. https://iranprimer.usip.org/resource/green-movement.

Morozov, Evgeny. 2009. "Iran: Downside to the 'Twitter Revolution.'" *Dissent* 56 (4): 10–14.

Mundt, Marcia, Karen Ross, and Charla M. Burnett. 2018. "Scaling Social Movements through Social Media: The Case of Black Lives Matter." *Social Media + Society* 4 (4). https://doi.org/10.1177/2056305118807911.

Shaban, Hamza. 2019. "Twitter Reveals Its Daily Active User Numbers for the First Time." *Washington Post.* February 7, 2019. www.washingtonpost.com/technology/2019/02/07/twitter-reveals-its-daily-active-user-numbers-first-time/?noredirect=on&utm_term=.93be38650988.

Shirky, Clay. 2011. "The Political Power of Social Media: Technology, the Public Sphere, and Political Change." *Foreign Affairs.* 28–41.

Sloan, Luke, and Anabel Quan-Haase. 2017. *The SAGE Handbook of Social Media Research Methods.* Sage.

Sohrabi-Haghighat, M. Hadi, and Shohre Mansouri. 2010. "'Where Is My Vote?': ICT Politics in the Aftermath of Iran's Presidential Election." *International Journal of Emerging Technologies and Society* 8 (1): 24–41

Stamati, Teta, Thanos Papadopoulos, and Dimosthenis Anagnostopoulos. 2015. "Social Media for Openness and Accountability in the Public Sector: Cases in the Greek Context." *Government Information Quarterly* 32 (1): 12–29.

Statista. 2019. "Leading Countries Based on Number of Twitter Users as of October 2019." Statista. November 19, 2021. www.statista.com/statistics/242606/number-of-active-twitter-users-in-selected-countries/.

Stebbins, Samuel. 2019. "These 15 Countries, as Home to Largest Reserves, Control the World's Oil." *USA Today.* May 22, 2019. https://www.usatoday.com/story

/money/2019/05/22/largest-oil-reserves-in-world-15-countries-that-control-the
-worlds-oil/39497945/.

Stroud, Natalie Jomini. 2010. "Polarization and Partisan Selective Exposure." *Journal of Communication* 60 (3): 556–76.

Sullivan, Andrew. 2009. "The Revolution Will Be Twittered," *The Atlantic.* June 13, 2009. www.theatlantic.com/daily-dish/archive/2009/06/the-revolution-will-be
-twittered/200478/.

Sunstein, Cass. R. 2001. *Republic.com.* Princeton University Press.

Tahmasebi-Birgani, Victoria. 2010. "Green Women of Iran: The Role of the Women's Movement During and After Iran's Presidential Election of 2009." *Constellations* 17 (1): 78–86.

The Twitter Rules. 2019. Twitter. Retrieved from https://help.twitter.com/en/rules-and
-policies/twitter-rules.

Thorson, Kjerstin. 2014. "Facing an Uncertain Reception: Young Citizens and Political Interaction on Facebook." *Information, Communication & Society* 17 (2): 203–16.

Treem, Jeffrey W., and Paul M. Leonardi. 2013. "Social Media Use in Organizations: Exploring the Affordances of Visibility, Editability, Persistence, and Association." *Annals of the International Communication Association* 36 (1): 143–89.

Twitter Help Center. 2020. Hateful conduct policy. help.twitter.com/en/
rules-and-policies/hateful-conduct-policy.

Valenzuela, Sebastián, Namsu Park, and Kerk F. Kee. 2009. "Is there Social Capital in a Social Network Site?: Facebook Use and College Students' Life Satisfaction, Trust, and Participation." *Journal of Computer-Mediated Communication* 14 (4): 875–901.

Warner, Michael. 2002. "Publics and Counterpublics." *Quarterly Journal of Speech* 88: 413–25.

Weinstein, Emily C. 2014. "The Personal Is Political on Social Media: Online Civic Expression Patterns and Pathways among Civically Engaged Youth." *International Journal of Communication (Online)*: 210.

Wiens, Brianna I., and Shana MacDonald. 2020. "Feminist Futures: #MeToo's Possibilities as Poiesis, Techné, and Pharmakon." *Feminist Media Studies* 21 (7): 1108–24.

Wolfsfeld, Gadi, Elad Segev, and Tamir Sheafer. 2013. "Social Media and the Arab Spring: Politics Comes First." *The International Journal of Press/Politics* 18 (2): 115–37.

Zhang, Weiwu, Trent Seltzer, and Shannon L. Bichard. 2013. "Two Sides of the Coin: Assessing the Influence of Social Network Site Use During the 2012 US Presidential Campaign." *Social Science Computer Review* 31 (5): 542–51.

Zimmer, Michael. 2010. "Facebook's Zuckerberg: 'Having two identities for yourself is an example of a lack of integrity.'" *Michael Zimmer.* May 14, 2010. www
.michaelzimmer.org/2010/05/14/facebooks-zuckerberg-having-two-identities-for
-yourself-is-an-example-of-a-lack-of-integrity/.

NOTES

1. Mir Hossein Mousavi is an Iranian politician, painter, architect, and reformist who was the last Prime Minister of Iran from 1981 to 1989.

2. Mehdi Karroubi held several key positions in the Iranian government, such as chairman of the parliament and head of the Imam Khomeini Relief Committee.

3. Even though most Iranian citizens were looking for a revolutionary change, the opposition leaders were not really intending to overthrow the Islamic regime. They published a manifesto of the Green Movement on February 22, 2011, on the *kaleme* website, indicating that the Iranian government should provide freedom of speech for its citizens, yet they emphasized that everyone should respect the Constitution of the Islamic Republic of Iran.

4. The "spiral of silence" theory is a mass communication and political science theory proposed by the German political scientist Elisabeth Noelle-Neumann. This theory states that a social group could isolate members because of the members' beliefs. Because individuals have a fear of seclusion, their fear accordingly leads to staying silent instead of expressing their thoughts.

5. Facebook (now Meta) allows users to change their profile name, but it warns the users that they cannot change it again for sixty days.

Chapter 5

Can Butches Be Feminists?

Unearthing the Complexities within Butch and Butch/ Femme Facebook Groups

Kristin Comeforo

Feminism does not have a great history of inclusion. As early as 1851, Sojourner Truth asked attendees at the Ohio Women's Rights Convention, "Ain't I a woman?," to call out Black women's exclusion from the Women's Movement. Later, lesbians, specifically butches, were similarly excluded. National Organization of Women (NOW) cofounder Betty Friedan famously coined the phrase "lavender menace" in 1969 when she worried out loud that the inclusion of "mannish" and "man-hating" lesbians would deter public support and undermine the movement. More recently, trans-exclusionary radical feminists (TERFs) question trans women's role in feminism, arguing that a "male at birth" assignment provides transwomen with a male privilege that is not only foreign to a woman's lived experience but also produces patriarchy that seeks to oppress all women. TERFs problematically worry that cis-women are being "erased" by trans and other nonbinary identities (Compton 2019), opening transwomen and nonbinary people up to violence.

Within the LGBTQ+ community there too is tension and exclusion. "Butch" and "femme" emerged as lesbian identities in the 1950s as working-class women adopted either masculine (butch) or feminine (femme) dress and role behaviors (Faderman 1991). Butch/femme created a lesbian social identity to both serve as an indicator of membership and to facilitate the romantic and sexual connections among working-class lesbians. In many ways, butch and femme meant a community that provided a personal safe haven and a political statement that usurped male privilege and challenged the patriarchy.

To the ire of middle-class lesbians, who were "less stereotypically obvious as homosexuals" (Faderman 1991, 184), butch/femme couples made lesbian identities visible and thus targets for vilification. Pulp novels of time presented butch/femme lesbians as outcasts and, by the end of the 1960s, the shifting demographics of women who were "beginning their lesbian careers" in college combined with a rise in feminism to push butch/femme identities out of fashion (Faderman 1991). This rejection of butch/femme continued into the 1970s and beyond, especially within mainstream feminism, which essentialized these identities as misogynist and mirrored the heteropatriarchy.

In many ways, groups excluded from mainstream feminism have fought back against discrimination. These struggles unfolded in the physical spaces of face-to-face "women's unions" of the Combahee River Collective (CRC), through which a salient Black feminism developed, and the direct-action protests of the Lavender Menace, the group formed by Rita Mae Brown and others to fight for inclusion of lesbians and lesbian issues within the feminist movement. More presently, social media have opened new spaces for excluded people to build community and develop identities, and also engage in activism. The Black Lives Matter movement and the LGBTQ+ anti-bullying "It Gets Better" project are just two that have found their footing through hashtag activism on Twitter, Facebook, YouTube, and Instagram, among others. As we continue to construct and practice feminism in the twenty-first century, this chapter considers whether Facebook groups offer a digital venue for feminist consciousness-raising, specifically within the lesbian butch/femme community. Through a grounded theory and textual analysis of butch/femme Facebook groups, I consider whether feminism is present within these groups, and whether the groups and content shared/produced therein create spaces for feminist expression and assembly.

Overall findings suggest that while there is an inherent feminism reflected by content posted in group pages and a subsequent empowerment/transformation of members, there are also feminist failings and a strident refusal to call what we are doing "politics" and/or "feminism." A cogent "butch feminism" was observed through butches' practice of alternative masculinities, such as "feminist masculinity" (hooks 2015) and "mas(k)ulinity" (Silverman and Comeforo 2019). While behaviors consistent with feminism and, indeed, a distinctive "butch feminism" were developed online, participation in these groups provided a "transformation" that can be predicted to carry forward into further online and offline practice of butch feminism.

A HISTORY OF STRUGGLES FOR INCLUSION

In 1851, Sojourner Truth, who had been previously enslaved, asked the infamous question "Ain't I a woman?" to highlight not only that women are as capable as men, but also that Black women had been systematically disqualified from the category of woman and therefore shut out of the women's movement. The Combahee River Collective (CRC) provided one response to the exclusionary politics of mainstream feminism. Founded by Black women in 1974, the collective was the first to use the term "identity politics" as a response to oppression based on identity. Identity, thus, was both the source of oppression and the source of political radicalization. It "was not just about who you were; it was also about what you could do to confront the oppression you were facing" (Taylor 2017, 9). Black feminism, through the CRC, took shape alongside "suddenly emerging information about the way that the state and the heteropatriarchal state had controlled and limited women's agency through their bodies" (Taylor 2017, 123). To confront this oppression, CRC proposed and practiced a feminism that was materialist, grounded in self-determination and intersectionality, and nonhierarchical. "Women's unions" were a way for Black feminists to "make a place for [themselves] and a way for [themselves]" (48) that was similar to, yet distinct from, the consciousness-raising meetings coordinated by mainstream feminists.

Lesbians were similarly marginalized and erased within this mainstream movement. The Lavender Menace was a direct response to the overt homophobia of Betty Friedan and NOW (Orleck 2015). The group used a tactic borrowed from the Gay Activist Alliance (GAA)—a "zap"— to make a bold statement and get attention. A zap was "a theatrical form of direct-action protest that typically involves the public shaming of an individual or organization to force them to change their ways or take a stance on a particular issue" (Iovannone 2018). The group wrote a manifesto and placed it on seats in the auditorium during the 1970 NOW Convention. Members donned Lavender Menace T-shirts under their clothes. The lights were cut in the auditorium. When the lights were turned back on, the Lavender Menace was standing in the aisles and on stage, revealing their T-shirts and their presence as being already among these feminists. The Lavender Menace encouraged feminists present who were lesbians to self-identify and to join them in a discussion of lesbian rights and issues within the movement. They were largely successful in their endeavor.

While honoring these disparate histories, growing attention to intersectionality was highlighting how race, gender, and sexuality work together to produce unique lived experiences that compound oppressions and privileges. Audre Lorde, for instance, identified as a "Black lesbian feminist" and held that gender oppression was not inseparable from other oppressive systems like racism, classism, and homophobia (Lorde 1984). We can see, thus, how Black women's ability to carve out a distinct Black feminism offers encouragement that butches can carve out a distinct butch feminism.

BUTCH AND BUTCH/FEMME THEORY

While there are, perhaps, as many ways of conceiving "butch" as there are butches themselves, two key terms are commonly invoked: masculine and lesbian. Indeed, butch is often used as "a receptacle [term] for all lesbian masculinity" (Halberstam 1998, 120). Much of the theorizing around butch speaks from an assumption of female/woman identification and a desire to maintain that female-body connection. Heidi Levitt and Katherine Hiestand (2004), for instance, found butches adamant in their contention that they do not want to be men and while they "may be read as [men]" they purport to live their lives as fully "embodied wom[e]n" (Browne 2004, 342). Sherrie A. Innes (1998) claims butches "lack belonging" because they are neither man nor woman; male nor female, a hybrid, perhaps, or "living in an incoherently sexed body" in the "uneasy borderland between man and woman" like Jess Goldberg, the protagonist in Leslie Feinberg's *Stone Butch Blues* (Prosser 1995). Further, butches are often defined through their relationship to femmes, while femmes are defined through their relationship to butches, both of which carry connotations in relation to traditional masculinity and femininity. Butch is thus, "not femme," meaning no "feminine[izing] [makeup], such as eyeshadow, lipstick" and no "skirts, stilettos, heels" (Younger Butch Facebook Group 2019).

Rapidly evolving lived experiences, however, prove that distinctions between genders, and performances of butch and femme are less discrete and more diffuse. Trans and nonbinary identities are opening spaces for new definitions of butch and femme and a radical rethinking of masculinity and femininity. Jian Neo Chen (2019), for one, distinguishes between cis- and trans- masculinity and femininity. Heteronormative cismasculinity and cisfemininity "[read] gender presentation as a binary sign for gender interiority and bodily essence" (37), while transmasculinity and transfemininity "appropriate semiotic resources to align or disalign themselves with a range of masculinities" (155) and femininities, thus allowing individuals to claim identities such as "trans guy" and "trans feminine," simultaneously (39). matthew heinz (2016) explores how "articulations of transmasculine experiences play off changes in understandings of masculinity and both reinforce and challenge social and cultural understandings of what it means to be a man" (10). Trans man Chaz Bono, for instance, was framed as "a different kind of

man" when he appeared on *Dancing with the Stars*, which provided both recognition and inclusion, and also a transphobic desexualization of Bono that
brought into question the very "manhood" it purported to present (Mocarski,
Butler, Emmons, and Smallwood 2013).

Within these slippages between binary connections of male/masculine and
female/feminine, Rachel Silverman and I (2019) theorize butch/femme as
"differential identities" that disrupt gender hegemony by "throwing recognition and misrecognition into play" through performances of "mas(k)ulinity"
and "fem(me)ininity" (3). Mas(k)ulinity and Fem(me)ininity are marked with
a "constant presence/absence of both masculinity *and* femininity within the
gender performance" (5). Mas(k)ulinity and fem(me)ininity work to break the
male/masculine, female/feminine binary and thus disrupt hegemonic patterns
of male/subject and female/object. In addition to mas(k)ulinity, bell hooks
(2015) offers a "feminist masculinity" that is grounded in self-esteem and
self-love rather than dominance, and that is not sexist (70). Along these lines,
S. Bear Bergman (2006) defines butch as "someone who has taken on the best
gendered characteristics of both woman and man, left a lot of the stuff born
of misogyny and heterosexism behind, and walked forward into the world
without apology" (64). The possibilities of other forms of masculinity that
are liberative rather than oppressive elevate butches, and the butch/femme
dyad, as prime locations for the analysis of sexism/feminism. Butches may
perform hegemonic masculinity in replication of patriarchy, or, they may not.
The question is which route will/do they take? I look to digital spaces, and
specifically Facebook groups, to find out.

DIGITAL MEDIA'S CHANGING LANDSCAPE

As media evolves, traditional structures of a top-down, elite-to-mass-media
production and distribution processes are being challenged by digital media
practices that have opened new spaces for user-generated content of all stripes,
including activism. Feminist activity and congregation on social media, for
instance, has become the "consciousness-raising" of the twenty-first century
(Rentschler and Thrift 2015; Kennedy 2007). Despite these openings, digital
spaces are not panacea for corporatized media control, as the most popular–
–Facebook, Twitter, Instagram, YouTube—are all owned by "tech giants"
who serve the dominant interests of capital and typically white, cisgender,
heterosexual men. Still, Sarah Jackson (2016) notes that these new technologies are used by activists to create "counterpublic communit[ies] that
center the voices of those most often at the margins" (375), such as women
in general, and butches more specifically. The internet thus has the "capacity

to create, find, and build interest-based communities" (Banet-Weiser and Miltner 2016, 173) which has not only helped produce "popular" and accessible feminisms, but also "alarming amounts of vitriol and violence against women in online spaces" that Banet-Weiser and Miltner call "networked misogyny" (171). One response to this new misogyny has been memes, which have been theorized as a form of feminist subjectivity and, thus, a way of "doing feminism in the network" (Rentschler and Thrift 2015, 331).

In addition to "doing feminism," digital spaces are key sites of identity development and expression. LGBTQ+ folk are more likely to be ostracized from the social and family groups within which they were socialized. Public discourse, a replacement for these narratives, thus becomes more important to the community. Participative digital technologies, such as YouTube, Twitter, and Facebook, increase LGBTQ+ access to public discourse and thus facilitate identity and community construction (Gal, Shifman, and Kampf 2016). Specifically, Mary Gray (2009) argues that digital content operates as a form of "queer realness" for rural youth who may not have local, IRL access to LGBTQ+ resources and culture. Much like the butches in the groups I participate in and study, Gray's rural youths "found comfort and familiarity in the narratives of realness circulating online" (1172). Many butches indicate that they lack a butch/femme community where they live, and perhaps the most often invoked praise point for these groups is that members love existing in a butch/femme–centered space and exclusively seeing representation of their (self) identity. In this way, the Facebook groups serve a purpose similar to the lesbian bars in the 1950s, where the butch/femme identity began to take hold as a cogent subculture (Faderman 1991).

METHOD

In engaging with Facebook groups, I set out to search for the presence of feminism in butch online communities through my own usage and participation. This research is highly personal and subjective, yet it is conducted with rigor through a grounded theory approach to textual analysis. Textual analysis considers media content as "texts" to be read (i.e., scoured for meaning by researchers who systematically uncover patterns and themes) (Phillipov 2013, 211) and allows for a thick description of what gets posted to these groups. Grounded theory is a highly inductive, qualitative approach in which data collection and analysis are simultaneous and interrelated, performed through continuous, structured close readings of texts and constant comparison (Corbin and Strauss 1990). This iterative process allows theory to emerge from the data and thus speak more truly to the lived experience of the butches and femmes participating in these groups.

Data was collected through participant observation within groups that I am a member. In total, I am a member of nineteen LGBTQ+ related groups. I found these groups using the "Search" tool on Facebook, as an everyday user of the social media site. These groups span the spectrum, ranging from the broadest most inclusive LGBTQ+, to lesbian, to butch/femme, to butch specific, and were chosen because they reflect different aspects of my identity. While all these groups inform my overall position as a participant observer, I chose to focus my analysis on the four groups I engage with most and that most effectively allow access to the butch identity I seek to study—"Butch/ Femme (Wholesome)," "Butch/Femme (Uncouth)," "Butch (Older)," and "Butch (Younger)." The following section describes each group quantitatively and qualitatively. Since all the groups I engage with are private, meaning that members must "request approval" to join and only members can see who is in the group and the content they post, I have chosen to use a descriptive name based on the community/members served and content themes rather than the actual name under which the group organizes and operates.

THE SAMPLING FRAME:
BUTCH AND BUTCH/FEMME GROUPS

The "Butch/Femme (Wholesome)" group was so named because group rules call for "a family/work friendly feed." It is the largest of butch/femme group on Facebook with a membership of 21,775. Administrators are a married butch/femme couple, one of whom uses she/her pronouns and one of whom uses they/them pronouns. The group also has two moderators, one of who uses she/her pronouns while the other uses they/them pronouns. This group has the most explicit sense of political awareness and engagement. According to the group's description: "This Group was created with the dynamics of Diversity in mind. The Butch-Femme Culture has evolved to make room for the most diverse set of gender and sexual identities than any other community under the rainbow canopy. We are a unique collective and when we use our differences to gather instead of divide, this Group along with other extended Butch-Femme Communities is what that kind of power looks like." On the other hand, the "Butch/Femme (Uncouth)" group, according to its self-description, was "created for Adult Lesbians," as a "place to have fun and relax." The group serves 17,157 members through fourteen Administrators and four Moderators. All eighteen group leaders use she/her pronouns. Content within this group is the most sexualized and oriented around memes and other flirtatious conversation starters.

The two butch-specific groups under analysis both focus on the butch aesthetic, largely through fashion and style. I distinguish between the two by referring to one as "Butch (Younger)," and the other as "Butch (Older)." The "Older" group embraces this distinction in its name, and how it describes itself on its "About" page. I assess the "Younger" group as such, through observation of pictures and posted content, along with the overall tone given off by group description, etc. According to the "Older" Butch group: "The goal for this group is to have a safe, supportive space for mature discussion and for members to share their passion for butch-centered fashion, styling, shopping, modeling and self-care. While you don't have to be butch to join-pls. be mindful that this is a lesbian-focused group with the primary purpose of sharing the butch lifestyle and supporting one another. Let's hold each other up . . . Pls. do keep it positive and Selfies are highly encouraged!!" The "Younger" Butch group self-describes as: "a space for butches to talk about clothes, outfits, accessories, styling, shopping, thrifting, diy . . . anything and everything butch fashion related. selfies are highly encouraged! you don't have to be a butch to join, but this is a lesbian-only group and primarily a butch space, so please do keep that in mind making posts."

Both groups are inclusive in terms of membership, suggesting that their definition of butch is immutable yet changeable, especially when it comes to cis- and transgender identities. Still, both carve out their groups as safe spaces for the butch identity to be presented, supported, and explored. The "Older" group is maintained by three administrators who all use she/her pronouns and two moderators, one of whom uses they/them pronouns while the other uses she/her. The "Younger" group has one administrator who uses she/her pronouns and four moderators who also all use she/her pronouns. The "Older" group has 8,100 members as of May 26, 2020, and the "Younger" group has 3,489.

DATA COLLECTION AND ANALYSIS

My data collection is naturalistic in that it comes largely from my participant observer status within the groups. That is, I collect data and observe content as it pops up during my everyday usage/experience of Facebook in my real life. This is consistent with both a "quare" studies approach and feminist methodology, which, while each focus on race and gender respectively, both value experience as evidentiary and call for a nonhierarchical/reciprocal relationship between the researcher and subjects (Johnson 2001; Hammersly 1992). My analysis was twofold. First, I used the grounded theory approach to perform a textual analysis, which allowed me to describe butch discourse and values in these Facebook groups. These findings are presented in the "How to Butch and How to Butch/Femme" section. Then, I used "key markers of feminism" collected from feminist literature and theory to look for the presence/absence of feminism in these butch and butch/femme spaces. The following section describes my approach to feminism and defines the "key markers" of feminism used for my analysis.

Defining and "Finding" Feminism

My preferred definition of feminism comes from bell hooks (2015): "Feminism is a movement to end sexism, sexist exploitation, and oppression" (xii). hooks reminds us that "all of us, female and male, have been socialized from birth on to accept sexist thought and action" (xii). Sexism is not just about women versus men, but rather an orientation toward dominance/ oppression, which privileges men but is not limited to men. That is, women can be, and are, sexist in how they view and treat both themselves and others and men can adopt a feminist masculinity, which is not sexist (hooks 2015).

To "find" feminism within the data, I looked for "key markers" as they coalesce around "everyday feminist activities" (Francis and Hey 2009; Schuster 2017); "feminist values" (duCoudray 2016; Grunig, Toth, and Hon 2009); "personal qualities" (Calder-Dawe and Gavey 2017); and "feminist pedagogy" (Webb, Allen, and Walker 2002). Everyday feminist activities include moral obligations to speak out and refusal moments (Francis and Hey 2009), along with resisting traditional gender roles, reclaiming/learning traditional feminized skills, and paying attention to/calling out sexism in everyday encounters (Schuster 2017). Feminist values include equality, civil/ human rights, and individualist choice/freedom (duCoudray 2016), along with cooperation, respect, caring, nurturance, interconnection, justice, equity, honesty, sensitivity, perceptiveness, intuition, altruism, fairness, morality, and commitment (Grunig, Toth, and Hon 2009). Personal qualities include self-knowledge, confidence, and nonconformity (Calder-Dawe and Gavey 2017). Feminist pedagogy refers to the organizational structure and most broadly calls for a nonhierarchical, democratic community of "cocreators," which values and respects difference, individual lived experience, and challenges traditional views (Webb, Allen, and Walker 2002). These findings are presented in the "Finding Butch Feminism" section.

How to Butch and How to Butch/Femme

Posted content revealed the ways members define, perform, and value their individual butch identities along with their relational butch/femme identities. Three key categories of content emerged—memes, advice seeking/giving, and the sharing/celebration of achievements.

Fe(meme)ism? While all posts can be read as "conversation starters" that encourage reaction and interaction, memes express more generalized perceived shared valued, or, habitus within the butch and/or butch/femme community. According to Rentschler and Thrift (2015), "feminist memes can create ad hoc feminist publics in some unexpected places" (332), that are decidedly nonpolitical, such as here within the butch and butch/femme groups. Memes may serve as "feminist interventions" that introduce feminism subtly through humor and/or habitus.

Habitus reflects an insider knowledge or cultural capital that allows, in this case, butches and femmes to recognize and belong with each other in a broader community sense (Rooke 2007). Memes in this instance can be considered accurate reflections of what posters believe to be cornerstones of butch and femme identities and values. For example, memes highlighted instantly recognizable facets of butch/femme and lesbian culture, such as butch chivalry, ruggedness, and mechanical skills; the inextricable pull toward, and need for, butch/femme pairings; and the challenges of being "nonconformists" in the cisgender heteropatriarchy, along with the struggles of negotiating bed space and sexual encounters given the presence of many cats and dogs.

Some memes were positive or neutral in terms of reflecting feminist values. Positive memes offered inspirational advice about self-love and self-care and often oriented around placing breakups in context and recognizing that it is for the best. These positive memes provide support within the community along with sensitivity and nurturing of one another through shared struggles. Neutral memes, such as animal and other "jokey" content, were regularly shared and warmly accepted by members as respite from the struggles of living transgressive lives in a patriarchal, heteronormative, cis-gendered world. Other memes were contradictory to feminist ideals and highly sexist. Butch/femme groups, the "Uncouth" specifically, included misogynistic content that by and large presented an objectified view of women—femme and butch alike. A meme of dessert brand mascot "Little Debbie" with the headline "FIRST B** I EVER ATE," for instance, garnered only positive reactions, as did another, which instructed us of "The right way to kiss a girl: Push her up against a wall, hold her arms above her head and kiss her like you mean it." Memes, like these, are far more complex than they look. They "act as a funhouse mirror for culture and society, reflecting and refracting the anxieties and preoccupations of a variety of social groups across a series of national contexts" (Miltner 2018, 413). In this way, butches and femmes may be responding to their experience of homophobia, or fear of it, by lashing out at women and performing the "networked misogyny" that Banet-Weiser and Miltner (2016) report as being largely accepted as the status quo.

While posting misogynistic content is anti-feminist and clearly problematic, the more egregious failure of feminism is the lack of calling out of such content. It is on this point that my participation in the groups, and my feminist identity, come into conflict. I recently reacted strongly to a post, "A group of femmes is called a maintenance," which I believe was meant as a fun conversation starter (as the group member also posted similar "taxonomies" for other butch/femme gender identities). As a butch and as a feminist, I felt the naming to be misogynistic and reductive/stereotypical in its description of femmes. My first comment was simply "nope," and I moved on. The post nagged at me, though, and I soon went back, heart pounding and sweating and posted:

> Really? These are people we love and who, by our identities, are who we choose as partners. How about holding them up, as they hold us up? A group of femmes = a FORCE. A f*ing beautiful force of women who get sh*t done, are sexy, and love us with all their hearts. [eight likes/loves; one positive comment]

While this is an instance of "calling out," I am no hero. I am most likely to grapple internally with the misogyny, get riled up, but ultimately "move along," as some groups' rules, and other members' policing posts, request members to do. I become complicit, much like in real life, when I don't call out sexism in meetings, or in class, or in other places. Group rules and the overall desire to "not rock the boat," or to "support all butches and femmes," have a chilling effect on feminist activity. Formal rules in all groups I am affiliated with forbid "discourse" and demand positivity/conflict avoidance. One group's rule on "no bullying" advises members that "if you don't like something, move along . . . don't try to make people feel bad [about their post]." These are well intentioned community pages that seek solidarity, love, and support, but in doing so they discourage critical discussion and counterpoints that are much needed for feminist growth within the community.

Words of Wisdom?

Another strong trend in the content was asking for advice. Areas of advice were broad, often revolving around the butch aesthetic, which includes a heightened attention to masculinized fashion, hair style, and other "accessories" that are part and parcel of the butch identity. Most typically, members used photos to ask for advice about how to perform their butchness through, specifically, what to wear (does this sweater work? which looks best––paisley, plaid, or solid tie?), which hairstyle to get, or which shoes go better with this outfit? In another way, members used advice-like posts to seek confirmation and reassurance that their *individual* choices were in line with, and appropriate for, successfully performing butch. What seems frivolous and vain, however, is what makes the butch identity inherently political—the transgressive performance of gender marked most visibly in our everyday lives through what we wear and how we fashion our bodies. Innes (1998), for instance, refers to butch as a "political statement," because the butch "refuses to accept her place as a 'properly feminine' woman in society" (236).

Butch fashion and presentation, however, can lead to very real political outcomes, namely, misgendering. Within the advice category, a subtheme of how to handle misgendering situations emerged. Many butches report "gender trouble" in their everyday lives in places and contexts ranging from mass transit, to at school/in the workplace, grocery stores, while shopping for clothes, and, of course, in the "Ladies" room. Members asked for "words of wisdom on how to handle situations such as this" and "what is your come-back when people call you a boy?" Phrasing of the question—i.e., aggressive as in a "comeback"—and answers—i.e., feeling complimented when called sir, or laughing it off—illustrate the complicated space that sex and gender occupy, specifically in relation to sex- and gender-related identities such as feminist and lesbian.

Butch Winning?

Achievements were shared often within the butch and butch/femme pages. Some exhibited strong self-confidence, a "personal quality" associated with feminism (Calder-Dawe and Gavey 2017), posting authoritative examples of ideal butchness and establishing themselves as "role models." As role models, butches gained cultural capital by responding to requests for advice, which made up another large portion of the interaction, specifically within the butch groups. Some achievement posts were less confident and more seeking vali-dation that they "got it right" and successfully achieved their butch identity.

The group feeds are full of achievements that celebrate butch success across a variety of areas. Good shopping finds, outfit selection, perfect haircuts, and "looks" are consistent with the butch pages focusing on butch style and care. These pages also included butches succeeding at work and in relationships, contributing to the framing of butch and butch/femme as pow-erful, ascendant identities. Posts about "asking" and "saying yes," along with wedding photos are prominent. These postings reveal the fruits of feminism's labors, which fought as part of the LGBTQ+ rights movement for marriage equality. In many ways, the achievement posts reveal a key function of the groups—allowing for, empowering, and inspiring a transformation or com-ing into oneself as a result of group content/support. Many posters who share their achievement include a note of gratitude to the group community, such as "I couldn't have done it without your support." This marks the achievement as not only personal, but rather collective, thus suggesting a salient feminism.

Trust/Respect

Content

Memes

Advice

Achieve-ments

Transformation

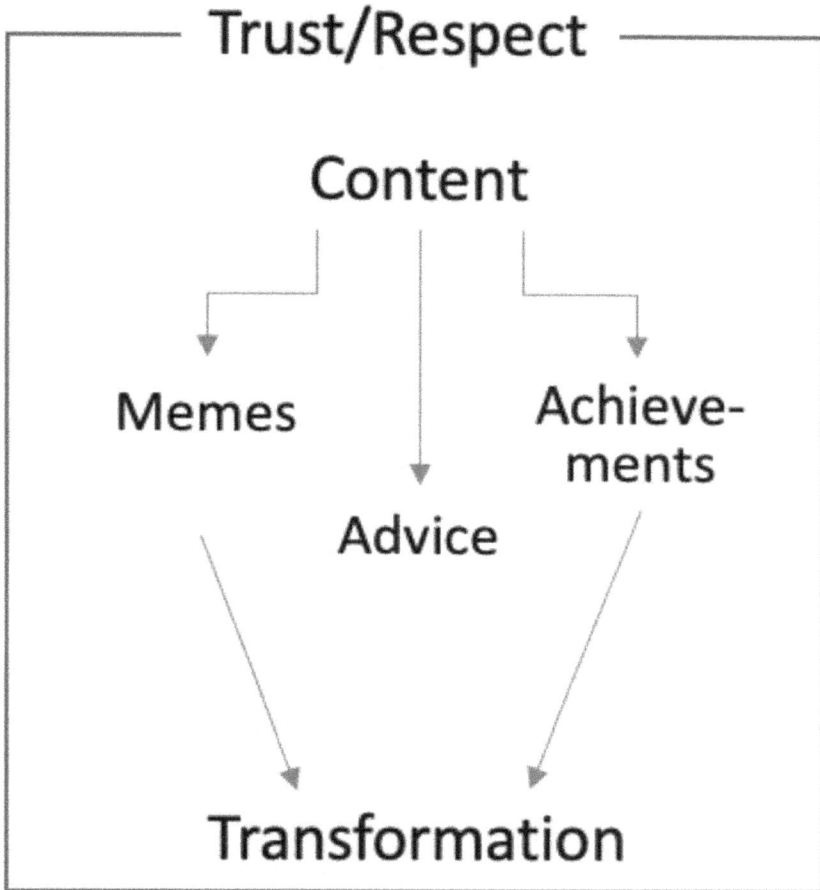

Figure 5.1. Butch performance and participation in Facebook Groups. *Courtesy of the author.*

A Model of Butch Performance and Participation

Based on the findings presented above, butch performance and participation in these butch and butch/femme groups can be visualized in figure 5.1.

Butches and femmes enter the groups with a trust and respect for one another that creates a safe space for identity performance and vulnerability. Within this environment, content is produced and shared that reflects the values of the community, which are centered around celebrating and honoring the distinct forms of mas(k)ulinity and fem(me)ininity that underpin butch/ femme relationships and identities. Likes and Comments reinforce group values and norms, which can have both a chilling effect on butch expression (i.e., I can't wear makeup and be butch) or a liberating effect from hegemonic norms (i.e., I can be masculine, butch, and still be a woman). Participation in this community through interaction with content allows for a transformation, which in these groups is the self-confidence of being true to oneself and also true to the shared identities of butch and femme. That is, butches reported, through posted comments and pictures within the group, as having the self-confidence to wear a tie in public for the first time, or, to wear a tank top that revealed their unshaven armpits, get a buzz cut or fade, ask someone out, and/or come out at work, etc. The online community opened a space for not only butch identity development and expression, but also the development of an inherent feminism that could be carried into the real world. This "Butch Feminism" is identified next.

Finding Butch Feminism

Overall findings suggest that there is an inherent "feminism" in the group pages as supported by the content posted, and subsequent empowerment and transformation of members. Butch emerged as a form of "embodied politics," which Fixmer and Wood (2005) define as "personal and often physical, bodily action that aims to provoke change by exercising and resisting power in everyday life" (237). Moreira (2017) goes further, describing embodied politics as a working-class practice that wrestle feminist activism from a white, privileged base and brings it into our everyday lives. Class generally intersects with other points of identity, but, more specifically, with the butch identity, as "butch" grew from working-class roots in the 1950s (Faderman 1991). According to Moreira (2017), embodied politics includes: (1) redefining identity by engaging the complexities of differences, ambiguities, and multiplicities in and between women; (2) building and working with coalitions to forge an inclusive solidarity; and (3) engaging in personal acts of resistance in local sites where injustices occur (237). Each of these are observed within butch activity in butch and butch/femme groups. The embodied politics of butch, however, rarely invoked the "f-word" (Peoples 2008) of feminism, yet was, for the most part, steeped in the feminist activities, qualities, values, and structural processes found in the literature, and described as "key markers" of feminism in the Method section of this chapter.

Most cogent in the content was connections to self-knowledge, confidence, and a commitment to each within the struggles of nonconformity (Calder-Dawe and Gavey 2017; Grunig, Toth, and Hon 2000) as well as valuing and respecting differences and individual lived experiences (Webb, Allen, and Walker 2002). As such, participation in the group, as evidenced through posts, provided for a sense of empowerment for members to be the butch they wanted to be. Posts indicated transformation, and finally "feeling myself," while also explicitly expressing thanks to the group for supporting and helping in their journey. As previously reported, many expressed that they "couldn't have done it without this group."

Thus, we can see a theory of "butch feminism" taking form. Butch feminism is the struggle against the gender hegemony and hetero-norm. It emphasizes the freedom for gendered lives beyond the binary male/masculine, female/feminine, and the valuing of distinctive butch/femme relationships that transcend gender and are anti-sexist. Butch feminism relies on butches performing a "feminist masculinity" based on self-esteem and self-love (hooks 2015) and/or a mas(k)ulinity (Silverman and Comeforo 2019) that at once obscures underlying sex and heightens the interplay between masculinity and femininity that are both constantly present/absent within butch and femme identities.

Yet Still, Feminist Failings?

Despite evidence of feminism, the groups still struggled with some of the basic tenets of feminism and feminist thinking. Failings occurred in two key areas: the structure of the groups and content.

Structure: A Bounded, Rather than Open, "Democracy"

Each of the four groups under analysis are "private" groups that potential members must request to join. They are created and managed through administrators and moderators who control group settings, make the rules, and enforce the rules by managing membership and posts on a daily basis. Membership requests require the "applicant" to answer a few questions and agree to abide by the group rules. Questions emphasize community membership and identity, asking things such as whether the applicant is butch or femme and what these identities mean to them. Some ask specifically about gender and sexual identities, either to exclude (i.e., "This is NOT a full spectrum lgbt group. It is specifically for Butch and Femme lesbians. That means we are for women only. No men, trans men, bisexuals/pansexuals or genderqueer. You can choose one option—Butch or Femme?") or include (i.e., "This Group includes Trans men as well as male identified Butches, Transmasculine and/or nonbinary folks. Transphobia is not tolerated. Do you agree?").

Each group is further governed by a set of rules, that not only bind members to standards in terms of posting, but also in terms of what it means to be butch, lesbian, and, even, a woman. Indeed, "the question of genitals and who 'really' counts as a woman, as well as debates over who counts as a lesbian"

(Weber 2015, 650) are on the minds of administrators of these groups as they write and seek to enforce rules for membership, both digitally in the group and socially more broadly. The groups actively avoid and restrict politics, which are called out as "discourse" and are forbidden according to the membership rules. Administrators and moderators manage the settings of the group (i.e., name, description, and rules) and group activity (i.e., reviewing posts and posting prompts to encourage interaction) respectively, and thus are the curators of both the group's intent/mission (what it stands for) and, more generally, what it means to be butch and oriented toward butch/femme. Informal reviews of demographics indicated that the groups included in my analysis are predominantly run by white, female-identified administrators and moderators. One of the groups was formed and is run by the founder of a known butch fashion brand. While this "corporate ownership" does not seem to impact group content, it does serve as a reminder of the intimate connections between media, culture, and capitalism that often leads to the privileging of elite ideals and the marginalization of all others (Herman and Chomsky 1988). Still, this does not say that the community members themselves are not politicized, and that the content posted apolitical. As mentioned earlier in this chapter, memes use humor to subtly inject politicized themes in unexpected places (Miltner 2018), and, as they allow for different readings of the same artifact, they provide a means for "negotiating" sociocultural norms (Gal, Shifman, and Kampf 2016), thus providing opportunity to subvert hegemonic systems of gender and sexuality.

Content: Explicit and Complicit Misogyny and Sexism

The butch/femme groups, rather than the butch "only" groups, struggled with misogynistic and sexist content. The content itself violates feminist ideals that seek equity and equality, that value women's experiences, and value women as whole people, rather than simply sexist objects. Compounding the feminist failure was that the misogynistic and sexist content was almost completely accepted by the group. That is, few, if any, comments called out the sexism and/or engaged in counter-discourse. This violates tenets of everyday feminism such as moral obligations to each other and speaking out (Francis and Hey 2009), while also indicating a refusal to participate in the "call-out culture" that is indicative of feminism's fourth wave (Lawrence and Ringrose 2018).

CONCLUSION

Butch and butch/femme groups on Facebook are ideal sites for studying and understanding how, or if, feminism permeates butch/femme lived realities and these butch/femme spaces. Overall, findings describe activities that can be considered politics without the "p-word," and feminism without the "f-word." Still, a discernible butch feminism emerged. Whether called feminism or not, transgressive gender presentation can be considered an "everyday feminist" practice. It is part of an "everyday feminism" that is incorporated into these butches' (and femmes') daily lives and is reflected through the performance of mas(k)ulinity and fem(me)ininity (Silverman and Comeforo 2019), which are further reflective of refusal moments/resistance to traditional gender roles and nonverbal forms of speaking out (Francis and Hey 2009; Schuster 2017; Webb, Allen, and Walker 2002). While butches in these groups don't use the "f-word" to describe their activity, this research has shown that their activity is marked by feminist tenets and ideals. If we consider Lawrence and Ringrose's (2018) assertion that "feminists are turning to social media sites to make visible marginalized voices and bodies, either through amplifying the stories of others or through drawing attention to their own experiences, which has opened up significant spaces for resistance to hegemonic femininities" (213), we can see that butches are performing all sorts of feminism in these butch and butch/femme Facebook groups. That is, like the 1970s lesbian activist group the Furies, these butches are "developing a lesbian feminist politic" (Sheir 2015).

Can butches be feminists? Yes. "A word doesn't will a movement into being. Action does" (Valenti 2014, 20). And that action, as accomplished through everyday feminism, provides us with "small victories" (Schuster 2017) that are important and critical to the movement nonetheless.

REFERENCES

Banet-Weiser, Sarah, and Kate M. Miltner. 2016. "MasculinitySoFragile: Culture, Structure, and Networked Misogyny." *Feminist Media Studies* 16 (1): 171–74.
Bergman, S. Bear. 2006. *Butch Is a Noun*. Arsenal Pulp Press.
Browne, Kath. 2004. "Genderism and the Bathroom Problem: (Re)materialising Sexed Sites, (Re)creating Sexed Bodies." *Gender, Place and Culture* 11 (3): 331–46.
Calder-Dawe, Octavia, and Nicola Gavey. 2017. "Authentic Feminist? Authenticity and Feminist Identity in Teenage Feminists' Talk." *British Journal of Social Psychology* 56: 782–98.

Chen, Jian Neo. 2019. *Trans Exploits: Trans of Color Cultures & Technologies in Movement.* Duke University Press.

Compton, Julie. 2019. "'Pro-lesbian' or 'Trans-exclusionary'? Old Animosities Boil into Public View." NBC News. January 4, 2019.

Corbin, Juliet, and Anselm Strauss. 1990. "Grounded Theory Research: Procedures, Canons, and Evaluative Criteria." *Zietschrift für Soziologie* 19 (6): 418–27.

duCoudray, Chantal Bourgault. 2016. "A 'Disappointing' Leader: The Postmaternalism of Public Feminist Commentary on Julia Gillard." *Continuum: Journal of Media & Cultural Studies* 30 (3): 274–83.

Faderman, Lillian 1991. *Odd Girls and Twilight Lovers: A History of Lesbian Life in Twentieth-Century America.* Penguin Books.

Francis, Becky, and Valerie Hey. 2009. "Talking Back to Power: Snowballs in Hell and the Imperative of Insisting on Structural Explanations." *Gender and Education* 21 (2): 225–32.

Gal, Noam, Limor Shifman, and Zohar Kampf. 2016. "'It Gets Better': Internet Memes and the Construction of Collective Identity. *New Media & Society* 18 (8): 1698–714.

Gray, Mary. 2009. "Negotiating Identities/Queering Desires: Coming Out Online and the Remediation of the Coming Out Story." *Journal of Computer Mediated Communication* 14: 1162–89.

Grunig, Larissa A., Elizabeth L. Toth, and Linda Childers Hon. 2000. "Feminist Values in Public Relations." *Journal of Public Relations Research* 12: 49–68.

Halberstam, J. J. 1998. *Female Masculinity.* Duke University Press.

Hammersly, Martyn. 1992. "On Feminist Methodology." *Sociology* 26 (2): 187–206.

heinz, matthew. 2016. *Entering Transmasculinity: The Inevitability of Discourse.* intellect.

Herman, Stuart, and Noam Chomsky. 1988. *Manufacturing Consent: The Political Economy of the Mass Media.* Pantheon.

hooks, bell. 2015. *Feminism Is for Everybody.* Routledge.

Inness, Sherrie A. 1998. "Flunking Basic Gender Training: Butches and Butch Style Today." In *Looking Queer: Body Image and Identity in Lesbian, Bisexual, Gay, and Transgender Communities*, edited by Dawn Atkins. Haworth Press, 233–37.

Iovannone, Jeffry J. 2018. "Rita Mae Brown: Lavender Menace." *Medium.* June 4, 2018.

Jackson, Sarah J. 2016. "(Re)imagining Intersectional Democracy from Black Feminism to Hashtag Activism." *Women's Studies in Communication* 39 (4): 375–79.

Johnson, E. Patrick. 2001. "'Quare' Studies, Or (Almost) Everything I Know About Queer Studies I Learned from My Grandmother." In *The Queer Studies Reader*, edited by Donald Hall and Annamarie Jagose, 96–117. Routledge.

Kennedy, Tracy L. M. 2007. "The Personal Is Political: Feminist Blogging and Virtual Consciousness-raising." *The Scholar and Feminist* 5 (2): n.p.

Levitt, Heidi M., and Katherine R. Hiestand. (2004). "A Quest for Authenticity: Contemporary Butch Gender." *Sex Roles* 50 (9/10): 605–21.

Miltner, Kate M. 2018. "Internet Memes." In *The SAGE Handbook of Social Media*, edited by Jean Burgess, Alice Marwick, and Thomas Poell. Sage, 412–28.

Mocarski, Richard, Sim Butler, Betsy Emmons, and Rachael Smallwood. 2013. "'A Different Kind of Man': Mediated Transgender Subjectivity, Chaz Bono on *Dancing with the Stars*." *Journal of Communication Inquiry* 37 (3): 249–64.

Peoples, Whitney A. 2008. "'Under Construction': Identifying Foundations in Hip-Hop Feminism and Exploring Bridges Between Black Second-Wave and Hip-Hop Feminisms." *Meridians: Feminisms, Race, Transnationalism* 8 (1): 19–52.

Phillipov, Michelle. 2013. "In Defense of Textual Analysis: Resisting Methodological Hegemony in Media and Cultural Studies." *Critical Studies in Media Communications* 30 (3): 209–23.

Prosser, Jay. 1995. "No Place Like Home: The Transgendered Narrative of Leslie Feinberg's *Stone Butch Blues*." *Modern Fiction Studies* 41 (3–4): 483–514.

Rentschler, Carrie A., and Samantha C. Thrift. 2015. "Doing Feminism in the Network: Networked Laughter and the 'Binders Full of Women' Meme." *Feminist Theory* 16 (3): 329–59.

Rooke, Alison. 2007. "Navigating Embodied Lesbian Cultural Space: Toward a Lesbian Habitus." *Space and Culture* 10: 231–52.

Schuster, Julia. 2017. "Why the Personal Remained Political: Comparing Second and Third Wave Perspectives on Everyday Feminism." *Social Movement Studies* 16 (6): 647–59.

Sheir, Rebecca. 2015. "Inside the HQ of D.C.'s Short-Lived but Influential Lesbian Separatist Collective." WAMU 88.5: American University Radio. November 6, 2015.

Silverman, Rachel E., and Kristin Comeforo. 2019. "Patriarchy Interrupted: Differential Realizations and Manifestations of Power in Butch/Femme Relationships." *Cultural Studies Critical Methodology* 20 (2): 1–13.

Taylor, Keeanga-Yamahtta. 2017. *How We Get Free: Black Feminism and the Combahee River Collective.* Haymarket Books.

Valenti, Jessica. 2014. "When Everyone Is a Feminist, Is Anyone? *The Guardian*. November 24, 2014.

Webb, Lynne M., Myria W. Allen, and Kandi L. Walker. 2002. "Feminist Pedagogy: Identifying Basic Principles." *Academic Exchange* 6 (1): 67–72.

Weber, Shannon. 2015. "Lesbian Communities." *The International Encyclopedia of Human Sexuality*: 649–719.

Chapter 6

"Please Send a Video of Yourself Breaking Shit"

The "Digital Assembly Video" and Networked Feminist Solidarities

Julie Ravary-Pilon

On February 21, 2012, five members of the collective Pussy Riot entered the cathedral of Christ the Savior in Moscow to perform a punk prayer. Wearing balaclavas and brightly colored clothes, a stone's throw from the Kremlin they denounced the collusion between the Orthodox Church and the political powers in place, asking the Holy Virgin to hunt Vladimir Putin for having violated the fundamental rights of marginalized sexual identities: "Virgin Mary, Mother of God, become a feminist, we pray thee [. . .] Freedom's phantom's gone to heaven Gay Pride chained in detention" (Pussy Riot 2012). The one-and-a-half-minute video recording of this action was uploaded online a few hours after the performance and quickly traveled the world. The video shows the performers beating their fists, playing the guitar, running, fleeing the security guards, being knocked to the ground, kicking the air, and, finally, being forced down the altar to the exit of the church. A few days after their performance, on March 3, 2012, three of the five members (Nadezhda "Nadia" Tolokonnikova, Maria Alyokhina, and Yekaterina Samutsevich) were arrested, and public reactions to the arrest culminated in August 2012 as the verdict was about to be announced. Official charges of hooliganism were made on August 17, 2012, when Tolokonnikova and Alyokhina were sentenced to two years in prison.

One of the actions made in support of the imprisoned members of the collective is the video *Free Pussy Riot* (2012) by Canadian multidisciplinary artist Peaches, cowritten with Simmone Jones. In early August, still waiting for the judgment, Peaches posted a message on Facebook inviting supporters of Pussy Riot to participate in collective actions: "If you are in Berlin, show up dressed as your best bad self and FREE PUSSY RIOT. [. . .] If you are not in Berlin, please send a 30-second video of yourself showing support by dancing, jumping on your bed, breaking shit, laughing, holding a free pussy riot sign, etc." (Peaches 2012). In this post, the musician asked people in Berlin to perform in the streets under her direction. She also invited internet users who could not gather at the physical place because of their geographical location, disabilities, financial situation, or otherwise to send auto-mise-en-scène—a self-staged video—that she would join, through editing, to clips of the Berlin walk: "Please send a second video of yourself showing support by dancing, jumping on your bed, breaking shit, laughing, holding a Free Pussy Riot sign" (Peaches 2012). This assembled video of the Berlin actions and global fan actions streamed online via Peaches' personal YouTube channel, PeachesTV, on Wednesday, August 15, 2012, and gathers clips of the event in Berlin as well as excerpts of seventy videos submitted by internet users. At the end of the video, the audience is invited to sign the petition "Free Pussy Riot" on the website change.org, a petition that accumulated more than 146,899 electronic signatures.

Peaches' video is one of the first manifestations of what I call "Digital Assembly Video" (DAV). DAV is distinguished from other activist art traditions, such as DIY (Do It Yourself) and zine aesthetics, by its political foundations and specifically aesthetic roots. This genre of video is part of what many have described as the dawn of a fourth feminist wave that emerged with the arrival of Web 2.0. This chapter will explore how Peaches, and DAV more broadly, convenes multimedia communication methods that are specific to social media platforms to create performative assemblies (Butler 2015), emphasizing Butler's exploration of the importance of media in recent political assemblies. This operative concept of media assembly allows scholars to consider the various potentials of the internet as a "decentralizer" of the new possibilities offered to collective creation that allows bodies to stage themselves when these people cannot appear in rallies or cannot take the streets. It is precisely this possibility of the self-constitution of these assemblies that is relevant to the collective-participatory aesthetic process used in the video *Free Pussy Riot*.

In order to make the argument that *Free Pussy Riot* is one of the leading works of the new tradition of DAV, this chapter considers how theories of media genres (drawing on Altman), fourth-wave feminisms' "affective temporalities" (drawing on Chamberlain), and the technologies of pop feminist activism (drawing on Stehle and Smith-Prei) offer a fuller understanding of DAV's emergence as a new genre of political video. Bringing these theories together, this chapter explores the genre of DAV as one that allows new modes of visibility for feminist network solidarities. Overall, I argue that these feminist solidarities work to take shape in a space that permits a collaborative construction of knowledge and a digital form of political protest that can be produced and broadcast in new ways, instantaneously.

TOWARD A SEMANTIC/SYNTACTIC APPROACH TO THE DAV

To delineate DAV as a new videographic genre, I first wish to consider Rick Altman's discussion of the "genre film" and his distinction between semantic and syntactic elements. I use this distinction to argue that DAV can be understood as a new videographic genre emerging through the specific technical development of digital video's democratization and opportunities for sharing that are encouraged by social media as a form of participatory culture. Altman's theoretical proposal reconciles the differing approaches within genre theory, which establish the narrative and aesthetic bases of narrative genres and genre history; this theory also focuses on the development, deployment, and disappearance of genres and their structure without considering the hybrid forms of such genres. Altman (1984) proposes that combining syntactic and semantic genres can reconcile the two. As he notes, "these two categories of generic analysis are complementary, and may be combined, and in fact, that some of the most important questions of the study may be asked when they are combined" (11). Altman defines the distinctions between the semantic elements, also known as "text materials," and syntactic elements, which he qualifies as the structure of the genre as the semantic. Here, the semantic is "building blocks," which include "common traits, attitudes, characters, shots, locations, sets" and the structural arrangements of the syntactical, or the "certain constitutive relationships between undesignated and variable placeholders" (10). Against this backdrop, I argue that DAV constitutes a genre in itself.

In the specific case of *Free Pussy Riot*, I suggest that the semantic elements include DIY cultural aesthetics, the symbol of the Digital Sign (Paveau 2017) and the use of conversational images (Gunthert 2014), with Butler's (2015) notion of performative assembly functioning as its syntactic structure. I will return to a more exhaustive definition of these semantic and syntactic elements in my analysis of *Free Pussy Riot* below. However, first it is important to note that the emergence of DAV as a genre takes place within the specific technical and technological conjuncture of Web 2.0. A brief overview of its emergence and its infrastructure will allow a clearer understanding of the development of the participatory culture interpellated by the DAV, as well as its relationship to what scholars have called the fourth wave of feminism.

A SOCIOTECHNICAL APPROACH
TO THE SOCIAL WEB

The history of the web is marked by its structural evolution from merely being a digital binary system connected by hyperlinks to a site of social networks. The Web 1.0, or the static web of the 1990s, connected information by relying on the "push" system of data distribution. It was a web of portals, a network in which the textual information was made available to the user by the webmaster without allowing extensive interaction between users and the central hub of dissemination. Web 2.0, also known as the social or participatory web, appeared at the beginning of the 2000s and is characterized both by the possibility given to users to create their own content but also by its potential to connect people using online digital platforms. In this version of the internet, users can participate in discussions, exchange information, and socialize. The distinction between content producer, as seen in the work of the webmaster in Web 1.0, and consumer is blurred in Web 2.0: one can both be producer and consumer of discourse; you can both code and decode its content. The phase of Web 2.0 ushered in the emergence of social networking platforms such as Facebook (2004), YouTube (2005), and Twitter (2006). In the early 2010s, however, digital culture moved to integrate Web 3.0: the semantic web based on highly sophisticated information gathering and data organizing. Currently, we are seeing the emergence of Web 4.0, also known as the intelligent web or Metaweb, which integrates smart devices that connect all elements of our living environment (Paveau 2017, 14–15).

Within this history and future of the web, I locate DAV as part of Web 2.0: the web of a so-called participatory culture. In *Web Social: Mutation de la Communication,* Florence Millerand, Serge Proulx, and Julien Rueff (2010) describe social networks, or what they term the "Social Web" as a "technical dimension" that can "provide programmers with functionalities encouraging users to collaborate with each other, with the aim to create and share content through tools such as blogs, wiki, social networking sites, music, image or video sharing sites, metaverse, content syndication or labeling" (2). The Social Web, through its "development of original mediated uses and its devices focused on the active participation of users in the production and dissemination of content circulating on the Web" (2), reflects clearly the ultimate goal of the internet's founders to connect billions of people. It is also within the rise of social networks that user-generated content begins to appear in unprecedented ways. For Millerand, Proulx, and Rueff, it is precisely the participatory dimension of this era that generates significant changes in communication practices. Their sociotechnical study on how technical devices allow new forms of social relations brings to light the particular context of the emergence of the DAV.

Building on this, it is important for scholars to then rethink our discursive analysis of the web because of its participatory nature. Marie-Anne Paveau (2017) argues that "these different realities of the web do not constitute equivalent grounds for linguistics because the communication, the interaction and the publication of content do not have the same characteristics and thus do not allow the same discursive forms. This is why the logocentrism of some approaches do not account for all aspects of online communication" (15).[1] In this way, we can understand the transformations of the web as akin to Russian dolls: the structural elements of each period of the web are always present in the era that follows it. Similarly, the structure elucidated by Russian dolls applies just as well to thinking through the waves of feminism.

FROM FOURTH-WAVE FEMINISM TO
FEMINIST TEMPORALITIES

Simply put, the first wave of feminism is characterized by the movement of suffragettes, while the second wave articulates the notion that "the personal is political" and the third wave insists that the relations of powers and privileges should be thought of as intersectional. Even though they are different claims, each of these waves exists in relation to the next. For instance, women's right to vote from earlier feminist waves was not given to all, and its legacies of racism and the centering of affluent white women's priorities are relevant to an intersectional approach a century later. Further, the MeToo movement from this most recent wave of feminism reminded us that power over women's bodies is always topical and is always both personal and political. The idea of feminist waves' coexistence is central to Prudence Chamberlain's (2017) argument in *The Feminist Fourth Wave: Affective Temporalities*. Chamberlain states, "When a new wave is declared, it emerges, it does not eradicate previous efforts of previous waves. In fact, it is simply adding a particular surge to an ongoing struggle for equality" (7). Many have examined this idea of the affective temporalities embedded within different waves of feminism (e.g., Sara Ahmed 2004; Clare Hemmings 2010), which, importantly, inform my reading of the production context of Peaches' video and the emergence of the DAV.

Since at least 2010, feminist media scholars have noted the role that Web 2.0 has taken in revolutionizing the way feminist activism discourses circulate (Baer 2016; Fotopoulou 2016; Garrison 2010; Maule 2016; Munro

2013; Wiens and MacDonald 2020). The effect of this technological revolution has precipitated what some have called the fourth wave of feminism. This technological shift in communication, which appears at the beginning of the 2000s but really takes off between 2008 and 2010, influenced the organization of feminist thinking and, by so doing, conveyed a new type of mobilization based on digital content sharing. An early example of feminist mobilizing online includes the Slut Walks, which began in April 2011 following a Toronto police officer's statement that female students should not dress promiscuously if they did not want to be assaulted on college campuses. In response, a feminist activist created a Facebook page calling for Torontonians to take the street to protest this public statement. This event became the first of many Sluts Walks to come; dozens of these events subsequently took place during the summer of 2011 in Canada first, then in the United States and subsequently in Switzerland, Bolivia, India, South Korea, and other countries. These marches are the first of this scale to be organized exclusively on the web.

In another example of web-based organizing, in 2014, in the wake of the debates over a legal definition of consent triggered by Jian Gomeshi's highly publicized trial,[2] Canadian journalists Antonia Zerbisias and Sue Montgomery created the hashtag #BeenRapedNeverReported to draw attention to the lack of reporting around rape and sexual assault. Eight million people took up the hashtag to share their experiences of sexual assault, making it a space of healing, testimony, and support for thousands of people who, without the technology of the web, could never have all been connected this broadly. The recent efforts of the #MeToo movement, originally created by Tarana Burke in the early 2000s, reflects the denunciations and mobilizations seen through #BeenRapedNeverReported and highlight the importance of the internet for calling attention to the rights of marginalized genders.

Like all forms of categorization of political or artistic movements that are not self-claimed, the idea of fourth-wave feminism is not accepted by all. One of the biggest criticisms of the fourth wave is the (in)accessibility of the internet. According to statistics from the International Telecommunication Union, in 2011, a few months before the creation of Peaches' video, only one-third of the population had the access needed to be considered an internet user (International Telecommunication Union 2011). By 2019, the accessibility of the web had expanded considerably. It is now estimated that one in two people currently use an internet network, with 4.1 billion people being active users on the internet, according to the International Telecommunication Union (2019). However, the production of content for the web is not available to everyone, either by geographical context (internet networks do not reach all locations), sociopolitical (censorship), or economic (an internet connection, computers, and recording devices such as cell phones remain expensive tools) factors.

As such, social networks are not as democratized a tool as some suggest. And yet, when it is accessible, the digital networks have unprecedented potential for connectivity and communicative immediacy. It is precisely these two characteristics that situate fourth-wave feminism as offering a new discursive method for the sharing of political ideas. Chamberlain (2017) notes that social media should be understood as a platform made available and used by a wide range of women, and that social media are not the exclusive tool of the younger generations: it is used by all age communities. This new development in feminist activism should not be understood as dividing generations of feminists, but as a point in history when these technological devices are creating new discursive apparatuses for feminists.

An understanding of the waves as representative of the historical conjunctures, rather than generationally determined, allows for a more inclusive conception of the waves; waves emerge when a younger group of women come to politics looking to shape a social movement that is more accommodating of, and tailored to, their identity. However, this is not to be confused with historical specificity, which speaks far more to my understanding of affective temporality. As Chamberlain (2017) writes, "historical specificity suggests that feminism as a social movement must adapt as times change. [. . .] The fourth wave is not a narcissistic declaration, nor is it a simple repetition of previous waves. Rather, it is the acknowledgment of an affectively intense period of feminist activism" (8–12). Wave imagery, therefore, cannot be defined according to the precise dates of their anticipated beginning and ends if we want a historical representation of feminist movements that, rather than foreground difference, highlight the forces that were maintained between each of them.

Chamberlain (2017) usefully proposes that we situate different feminist waves as "affective temporalities," encouraging an understanding of these different periods as being tied into an "intense affective response to specific social context[s]" (38). Distancing herself from a definition of the wave's imagery as a succession of independent blocks following one another according to a numerical delimitation, Chamberlain presents these movements as being part of the same "ocean," generated by affective impulses shared by communities in front of a common feeling. Within this framework, the fourth wave can be seen as a networked solidarity that unfolds simultaneously through both online and offline activism that is organized in public spaces. These elements of affect, connectivity, and immediacy lie within the aesthetics of DAV and are important parts of Peaches' video creation. In the following section, I offer a closer analysis of the Canadian artist Peaches' work to offer insights into the ways in which protest is visualized in *Free Pussy Riot*.

PEACHES, PUSSY RIOT, AND THE DAV AESTHETIC

Since her debut, Peaches' multidisciplinary body of art has been associated with punk culture. Whether it is the rhythm and lyrics of her music or her extravagant mise-en-scène using a typically punk fashion, Peaches' art has always been linked to this culture of resistance. Stacy Thompson, in her text "Punk Cinema" (2004), describes the punk cinematic aesthetic as a genre that "mimics punk music's speed, frenetic energy, anger, anti-authoritarian stance, irony, style, anomie, or disillusionment" (47). This energy crystallizes in the demand to don bright colors, emitted in Peaches' message to internet audiences: PLEASE WEAR BRIGHT SOLID COLORS (Peaches 2012), in tribute to the costumes and colorful balaclavas of Pussy Riot and in the fast pace of the visual editing.

The editing chosen by Peaches is much faster than the average montage of films and videos of the time. The average shot length of *Free Pussy Riot* is twice as short as the rhythms of popular trends videos in 2012.[3] Rhythmic cadence is an integral part of punk music and cinema, but punk culture is above all characterized by an ethic of liberation from the commodification of art whether in music, fashion, zine, or in cinema.[4] Punk artists put forward this duality between creative practices and economics. It is for this reason that one of the maxims of punk culture is "do it yourself" (DIY). It is this sort of democratizing dictum that an inscription of this culture outside of the system would be made possible. Peaches' invitation to users is accompanied by a set of guidelines to ensure continuity between self-filmed scenes via a post on her open Facebook page, which testifies to this public encouragement of DIY:

> THIS IS A CALL TO ALL PUSSY RIOT SUPPORTERS, whether you are in Berlin or anywhere in the world. Peaches and Simonne Jones are writing a FREE PUSSY RIOT SONG today and shooting a video for it on Wednesday. If you are in Berlin, show up dress as your best bad self and march down the streets and in the park with us singing FREE PUSSY RIOT. The more the better so bring supporters with you. We will meet at 5pm outside rain or shine, Glory Whole cafe. PLEASE WEAR BRIGHT SOLID COLORS . . . If you are not in Berlin or can't make it, please send a 30 second video of yourself showing support by dancing, jumping on your bed, breaking shit, laughing, holding a free pussy riot sign, etc. Send a link to your video to my email . . . we will edit this on the weekend and get it out to the world by Monday. We have to do this!!!!! Thxxx to you all and FREE PUSSY (August 8, 2012).

In their book *Awkward Politics: Technologies of Popfeminist Activism*, Maria Stehle and Carrie Smith-Prei (2016) specifically comment on the written form of this invitation message, writing that "In its grammatical and lexical missteps, its running together of sentences, its text messaging-like shortening of words or preference for lower case, and its excessive use of exclamation marks, the call communicates a sense of immediate urgency pushed forward by emotion" (4). Undoubtedly, the text seems to take the shortcuts offered by digital exchanges between people and transmits to audiences the urgency to act through its tone. What is particularly interesting is that the "grammatical and lexical missteps" seems to be quite conscious on the part of the artist. She inscribes her language register in a linguistic and lexical form that does not conform to institutional English and therefore takes place outside of dominant linguistic systems, offering again a form of resistance that could be seen as part of punk culture. Teal Triggs' (2006) work speaks to this when Triggs describes punk aesthetics as a "graphic language of resistance in contemporary Western culture" (72). According to Triggs, this resistance would occur through a return to an era of handwriting. The DIY aesthetic of Peaches' video thus reveals an extension of a cultural form of resistance developed specifically in the potentials of the participatory web.

THE DIGITAL SIGN

The iconography of a handwriting, central to the culture of punk zines, joins the envisioned effect of what Paveau (2017) called *pancarte numérique*, a term that can be translated to "digital sign." The digital sign consists of a person addressing the camera with a written sign in her hand. The photographic or audiovisual recording is then uploaded to an online space. Paveau describes the digital sign as a socio-discursive practice that puts forward the corporeality of the interlocutor: The manuscript writing of the digital sign "ensures the commitment of the interlocutor. In any case, the sign proves that with digital, we are far from the myth of dematerialization and the lack of physicality on the web" (330–31).[5]

The digital sign adapts traditional uses of political signs and slogans used in street protests of the twentieth and translates them to the twenty-first-century public spaces created by the web. Digital sign imagery emerged with the beginning of social networks in the mid-2000s. Today, it has become a staple for many online social campaigns. According to Paveau, the digital sign is now "the central semiotic tool of digital campaigns with humanitarian, social or political dimensions, innumerable on the internet" (Paveau 2017, 328). Examples of campaigns that use the digital sign include the Unbreakable Project by activist and photographer Grace Brown who, in 2011, set up an email address where survivors of sexual assault, child abuse, and domestic violence could send a photo of their experience, their wish for the future, or their encouragement to other survivors. One can also think of the "*Je désobéis à la Loi 128/* I Disobey Law 78" campaign as part of the protest against public assembly bans issued by the provincial government of Jean Charest's Liberal Party during the Quebec student strike in 2012.

Here, in figure 6.1, the digital sign is a semantic element of the genre DAV. Its use of handwriting foregrounds the corporeality of the person onscreen via the frame of the sign that they surround. The message created or endorsed by the onscreen body is thus accompanied by a face (masked or not) and hands. In the case of the video *Free Pussy Riot*, some internet users wrote their message directly on their body thus producing a reconfiguration of the digital sign that places the body at the center of the speech. These types of inscription on the body also testify to an even more personal and intrinsic commitment to collective political action.

In figure 6.2, by employing the digital sign as a discursive device, this type of DAV aesthetics ensures that the words of the individual are joined to her personal body via a self-conceived mise-en-scène. One can also put a face or identify the bodies constituting the collective. This maneuver counters the bad reputations of collective movement on the web believed to be unrepresentative (fake accounts) or not being as involved as other methods of support (distant or aloof "likes"). In short, it breaks the myth of dematerialization and the lack of physicality on the web that Paveau (2017) refers to and that I quoted earlier. It is important to note that these formal traits used by current DAV practices (i.e., aesthetics of the resistance and DIY culture, handwriting, and political relations to the bodies) are reminiscent of the semantics elements of feminist political media from preceding decades. They illustrate an important migration of long-standing formal elements for new uses according to the aesthetic and discursive potential of the web. Moreover, the semantic

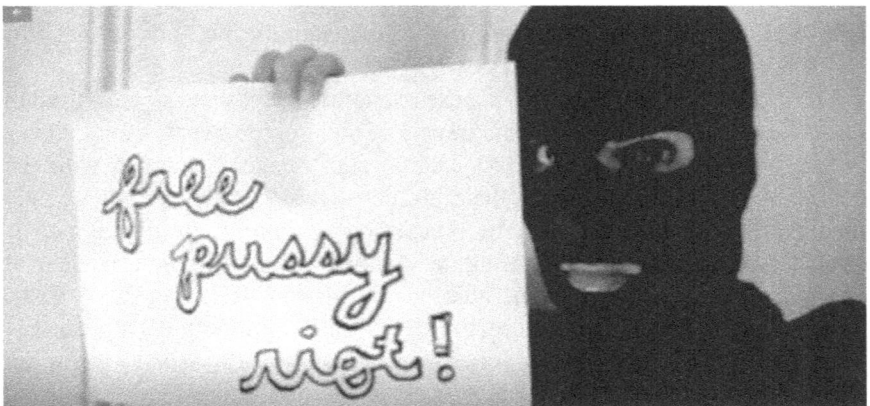

Figure 6.1. Screenshot from Peaches TV on YouTube showing a person wearing a bala-clava with the handwritten sign "free pussy riot!" *Source:* https://www.youtube.com/watch?v=SaJ7GzPvJKw

Figure 6.2. Screenshot from Peaches TV on YouTube showing three people, faces obscured by homemade balaclavas, with the words "free pussy riot" written across their fingers. *Source:* **https://www.youtube.com/watch?v=SaJ7GzPvJKw**

element of the "conversational image," which I will outline further below, emerges in its current format because of recent digital innovations, such as the democratization of content sharing with the arrival of social media platforms.

THE CONVERSATIONAL IMAGE

The concept of the conversational image comes from André Gunthert's (2014) proposal that special attention should be paid to the digitization of images beyond their quality or the precision of the image, thinking instead in terms of their fluidity and "conversationality." Gunthert notes, "the digitization, by reducing the materiality of the images, confers them a new plasticity and mobility. Under the kind of files that are easy to copy or manipulate, the iconic object becomes a fluid image" (2).[6] This observation is also in line with the observations of Stehle and Smith-Prei (2016) who understand this "poor" form of conversational visual as one of the elements constituting what they describe as awkward feminist political practices: "Awkwardness, therefore, also describe politics as an aesthetic form of becoming, of defiance, and of disruption. In this sense, our readings of popfeminist protest events in the digital age propose that exploiting, using, and keeping with the awkward—instead of smoothing it over or explaining it away—is a mode of politics" (12). This blurring of the images also allows a better fluidity between the sequences uploaded by internet users, being that this loss of specificity allows their aesthetic to be porous to one another. This fluidity of formats is transmuted on the sequences of self-represented bodies uploaded by users at the request of Peaches. The bodies become fluid because of the porosity of the conversational images, putting forward the relation between digital image materiality and the materiality of the body.

To this point, Judith Butler, in *Bodies That Matter* (1993), recalls the importance of considering the materiality of bodies. Butler writes, "[Matter] is productive, constitutive, one might even argue performative, inasmuch as this signifying act delimits and contours the body that it then claims to find prior to any and all signification. [. . .] This unsettling 'matter' can be understood as initiating new possibilities, new ways for bodies to matter" (30). Our understanding of mediated bodies and their representation needs also to be informed by a consideration of their respective materiality, that is, in this case, how user-creators decide to materialize their bodies through self-representation.

In *Free Pussy Riot*, body-matter is blurred into a conversational image. A fluidity of bodies resembling the reflection behind Pussy Riot's costume choices. Unlike FEMEN, for example, who uses nudity and perform with open faces, the use of balaclavas by Pussy Riot's performance-action erases individualism for the benefits of collective solidarity. An idealized feminine hegemony is refuted by a diversity of body size, but faces are never identifiable. Peaches' *Free Pussy Riot* pays homage to this aesthetic by borrowing the fashion style of Pussy Riot itself. This borrowing is encouraged in the invitation posted by Peaches and adopted in several users' self-mise-en-scène. Further, *Free Pussy Riot* is edited so as to alternate between the sequences captured during the rally-performance in Berlin and the short video submitted by internet users. Because Peaches did not mention at any point a format of a minimum of visual definition, users had recourse to different recording techniques and chose various technological devices. The result gives a mosaic effect oscillating between multiple visual styles, thus allowing conversational moving images to emerge.

According to Gunthert (2014), it is this encounter between the digitization of visual content and the documented interaction of exchanges between users that constitutes the aesthetic basis of the conversational image since it "depends on appropriative mechanisms where user choices have played a major role" (1). The conversational image thus belongs specifically to the participative character of social networks: "While the first period of the static web was characterized as an 'author society,' the symmetric interaction capabilities promoted by Web 2.0 instead lead to describing online publishing activity as a conversation" (Gunthert 2014, 5). Thus, within the digital era of participatory culture, digital videos are not only the subject of conversation, but they become new ways to communicate: a new apparatus to participate in a cultural or political movement. This important participatory dimension, peculiar to this new form of visual language, requires a new form of analysis. In sum, interacting with the conversational image of Gunthert with *Free Pussy Riot* allows us to note that the DAV, by its semantic element that constitutes the conversational image, operates a blurring of images for an appropriative visual language and participatory questioning the "good" and "bad" uses of the technological devices of video recording for urgent political actions.

SOCIO-DIGITAL ASSEMBLY, OR THE IMAGE OF A PARTICIPATIVE POLITICAL CULTURE

This chapter has thus far explored a new mode for feminist activists to foster network solidarities in a space that allows for a collaborative construction of knowledge through digital forms of political protest. Through an analysis of the semantic elements of the Digital Assembly Video, we have seen how the iconographies favored practices of feminist worldmaking through social media networks have been gestured toward via the example of *Free Pussy Riot*. Together, I have suggested that these semantic elements (DIY aesthetic, digital signs, and conversational images) create what Altman (1984) calls syntactic leaps: "The distinction between the semantic and the syntactic, in the way I have defined it here, thus corresponds to a distinction between the primary, linguistic elements of which all texts are made, and the secondary, textual meanings which are sometimes constructed by virtue of the syntactic bonds established between primary elements" (16). It is through this study of the semantic elements that we can understand the syntactic structure, and the analysis of *Free Pussy Riot*'s DIY aesthetic and its use of digital signs and conversational images allows the foundations of the syntactic structure to reveal itself.

Going one step further, it is through the bonds between semantic elements in Peaches' video that I detected the syntactic structure of the digital performative assembly. My use of the term "assembly" and my consideration of its ties to media practices are borrowed here from Butler's (2015) understanding of assembly. Because my focus specifically addresses the participatory and self-staging in the DAV, I focus below on the sequences uploaded by supporters of *Free Pussy Riot* and less on the film footage from the event in Berlin. In reflecting on the media reproductions of political demonstrations taking place in the street, I turn to Butler's text "Bodies in Alliance and the Politics of the Street" (2012), which suggests that what bodies perform on the street when they demonstrate is fundamentally related to what devices and communication technologies do when they tell what is happening on the same streets:

"The street scenes," Butler writes, "become politically potent only when and if we have a visual and audible version of the scene, or the media does not just report the scene, but is part of the scene and the action; Indeed, the media is the scene or the space in its extended and replicable visual and audible dimensions [. . .] At least in some instances, the media not only reports on social and political movements" (130–31). Manifesting in the street and recording these manifestations are certainly different actions, but they both reveal the implications of the bodies taking the street.

Building on this, Butler (2015) asserts that assembly is a concerted bodily enactment, a plural form of performativity. When bodies appear as an assembly in public places including digital spaces, they claim together their right to appear and make visible a collective resistance, a resistance against the risks of policies that allows for bodies to be precarious: "when bodies assemble on the street, in the square, or in other forms of public space (including virtual ones) they are exercising a plural and performative right to appear" (Butler 2015, 11). She goes on to argue that this right to appear is "one that asserts and instates the body in the midst of the political field, and which, in its expressive and signifying function delivers a bodily demand for a more livable set of economic, social and political conditions no longer afflicted by induced forms of precarity" (11). For Butler, the media are an increasingly integral part of these assemblies, giving rise to the emergence of new forms of actions. These forms of bodily and plural performativity are of great importance for any understanding of what the "people" are. Not everyone can appear in a physical bodily form, and many people who are prevented from appearing and who decide to do so through digital networks, via a DAV for instance, are no less part of the "people." Being prevented from appearing in street rallies forces us to reconsider the exclusive dimensions of some public spaces and the political mobilization taking place in them.

CONCLUSION

Self-staging in DAVs allows people to overcome a range of restrictions associated with street assembly and to find forms of public gathering spaces in which more bodies can appear. The use of the web is a tool by which we can reveal bodies that could have been excluded before from rallies—a tool used by an artist like Peaches through precise semantic elements, such as participatory DIY aesthetics, digital signs, and the conversational image in the creation of a clear example of DAV. These formal elements reveal important ties to Butler's concept of the performative assembly. The collective-participative process used in *Free Pussy Riot* speaks loudly to the potentials of the web as a space that can offer multiple creative possibilities for bodies to stage themselves, as well as major opportunities for people prevented from appearing in flesh in street rallies. The Digital Assembly Video thus unveils an important extension of a cultural form of resistance developed specifically within the potential of the online social networks and the bodies that need, and deserve, to appear.

REFERENCES

Ahmed, Sara. 2004. *The Cultural Politics of Emotion*. Routledge

Altman, Rick. 1984. "A Semantic/Syntactic Approach to Film Genre." *Cinema Journal* 23 (3): 6–18.

Baer, Hester. 2016. "Redoing Feminism: Digital Activism, Body Politics, and Neoliberalism." *Feminist Media Studies* 16 (1): 17–34.

Butler, Judith. 1993. *Bodies that Matters: On the Discursive Limits of Sex*. Routledge.

———. 2012. "Bodies in Alliance and the Politics of the Street." In *Sensible Politics: the Visual Culture of Nongovernmental Activism*, edited by Meg McLeagan and Yates McKee. Zone Books.

———. 2015. *Notes Toward a Theory of Performative Assembly*. Harvard University Press.

Chamberlain, Prudence. 2017. *The Feminist Fourth Wave: Affective Temporalities*. Palgrave Macmillan.

Fotopoulou, Aristea. 2016. "Digital and Networked by Default? Women's Organisations and the Social Imaginary of Networked Feminism." *New Media and Society* 18 (6): 989–1005.

Garrison, Ednie Kaeh. 2010. "U.S. Feminism—Grrrl Style! Youth (Sub)Cultures and the Technologics of the Third Wave" in *No Permanent Waves: Recasting Histories of U.S. Feminism*, edited by Nancy A. Hewitt. New Brunswick: Rutgers University.

Groeneveld, Elizabeth. 2015. "Are We All Pussy Riot? On Narratives of Feminist Return and the Limits of Transnational Solidarity." *Feminist Theory* 16 (3): 329–59.

Gunthert, André. 2014. "L'image conversationnelle: Les nouveaux usages de la photographie numérique." *Études photographiques* 31: histoirevisuelle.fr/cv/icones/2966.

Hemmings, Clare. *Why Stories Matter: The Political Grammar of Feminist Theory*. Duke University Press.

International Telecommunication Union. 2011. Facts and Figures 2011. www.itu.int/en/ITU-D/Statistics/Documents/facts/ICTFactsFigures2011.pdf.

———. 2019. Facts and Figures 2019. www.itu.int/en/ITU-D/Statistics/Documents/facts/FactsFigures2019.pdf.

Maule, Rosanna. 2016. *Digital Platforms and Feminist Film Discourse*. Palgrave Macmillan.

Millerand, Florence, Serge Proulx, and Julien Rueff. 2010. *Web Social: Mutation de la Communication*. Québec: Presses de l'Université du Québec.

Munro, Ealasaid. 2013. "Feminism: A Fourth Wave?" *Political Insight* (September 2013): 22–25.

Paveau, Marie-Anne. 2017. *L'analyse du discours numérique: Dictionnaire des formes et des pratiques*. Paris: Édition Hermann.

Peaches. 2012. "This Is a Call to All Pussy Riot Supporters." Facebook, August 8, 2012. https://fr-fr.facebook.com/officialpeaches/.

Peaches and Simonne Jones. 2012. "Free Pussy Riot." *Change*. August 15, 2012. www.change.org/p/free-pussy-riot.

Pussy Riot. 2012. "Pussy Riot-Punk Prayer." YouTube. Video. March 10, 2012. www.youtube.com/watch?v=ALS92big4TY.

Stehle, Maria Stehle, and Carrie Smith-Prei. 2016. *Awkward Politics: Technologies of Popfeminist Activism*. Montreal: McGill-Queen's University Press.

Thompson, Stacy. 2004. "Punk Cinema." *Cinema Journal* 43 (2): 47–66.

Triggs, Teal. 2006. "Scissors and Glue: Punk Fanzines and the Creation of a DIY Aesthetic," *Journal of Design History* 19 (1): 69–83.

Wiens, Brianna I., and Shana MacDonald. 2020. "Feminist Futures: #MeToo's Possibilities as Poiesis, Techné, and Pharmakon." *Feminist Media Studies* 21 (7): 1108–24.

NOTES

1. The original French text reads: "Ces différentes réalités du web ne constituent pas des terrains équivalents pour la linguistique car la communication, l'interaction et la publication de contenus n'y ont pas les mêmes caractéristiques et ne permettent donc pas les mêmes formes discursives. C'est la raison pour laquelle le logocentrisme de certaines approches ne permet pas de rendre compte de tous les aspects de la communication en ligne" (Paveau 2017, 15).

2. Jian Ghomeshi was a Canadian radio and television host who was one of the Canadian Broadcasting Corporation's most popular on-air personalities. In 2014, he was arrested and charged with four counts of sexual assault, and one count of overcoming resistance by choking, in relation to three complainants. Ghomeshi pleaded not guilty to all counts. He was acquitted of all five charges on March 24, 2016, which led to widespread criticism of the Canadian legal system by women's groups.

3. Comparing the number of shots during the first thirty seconds of the most-watched music video in 2012, the Korean electronic music video "Gangnam Style" (Psy 2012), with *Free Pussy Riot*, we see twenty-six shots for the first thirty seconds of Peaches' video (excluding the opening shot of the title "FREE PUSSY RIOT" flashing in nine different colors) and thirteen shots for Psy's video. Peaches' video's average shot length is two times faster. In all, the video of Peaches counts 166 shots for two minutes and forty-seven seconds, which is almost exactly one shot per second.

4. For a study on feminist zines, refer to Elizabeth Groenveld's (2016) *Making Feminist Media: Third-Wave Magazines on the Cusp of the Digital Age*.

5. The original French text reads: "assure l'engagement des locuteurs. En tout état de cause, la pancarte prouve qu'avec le numérique, on est bien loin du mythe de la dématérialisation et de l'absence de physique sur le web" (Paveau 2017, 330–31).

6. The original French text reads: "La numérisation, en réduisant la matérialité des images, leur confère une plasticité et une mobilité nouvelles. Sous l'espèce de fichiers faciles à copier ou à manipuler, l'objet iconique devient image fluid" (Gunthert 2014, 2).

Chapter 7

One Taught Me Action

The Digital Meta-Lives and Affective Resonances of Pop Protest Signs

Morgan Bimm

One notable tactic at play in the optics of contemporary protest is the use of popular culture, with music, in particular, playing a key role in contributing to the shareability and spreadability of protests' digital footprint. Protests have always had a soundtrack; in many ways, imagining a history of political organizing disentangled from popular music is as foreign as imagining its absence at cultural occasions like weddings or birthday celebrations. What is unique about the current invocation of music and pop culture in protest (and protest signs in particular) is that it takes place in a closed loop of digital mediation: the content, memes, and music that inform protest signs are gathered via various digital networks and, similarly, are reproduced and performed in the political space of the protest with the knowledge that further sharing and mediation is inevitable. In such hyper-self-aware economies of visibility (Banet-Weiser 2018), it is useful to question the affective and political impact of those signs that go on to be circulated in digital space, both by attendees and, in a growing number of cases, by the artists themselves.

Using the case of the 2019 Women's March protest signs featuring the words of singers Ariana Grande and Cardi B, this chapter sets out to explore the presence of celebrity feminisms via activists' signs. It examines the sharing of logics and social media practices that inform these signs and their digital meta-lives. The politics of the Women's Marches rely on the circulation of particular affects—rage, melancholy, joy—that become attached to certain figures and refuse to adhere to others, always mediated by the digital remix practices responsible for spreading the singular March beyond its initial temporal and geographical bounds. The inevitability of this digital spread, I argue, along with the communal understanding found in culturally savvy remix practices, are central to discussions of how feminism is networked in the aftermath of singular political events. I first consider the ways that Ariana Grande and Cardi B's feminisms are shaped by how the public read race and class into their actions. Individual feminisms are reflected and refracted through economies of visibility and, as I will expand upon shortly, the question of whether Ariana Grande and Cardi B's actions are legible as feminism at all frequently hinges upon their place in celebrity culture. Celebrity feminism can be broadly defined as the manner in which celebrities deploy their capital and privilege to articulate feminist positions (Taylor 2014). To this end, within a celebrity feminist frame, this chapter asks what are the benefits and limitations to Ariana Grande and Cardi B's individual brands of pop feminism? Why do musical artists embrace a political identity, and how can we see these choices reflected in the ways these celebrity feminists figure into activists' signs? What does this tell us about the affective "use" of celebrity feminism in digital remix cultures, and why does it matter?

WHO GETS TO MAKE "PROTEST" MUSIC?

Every historical period of social and political upheaval has given birth to songs of discontent. The ongoing relationship between music and politics remains relatively under-researched, with fields such as ethnomusicology and popular culture studies only recently seeking to expand their study of protest music beyond the normative bounds of American culture and the late twentieth century (Damodaran 2016; Friedman 2013). Where conversation on the politicization of musical artists abounds, instead, is in popular cultural writing and journalism, in publications as varied as *Teen Vogue*, *Vice*, and *Flare*. These texts are central to this chapter as their celebrity feminist methodologies are frequently political, unafraid to grapple with nuance, and—due to the slow time lines of academic publishing—often much more timely than traditional theory could ever hope to be. Even these conversations, however, can occasionally miss the mark.

The confluence of a social media-saturated culture and the ongoing pressure for pop musicians (and particularly female pop musicians) to perform to a new standard of political engagement can result in politics being read into celebrities' persona and creative output in some questionable ways. The collapsed publics of digital spaces enable a kind of one-sided closeness between fans and artists that go beyond Sandvoss' (2005) "fandom as mirror" (126), conceived in the early days of the networked internet—these days, fans don't want mere mirrors and empty signifiers, but comprehensive insight into celebrities' politics that align with their own (Click, Lee, and Holladay 2017; Sandvoss 2005). In the absence of this insight, fans may be prone to project upon celebrities their own hopes for activism, "projecting into the void" (Gross 2018, 32). This is abundantly clear in the wave of internet praise for Taylor Swift's 2019 album *Lover*. A *Variety* article heralded one of the album's deep cuts, "Miss Americana and the Heartbreak Prince," as "the great protest song this generation has needed" (Willman 2019). In her response, published in the increasingly political *Teen Vogue*,[1] Anjana Pawa links the praise for Swift to similar accolades bestowed upon Lana Del Ray, whose single "Looking for America" earned her comparisons to Bob Dylan's anthemic songwriting from *Rolling Stone* (Dolan 2019). As Pawa states (2019), "all of this praise for [white pop stars'] political commentary provides a glaring reminder of how differently the public often responds toward inherently political songs by black [sic] artists," noting political songwriting by female artists of color such as Beyoncé and Janelle Monáe rarely receive the same recognition. The visibility and mediation of protest and its artifacts in popular media culture is always operating against that culture's investment in whiteness and a respectability politics that is committed to ensuring legibility for a white audience first and foremost.

In recent years, a particular kind of neoliberal feminism has become a normalized aspect of celebrity culture. Increasingly, aligning oneself with feminism in today's pop culture climate is (re)inscribed as a necessary step toward what internet scholars Alice Marwick and danah boyd (2011) have termed "the construction of a consumable persona" (140). The labor that goes into this construction, of course, is almost always done on social media and in other digital space, as this is where reputation economies and economies of visibility live and die (Banet-Weiser 2018). Given this ongoing push for musicians to align themselves with a certain degree of political action, it makes sense that celebrity feminisms should play a significant role in the Women's Marches, even if the singers themselves were not physically present. This chapter turns now to a discussion of two specific artists, Ariana Grande and Cardi B, whose lyrics were widely taken up at the 2019 Women's Marches across the United States and around the world to ask: what is significant about these artists' words and the affect they invoke?

"THIS SHIT IS SERIOUS"

Cardi B made history in early 2019 for being the first solo woman to win a Grammy for best rap album of the year, but the Bronx-born singer has made just as many headlines for her unapologetic political views and posts in the months leading up to and since the 2019 Women's Marches.[2] In an April 2018 interview with *GQ Magazine*, Cardi B touched on topics as varied as gun control, Social Security, and her preferred political candidates for the upcoming midterm elections. She stated, "I hate when you talk about something that's going on in the community, people think because you're famous, you doing it [sic] for clout. But you concerned [sic] about it because you are a citizen of America; you are a citizen of the world" (Feller 2019). Her concern, Cardi B assures us, is not a performance, but genuine despair.

These same frustrations appear in another piece of content produced just days before the 2019 Women's March. In the midst of the United States' longest government shutdown to date, Cardi B posted a video to her Instagram urging her more than forty million followers to pay attention: "This shit is really fucking serious, bro [. . .] We really need to take this serious [sic]. I feel like we need to take some action. I don't know what type of action, because this isn't what I do, but [. . .] I'm scared." Just days after her Instagram post went viral, Cardi B's call to action was amplified and spread in real time. Whereas Cardi B's presence at previous Women's Marches had been limited to her lyrics (signs from Marches the previous year referenced her hit "Bodak Yellow"), many of the signs from the 2019 March quote from her government shutdown video or other political statements Cardi B had issued via social media over the previous year.

The singer retweeted a number of the signs, noting that she wished she could have been there (she was busy rehearsing for the first ever Super Bowl Music Fest in Atlanta, Georgia) and expressing that she felt "so honored." Less than a week later, Stephen Colbert tweeted about starting a petition to have Cardi B deliver the rebuttal to Trump's State of the Union address (Feller 2019). The singer was also invited by a group of Iowa Democrats to speak at "a reception of her choice" when she passed through the state on tour later in the year (Griffith 2019). Cardi B responded to both calls with her usual pointedness. To Colbert, she replied: "Why not? I get straight to the point." And to the Iowan Democrats, she simply tweeted out: "Should I?" The latter tweet received over 200,000 likes in a matter of hours.

Regardless of Cardi's physical absence from protests and Democratic receptions, then, it seems the singer's calls to action (despite it not being "what she does") were answered. Cardi's absence from the physical space of the Women's March becomes almost irrelevant in the face of her sustained engagement with activists who did attend, granting her a digital presence bolstered by the myriad protest signs referencing her words. In the same way the "streets" where protest takes place in the 2010s can be conceived as digitally freed from geographic constraints, the March bypasses other barriers to access with each passing retweet. According to Sarah Banet-Weiser (2018), "with its social media origins and wide circulation on all media platforms, the

March [is] an important illustration of the *potential* of the circulation of popular feminism within an economy of visibility to have a broader reach" (179). This potential means greater visibility and reach, certainly, but it also means that political actions today are more accessible than ever before. Disability activist Johanna Hedva (2016) writes that individuals who are "not able to physically get their bodies into the street" have often been understood as apolitical because of the multiple barriers to forms of legible, visible protest. The transmedial nature of Cardi B's words at the 2019 Women's Marches point to how we might reimagine engagement in the context of a digitally literate protest culture.

Cardi B's Instagram video lent its momentum to the current wave of online activist artifacts in the form of protest signs whose digital meta-lives grow the conversation beyond its original form. That recognition of Cardi B's feminism has taken so long to reach the mainstream (and only now via white gatekeepers of leftist culture such as Colbert and those Iowa Democrats) only serves to underscore the ways in which celebrity feminisms' legibility follows from distinctly racialized and classed logics of exclusion. In Susana Loza's (2013) scholarship on #SolidarityIsForWhiteWomen, she notes that digital activism provides more space for racialized women "to speak to each other across borders and boundaries." Cardi B's outspoken social media presence is in keeping with Black feminist media scholars' notions of capacious digital, networked spaces being well-suited for germinating Black feminist action, for as long as the mainstream continues to include Black feminists only as an afterthought.

"LET'S KEEP OUR VOICES LOUD"

While perhaps not as explicit in her political views as Cardi B, singer Ariana Grande has her own unique brand of celebrity feminism that has thrust the Italian American pop singer into the spotlight on numerous occasions over the past several years. These moments have been compiled in any number of *Buzzfeed*-style articles around the internet, including a list of Grande's best-known "feminist moments" compiled by Global Citizen (Rueckert 2017) and a tribute to the singer as part of *Flare*'s "12 Days of Feminists" in 2018 (Wray). Grande also attended the inaugural anti-Trump DC Women's March in 2017, posting a photo to her Instagram account with a lengthy caption that read: "We are so much stronger and louder than hatred, ignorance, sexism, racism, ageism, homophobia, transphobia, body shaming, slut shaming, prejudice, discrimination of all kinds, patriarchal conditioning and the backwards expectations of what a woman should be [. . .] let's keep our voices loud, passionate, and peaceful!" (arianagrande 2017).

While Grande has yet to discuss the specifics of her political views to the extent that Cardi B has, she clearly aligns herself with a version of celebrity feminism invested in body and sex positivity, solidarity between women, and equal opportunity. Grande's feminism is in many ways akin to the kind of white celebrity feminism espoused by figures like Emma Watson (of HeForShe fame) and Taylor Swift; it is both an acceptable brand of feminism because of Grande's conventional femininity, and undeniably beneficial to her public image as a role model for young fans. Her commitments to feminist ideals of equality and body positivity are palatable in a way that Cardi's impassioned rants on government shutdowns are not. Grande's less-radical political image means that her clapbacks are archived into feel-good *Buzzfeed* articles while Cardi's viral video found her embroiled in a Twitter feud with conservative pundit Tomi Lahren (iamcardib, "You're so blinded . . . "). Such inequitable reactions are consistent with how many Black women experience social media activism; according to Mirama Kaba and Andrea Smith, Black women's stories are "easily dismissed" and "made illegible," while white women are seen as sympathetic subjects "worthy of our concern" (2014). To elevate Black women's voices beyond the social media platforms where their politics tend to flourish, writes Susana Loza (2013), "[we] will have to learn to see the potential of anger." The mainstream press continues to project feminism *onto* white celebrities, while Black celebrity feminists can only access the same celebratory reception once their actions have hit a kind of critical mass (and only then while being forced to manage expectations and perform damage control).

In the absence of candid political content like Cardi B's government shutdown video, Grande's primary presence at the 2019 Women's Marches was in the form of her lyrics themselves. In the dozens of signs from the 2019 Marches that were retweeted and shared in the hours and days that followed, the most popular by far were variations on the lyrics of Grande's hit single "Thank U, Next." Grande's take on the popular "catalog song" was originally written as a breakup anthem following the dissolution of Grande's engagement to *Saturday Night Live* comedian Pete Davidson. She spends the first verse listing exes, thanking them for teaching her various lessons, before taking the second verse to enthuse that spending time with herself has taught her most of all. The most frequent reinterpretation of the hit single at the 2019 Women's March featured images of former president Barack Obama, Democratic presidential candidate Hillary Clinton, and President Donald Trump alongside the lyrics, "one taught me love, one taught me patience, one taught me pain."

Similar to Cardi B, the singer retweeted a collage of signs referencing her words culled from across the internet, captioning the images with a single black heart emoji. Thus, while Grande has refrained from being as outspoken as Cardi B around political issues, her commitment to politics extends far enough that she was aware of and clearly supported Marches initially founded on explicit anti-Trump political sentiments. This follows from what we know about the ways in which celebrities are pressured to take up feminist politics. Economies of visibility, Sarah Banet-Weiser (2018) tells us, fundamentally shift the politics of visibility so that visibility becomes *the end* rather than a means to an end. She writes, "political categories such as race and gender have transformed their very logics from the inside out, so that the visibility of these categories is what matters, rather than the structural ground on and through which they are constructed" (23). Identifying as someone who "looks like" a feminist becomes sufficient political action; the identification and the announcement is "both the radical move and the end in itself" (Banet-Weiser 2018, 23). To what degree does this pressure to 'look like' a feminist take the place of embodied politics when it comes to celebrity feminists such as Ariana Grande and Cardi B?

In revisiting this question of economies of visibility, it is important to note that economy is not a mere metaphor when we speak about the choices that celebrities make in performing a particular type of feminism. As Banet-Weiser (2018) points out, the visible body is also the commodifiable body (25), and all bodies are not commodifiable in the same way, mediated as they are by categories of race, class, sexuality, age, and ability. If the celebrity body is a commodity, then we can think of things like confidence, competence, and even feminism as assets; discursive themes and "goods" that, when attached to the "right" kind of body and in the right social context, elevates that celebrity to make her even more marketable. If Cardi B manages to be politically explicit even in her literal absence from political spaces, then Grande in many ways allows her association with a notably safer, more implicit brand of celebrity feminism (a single off 2018's *Sweetener* was notably titled "God Is a Woman") to speak for itself. Beyond the ways that race and class affect the legibility of celebrity feminisms, the political resonances of Cardi B and Ariana Grande also speak to expectations held by audiences when it comes to the tone they expect young female musicians' feminisms to take.

ON RAGE, RESILIENCE, AND INTERSECTIONALITY

Much has been written about the affect that gets attached to girls and, by extension, to girl feminists. Girl studies scholars such as Monica Swindle (2011) and Natalie Coulter (2018) have both written about the drive for girls to associate or align themselves with a particular kind of happy or fun affect, and many scholars who have taken up Sara Ahmed's figure of the feminist killjoy (2010) have observed that the killjoy spirit does not always sit well with girl feminists and, by extension, many versions of celebrity feminism. Angela McRobbie (2009) writes that women are only rendered visible if they embody what she refers to as the "spectacularly feminine" (60); that girls are held to a similar standard to "sparkle" (Kearney 2015) speaks to this same broader distrust of negative or "ugly" affect (Ngai 2005), particularly when embodied by women and girls. Even within purportedly feminist spaces, girls are often constituted in very particular ways that serve very particular functions. For many, girls come to embody hopeful futures and potential and are thus frequently positioned as a generation who can come to be the "good, resistant subjects of feminism" if they would only take up feminism in particular ways (Harris and Shields Dobson 2015, 146).

In this sense, feminism can work to naturalize young women's agency as innately progressive and, similar to Ahmed's killjoy, the affective impact of their disavowal or resistance to sanctioned ways of taking up feminism can cause what some girl studies scholars have termed a "feminist melancholia" (Harris and Shields Dobson 2015, 146). In such a scenario, young women (or celebrity feminists) come to be positioned as the source of an acute melancholia over the loss of generational hope when they fail to live up to older or other feminists' expectations of resistance. Young, female celebrities are therefore expected to align themselves with specific kinds of feminist embodiment and, if they fail to do so by choosing alternative modes of resistance or by rejecting a feminist ideology altogether, they are cast as disharmonic actors within the grander feminist progress narrative. In the case of Ariana Grande and Cardi B, such performances become central to unpacking how and why the singers' feminisms are received. Although both singers' politics are powerful enough to inspire young girl fans to follow politics and engage in actions like the Women's March, the degree, specificity, and mobilization of that politics varies.

Feminist musicologist Robin James' notion of resilience as the primary mode by which contemporary pop music tends to engage with resistance is also useful here. Resilience, according to James, is a quintessentially neoliberal logic that works to individualize trauma: "We now expect individual women to overcome the damage wrought by traditional femininity: they need to 'lean in' and be tough, be 'all about that bass,' [and] just 'shake it off'" (James 2019). James' tongue-in-cheek references to pop anthems of the last few years (by Meghan Trainor and Taylor Swift, respectively) is deliberate; this ethos of resilience and embodying strength by "just getting over it" is a narrative that has found its way into a surprising number of Top 40 hits in recent years. If we look to the lyrics of the songs that have most frequently made their way onto the signs of the Women's Marches, this much is clear. Ariana Grande's "Thank U, Next" is the most obviously resilience-fueled; as James (2019) puts it, the song presents "an already-resolved narrator who's fully accepted all of her past breakups and, more importantly, herself [. . .] overcoming is like the assumed prequel to the actual song, which focuses [instead] on the pleasure and profit of having overcome." But even Cardi B's "Bodak Yellow," a popular choice for signs at the 2018 Marches, indulges in this same neoliberalism-fueled resilience at times: "Dropped two mix-tapes in six months/What bitch working as hard as me?" and "Look, I don't dance now/I make money moves" both refer to Cardi B's experience as a sex worker and her break into the music industry, where she continues to "make money moves" by virtue of her tireless work ethic and industry smarts. In this way, both Cardi B and Grande have modeled a kind of individualized resilience narrative in their music—one that exists at odds with the collective affect and digital sharing cultures these lyrics enter into via actions like the Women's March.

Resilience, like the happiness and fun that is regularly attributed to celebrity feminists, is "a blooming bouquet of positive affect" (James 2019). So, what is the opposite of resilience? James tells us that in terms of the sonic resonances of the pop music she analyzes, resiliency is frequently shadowed by melancholy. Melancholy can look like anger or anxiety—"a kind of staying with and intensifying the trouble rather than overcoming it" (James 2019). James draws comparisons between her musicology-informed vision of melancholy and what Ahmed (2018b) identifies as the work of complaint and giving voice to negative affect that is "not supposed to happen." Under this framework, Ariana Grande's celebrity feminism is difficult to read as anything but straightforward resilience: she writes candidly in her lyrics of the struggles she has overcome and, when she does speak explicitly about politics, the rhetoric she invokes privileges solidarity and "keep[ing] our voices peaceful" (Woodward 2017). Cardi B's political analysis might be more nuanced, but the same race and class markers that temper the legibility of her feminism for her white fans also align her with a particular type of angry or anxious affect[3] that exists in direct opposition to friendlier narratives of resilience and neoliberal triumph.

This affect is of course often racialized, as evidenced by the frequency with which the trope of the "angry Black woman" is alternatively invoked, critiqued, or parodied in media. The same way that we can complicate understandings of individualized resilience narratives transposed into collective action via protest signs, we can also complicate the directions that melancholic affect takes. In the context of protest optics, what becomes particularly troubling is when melancholic rhetoric originated by women of color is taken up by white protestors. In an article published in the months following the

2018 Marches, writer Ashley Nash (2018) questions the use of lyrics from artists of color on white protestors' signs and social media posts. Nash notes that these same protestors likely contribute to systems that keep people of color and especially women of color at the margins, a kind of cognitive dissonance that reflects what Black feminist scholar Mariana Ortega (2006) has called "loving, knowing ignorance." According to Nash, "It's important . . . for 'pink hats'[4] to put respect on the backgrounds and identities of Black women the same way they revere their creativity; to put respect on all Black women regardless of fame or fortune" (2018). In other words, the representational politics of white women's protest signs is a poor substitute for an engaged and sustained intersectional feminist praxis.

PRIMING THE COMMONS FOR TWITTER AND TIKTOK

The optics and rhetoric of the 2019 Women's Marches were, at every level, impacted by digital forms of mediation. Tension between corporeal protest "in the streets" and these events' online meta-lives, however, are complicated by questions of what "counts" as activism, visibility, and participation in an age when these terms are in seemingly never-ending flux. According to Rianka Singh and Sarah Sharma (2019), who use the term "platform feminism" to describe a kind of activism where one's engagement can be as straightforward as using a predetermined hashtag, "under the logic of the platform, different histories of visibility are rendered illegible" (302). Platform logics, founded on a kind of neoliberal individualism not dissimilar to James' notions of resilience, preclude community action, and collective meaning-making. "The very structure of platform feminism," write Singh and Sharma (2019), "straightens and whitens the movements because they privilege rising up as the dominant spatial tactic" (303). This goes against understandings of digital engagement with activism that foreground its accessibility for those unable to make it out into the streets (Hedva 2016; brown 2017; Piepzna-Samarasinha 2018). Extending these discussions, I want to suggest that the platform logics surrounding the invocation of celebrities' words and lyrics on protest signs also evoke an act of what Sara Ahmed (2018a) names "queer use": an opening up of spaces for thinking through the legibility of online activism in terms of its potential for inspiring community, mutual aid, and a certain kind of hopeful affect necessary to build sustainable movements.

At its core, the historical tradition of making, documenting, and sharing images of protest signs is a form of remix culture, made all the more transmedial with the rise of digital networks and social media sharing economies.[5] The space of the March is one that encourages meme culture and relies on the innate spreadability of an idea or phrase to inspire, on the one hand, what might be interpreted as a certain degree of humor or levity, but on the other, often draws attention to the innate everydayness of politics and political experiences. In her treatise on "Queer Use," Ahmed (2018a) interrogates the notion of reuse as queer use. The innate queerness of reuse does not mean that all raw materials qualify as open to reclamation or politicization; in Ahmed's words, "something can not be used for anything."[6] Indeed, queer uses, or "when things are used for purposes other than the ones for which they were intended, still reference the qualities of a thing; queer uses may linger on those qualities, rendering them all the more lively." Following this, protest signs taking up the words of celebrity feminists may indeed be the ultimate act of activist remix culture—a text primed for retweeting—but there is still a reason that certain celebrities feature more prominently than others. In other words, what is the something "lively" about Cardi B and Ariana Grande's star texts that contributed to their overrepresentation on the protest signs of the 2019 Women's Marches? The answer, I suspect, is the same identificatory impulse that inspired all of those *Buzzfeed*-style listicles about Grande and spiked Instagram engagement metrics on Cardi B's government shutdown rant: a kind of relatably messy, "bad,"[7] or complicated feminism that resonates with an audience and works to expand that celebrity's fandom beyond those individuals interested solely in her music. Similar to the narrow affective embodiments available to young feminist fans discussed previously (i.e., girl = happy), the experience of coming into one's activist impulses is often rife with gatekeeping. Celebrity feminists will never be wholly unproblematic figures, as Jessalyn Keller and Jessica Ringrose (2015) have explored; young fans are often all too aware of just how fallible their heroes can be. As such, the remixing of these pop star feminists' words on protest signs points to a kind of playful, savvy investment in celebrity feminism, underscoring these figures' usefulness and reliability as key touchstones in a culture obsessed with doing feminism right.

Thinking of the celebrity musician lyrics on protest signs as remix culture complicates Singh and Sharma's (2019) assertion that the vast majority of platform feminism and #hashtag activism serves to center a single person, figure, or voice (302). When these words and lyrics enter into meme and protest culture, used queerly by people at the Marches and remixed further by those sharing and reimagining their use in digital space, it becomes impossible to imagine them as belonging to a single author. Rather, celebrity feminists' physical absence (or, perhaps more accurately, their non-presence) at the 2019 Marches positions them as participants in those same processes of remix and reuse. Ariana Grande might still be the most visible person to retweet the imagery of the "Thank U, Next" signs, but ultimately, she is neither more nor less invested than anyone else engaging with the digital afterlife of those lyrics. Indeed, her response to this new use—a single heart emoji—may signal less.

If we reimagine the digital meta-lives of protest signs as remix culture, it also introduces the possibility of imagining the sharing of these images online as a kind of community formation in and of itself. Nancy Baym (2015) posits that there are certain qualities that help define online communities: space, practice, shared resources, shared identity, and interpersonal relationships (76–90). To return to an earlier assertion that the digital meta-lives of Marches expand the spatial and temporal bounds of the March, what we find in them is shared space. The routinized or even performative act of sharing images of protest signs becomes a communal, community practice, and the meme culture that allows community members to interpret and understand the content of those signs represents a kind of shared resource. The final two markers of shared identity and interpersonal interaction are embedded in the logic of online sharing economies; to participate in the March as an event is to add one's voice to the digital cacophony and feel connected, in some small way, to others engaged in similar conversations. Accounting for continuously newer, queerer, and messier modes of protest opens up space for imagining how the digital might undermine the spatial, temporal, and racial logics that narrow the possibilities of more corporeal modes of protest (like the sit-in, the walkout, or the march) that remain confined to the literal street.

ACTIVISM, ITS AFFECTS AND AFTERLIVES

This chapter has thus far been primarily concerned with the exploration of what Banet-Weiser (2018) named as "the potential of the circulation of popular feminism within economies of visibility" found in digital space, but I also hope to impart a new appreciation for the affective dimensions of pop protest signs. Coverage of pop music lyrics on protest signs at the Women's Marches seems to discount or simply forget the pleasure that can be found in remixing song lyrics or a favorite singers' words into a reflection of one's politics (see Gross 2018). Self-described pleasure activist adrienne maree brown (2017) writes against the tendency toward "rigid radicalism" in the post-Trump political landscape, wherein activism must be difficult, exhausting, and necessarily filled with cynicism (Bergman et. al 2017; brown 2019). brown posits that there must be another way forward: "I suspect that to really transform our society, we will need to make justice one of the most pleasurable experiences we can have" (2017). The importance of celebrity culture and fandom for empowering and invigorating activists is part of a larger conversation around naming joy as a structuring affect of protest, even as that conversation is complicated by the politics of who gets to stake a cultural claim to this pleasure (recalling, for instance, James' discussion of the racialized aspects of resilience and melancholy). Still, might it be radical to find joy in one's melancholy? It doesn't seem all that far-fetched to conclude that making reference to one's favorite singer might be an easy antidote to the anxiety, sense of being overwhelmed, and other "ugly feelings"[8] that often mark the experience of participating in large-scale public marches.

The optics and archival practices of twenty-first century protest have been, in many ways, irrevocably shaped by the ongoing integration of digital networks. With the possibility of seemingly endless Twitter threads, reblogs, shares, and likes comes the distinct possibility that the geographically and temporally bound notion of *the event* as we know it no longer exists. In its place, as this chapter has explored, is an ever-expanding remix culture, the legibility of which is predicated on one's fluency in popular culture, musical references, memes, and a distinctly generational humor that often combines those first three categories. Cardi B and Ariana Grande embody two notably different types of celebrity feminism, shaped by factors as varied as their race, class, political engagement, and respective audiences, yet both musical artists had starring roles in the signs and rhetoric of the 2019 Women's Marches. That images of these signs and slogans continue to circulate in digital space so many months after the Marches seems inevitable, and new trends for signs founded in the popular culture of the moment will no doubt continue to proliferate in those actions and marches yet to come (but seemingly inevitable in today's politically turbulent times). In this way, the sharing economies that shape and grow the digital meta-lives of activist artifacts such as protest signs signal the key role the digital plays in amplifying particular aspects of historical events, even—and perhaps especially—as they unfold.

REFERENCES

Ahmed, Sarah. 2010. "Killing Joy: Feminism and the History of Happiness." *Signs* 35 (3): 571–94.

———. 2018a. "Queer Use." *Feminist Killjoys.* November 8, 2018.

———. 2018b. "The Time of Complaint." *Feminist Killjoys.* May 30, 2018.

arianagrande. "today filled my heart with so much hope . . . " Instagram. January 21, 2017. Accessed April 1, 2020.

Banet-Weiser, Sarah. 2018. *Empowered: Popular Feminism and Popular Misogyny.* Duke UP.

Baym, Nancy. 2015. *Personal Connections in the Digital Age.* Polity Press.

Bergman, Carla, Nick Montgomery, and Hari Alluri. 2017. *Joyful Militancy: Building Thriving Resilience in Toxic Times (Anarchist Interventions).* AK Press.

brown, adrienne maree. 2017. *Emergent Strategy: Shaping Change, Changing Worlds.* AK Press.

————. 2019. *Pleasure Activism: The Politics of Feeling Good*. AK Press.

Click, Melissa A., Hyunji Lee, and Holly Wilson Holladay. 2017. "'You're born to be brave': Lady Gaga's Use of Social Media to Inspire Fans' Political Awareness." *International Journal of Cultural Studies* 20(6): 603–19.

Coulter, Natalie. 2018. "'Frappés, Friends, and Fun': Affective Labour and the Cultural Industry of Girlhood." *Journal of Consumer Culture*. DOI: doi.org/10.1177/1469540518806954.

Damodaran, Sumangala. 2016. "Protest and Music." *Oxford Research Encyclopedia of Politics*. August 5, 2016.

Dolan, Jon. 2019. "Song You Need to Know: Lana Del Ray, 'Looking for America.'" *Rolling Stone*. August 9, 2019.

Doyle, Sady. 2016. "The True Story of How Teen Vogue Got Mad, Got Woke, and Began Terrifying Men Like Donald Trump." *Quartz*. December 19, 2016.

Feller, Madison. 2019. "A Comprehensive Guide to the Political Leanings of Cardi B." *Elle Magazine*. February 26, 2019.

Friedman, Jonathon. 2013. *The Routledge History of Social Protest in Popular Music*. Routledge.

Gay, Roxane. 2014. *Bad Feminist: Essays*. Harper Perennial.

Griffith, Janelle. 2019. "Cardi B Invited to Speak to Influential Democratic Group in Iowa." NBC. January 31, 2019.

Gross, Allyson. 2018. "Sign(ifier) of the Times: On Pop Stars, Populism, and the Harry Styles Fandom." MA thesis. University of London, Goldsmiths.

Harris, Anita, and Amy Shields Dobson. 2015. "Theorizing Agency in Post-Girlpower Times." *Continuum: Journal of Media and Cultural Studies* 29 (2): 145–56.

Hedva, Johanna. 2016. "Sick Woman Theory." *Mask Magazine*. January 19, 2016.

James, Robin. 2019. Resilience, Sonic Patriarchy, and Melancholies. Presented at the CTM Festival, Berlin. http://www.its-her-factory.com/2019/01/berlin-talks-january-2019/.

Kaba, Mirama, and Andrea Smith. 2014. "Interlopers on Social Media: Feminism, Women of Color and Oppression." Truthout. February 1, 2014.

iamcardib. 2019. "You're so blinded by racism that you don't even realize the decisions the president you root for is destroying the country you claim to love so much. You are a perfect example on no matter how educated or smart you think you are you still a SHEEP!" *Twitter*, January 20, 2019. twitter.com/iamcardib/status/1086990411770384384.

————. 2019. "Should I?" *Twitter*, January 31, 2019. twitter.com/iamcardib/status/1090990439406767623936.

Kearney, Mary Celeste. 2015. "Sparkle: Luminosity and Post-Girl Power Media." *Continuum: Journal of Media and Cultural Studies* 29 (2): 263–73.

Keller, Jessalynn and Jessica Ringrose. 2015. "But then feminism goes out the window!': Exploring Teenage Girls' Critical Response to Celebrity Feminism." *Celebrity Studies* 6 (1): 132–35.

Keller, Jessalynn. 2015. *Girls' Feminist Blogging in a Postfeminist Age*. Routledge.

Lang, Cady. 2020. "A Comprehensive Guide to All the Times Cardi B Sounded Off on Politics." *Time Magazine*. January 17, 2020.

Loza, Susana. 2013. "Hashtag Feminism, #SolidarityIsForWhiteWomen, and the Other #FemFuture." *Ada: A Journal of Gender, Media, and Technology* 5. https://adanewmedia.org/2014/07/issue5-loza/.

Marwick, Alice, and danah boyd. 2011."To See and Be Seen: Celebrity Practice on Twitter." *Convergence* 17 (2): 139–58.

McRobbie, Angela. 2008. "Young Women and Consumer Culture." *Cultural Studies* 22 (5): 531–50.

Nash, Ashley. 2018. "White Women: Your Hip-Hop Inspired Protest Signs Are Questionable." *Afropunk*. March 22, 2018.

Ngai, Sianne. 2005. *Ugly Feelings*. Harvard University Press.

Ortega, Mariana. 2006. "Being Lovingly, Knowingly Ignorant: White Feminism and Women of Color." *Hypatia* 21 (3): 56–74.

Pawa, Anjana. 2019. "If You Think Taylor Swift Is the Only Artist Making Protest Songs, You're Just Not Listening." *Teen Vogue*. September 10, 2019.

Piepzna-Samarasinha, Leah Lakshmi. 2018. *Care Work: Dreaming Disability Justice*. Arsenal Pulp Press.

Rueckert, Phineas. 2017. "These 7 Feminist Quotes Show Why Ariana Grande Is the Hero We Need." *Global Citizen*. March 17, 2017.

Sandvoss, Cornel. 2005. *Fans: The Mirror of Consumption*. Polity Press.

Schwartz, Andi. 2019. "Ariana Grande's 'thank u next' Is the Queer Break-up Track We Need." *Xtra Magazine*. March 4, 2019.

Singh, Rianka, and Sarah Sharma. 2019. "Platform Uncommons." *Feminist Media Studies* 19 (2): 302–3.

Swindle, Monica. 2011. "Feeling Girl, Girling Feeling: An Examination of 'Girl' as Affect." *Rhizomes* 22. www.rhizomes.net/issue22/swindle.html.

Taylor, Anthea. 2014. "'Blockbuster' Celebrity Feminism." *Celebrity Studies* 5 (1–2): 75–78.

Willman, Chris. 2019. "Is Taylor Swift's 'Miss Americana' the Greatest Protest Song of Our Time?" *Variety*. August 28, 2019.

Wray, Meaghan. 2018. "12 Days of Feminists: Ariana Grande." *Flare Magazine*. December 20, 2018.

NOTES

1. For a detailed explanation of *Teen Vogue*'s shift toward political journalism, see Doyle 2016.

2. See Madison Feller's 2019 time line in *Elle* for a sense of the scope of Cardi B's activism and interest in politics prior to January 2019. Cady Lang's 2020 article in *Time* provides an updated account; the fact that this coverage is now deemed worthy of *Time* is a further signal that Cardi B's celebrity feminism has reached a particular level of mainstream acceptability.

3. James also observes that we resist this kind of affect *because* it is not easily fixed, and instead requires us to grapple with harder truths: "This melancholy is the effect of pointing out and being mad at ongoing sexism, racism, and the like. . . . It

grates at people both because it forces us to face the reality that we aren't the good post-racial, post-feminist subjects we want to present ourselves to be, and because anger and anxiety interfere with productivity" (2019).

4. Nash's reference here refers to the "pink pussy hats" that became popular at the inaugural anti-Trump Women's Marches in 2017, which have been roundly critiqued for the ways in which they reinforce a narrow, cisnormative, and unapologetically white feminism.

5. This calls to mind the notion of "spreadable media," popularized in Jenkins, Ford, and Green's edited volume of the same name (2013). The variable "speed" of online content is intimately connected to its value as part of what Grant McCracken terms "fast culture," or that which moves at such a rapid rate that its digital spread is simultaneously more visible and trackable (Jenkins et al. 2013, 95).

6. That said, there does seem to be something in particular about "Thank U, Next" that marks it for queer use. In a 2019 article, femme scholar Andi Schwartz writes that the song "operates on queer logics," espousing treating one's exes as valuable relationships, rethinking kinship forms, and other relationship practices typically associated with queer culture.

7. Roxane Gay popularized the term "bad feminist" in her 2014 essay collection of the same name to describe the complications of identifying as feminist while loving things and engaging in practices that could seem at odds with feminist ideology.

8. In Sianne Ngai's book of the same title, she offers an exploration of affects that act as indexes of frustration borne of societal powerlessness, or what she calls "obstructed agency" (2005).

Chapter 8

Meme Feminisms

Tactical Irony on Social Media

Keren Zaiontz and Kristen Cochrane

Digital feminism is a warren of subcultures and social movements that, like everything on the internet, unfolds in the standardized "radically indifferent" space of networked platforms.[1] The writers, editors, designers, and influencers that contribute to feminist discourses forge communities and cobble together earnings within the normative machinery of social media. These cultural workers rely upon the same self-generated platforms that contribute to the herding effects of market-led, prescriptive femininity. The same feeds in which content is so relativized that forgeries flow in the same stream as fact. Digital feminism in all variations was never born free, and unlike the coterie of largely male abstract expressionists who negated the barbarism of war and capitalist markets by focusing on the formal power of brushstrokes, the feminists we discuss here must claim autonomy over their craft (i.e., memes, blogs, podcasts) by other means. We use this chapter to consider some of those other means by focusing on a subset of feminist memers and the platforms and personalities to which they are connected. We intersperse screen captures of memes throughout that circulated between 2019–2022 with an express focus on the work of coauthor Kristen Cochrane, whose role here straddles media theorist and situated expert. As such, she is sometimes directly quoted as a subject in and of the field.[2] When we wrote this chapter before the COVID-19 pandemic, Cochrane was putting herself through graduate school as an author and influencer. On Instagram, she goes by the handle ripannanicolesmith where, since 2016, she has generated feminist memes and posts for her now nearly 88,000 followers.[3] A number of Cochrane's Instagram followers also subscribe to her bimonthly newsletter, a hybrid text of feminist popular culture and critical analysis published through crowdfunding membership platform Patreon. At the time of writing, Cochrane was just shy of five hundred readers ("patrons") who were paying a monthly sliding- scale subscription to her scholarly essays and videos. This digital labor is a means of survival and a complex distribution of self to readers and followers who are intimately bound up with her everyday life.

Cochrane is transparent about the pleasures and perils of self-branding and what this work affords her in terms of (modest) livelihood and friendship. This is not digital feminism as a mechanism for political action—we are proponents of feminist bases of power; however, that is not what we are examining here—but a means of economic survival and the strengthening of affective bonds between creatives and their followers and/or subscribers. Cochrane considers herself a tenant of a disposable neoliberal culture in which cultural workers are expendable and their physical and mental health collateral damage. But she is also continually buoyed by the online experience of meeting other people who share her interests, and sometimes, people who become her friends. There is an especial excitement—and deep affinity—to meeting people who also enjoy forms of humor that have historically been considered lowbrow or a "bad object" (not worthy of serious scholarly study), including memes circulated on Instagram. This humor and friendship unfold within the realm of social media in which selfhood and self-promotion are often part and parcel of the same practice.

The multiplicity that is digital feminism never experienced a moment outside co-option, because online content was engineered, particularly following the rise of Web 2.0 platforms such as Facebook and search engines such as Google, to be "captured."[4] In her book *Blog Theory*, first published in 2010, political scientist Jodi Dean uses "capture" to not only describe traditional blogs, but other forms of online content production. The practices of what she calls "mediated reflexivity" or "posting, linking, commenting, reacting, measuring, and circulating" are medium-specific to the internet. And the internet is driven by profit and plunder. The act of publicly registering our tastes and desires is tied to practices of data mining, algorithmic predictions, and personalized advertisements (Dean 2010, 7).[5] That inescapability or "capture" is the "default mode" of what it means to post and tweet, to live and work on the internet (7).

There has long been a healthy skepticism among feminist and digital media critics who have grappled with the effects of this capture (see, e.g., Banet-Weiser 2018; Rottenburg 2018). This is not only because status updates and tweets form part of the data flow of platforms that trade for billions of dollars in private earnings on global stock exchanges, but because feminism itself has been reformatted with inductions by former Facebook COO Sheryl Sandberg to "Lean In" and by cosmetic giants whose advertising campaigns, such as Dove's Project #ShowUS, mimic feminist direct actions. In other

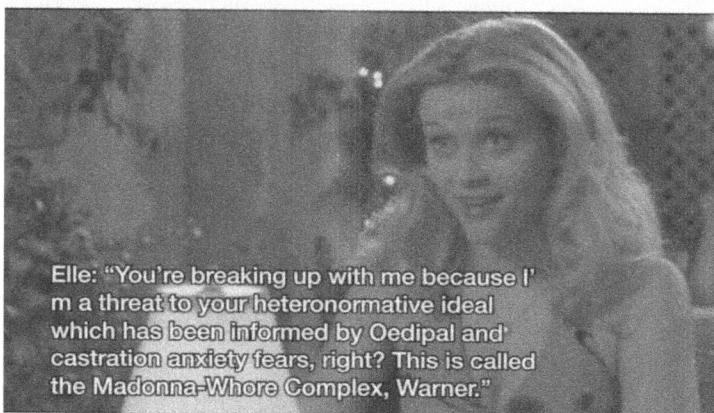

ripannanicolesmith
Bel Air, Los Angeles

• • •

Elle: "You're breaking up with me because I'm a threat to your heteronormative ideal which has been informed by Oedipal and castration anxiety fears, right? This is called the Madonna-Whore Complex, Warner."

View Insights   Promote

♡ ◯ ◁   ⊓

👥 Liked by **sukiwaterhouse** and **6,424 others**

ripannanicolesmith What's Elle Woods' birth chart looking like

View all 123 comments

gwblue1970damba2 Everyday on the bus i see oedipus at least once   💜

karleyslutever 💜   ♡

OCTOBER 7, 2018

⌂   Q   ⊕   ♡   👤

Figure 8.1. This meme was very popular, and Cochrane sees it as a fragment of an imagined screenplay or television show she would write if *Legally Blonde* were set in her milieu. The memes have attracted people who have similar interests to her own, who grew up enjoying *Legally Blonde* but also want to see feminist, queer, and psychoanalytic recuperations of regressive narratives. It is satisfying to imagine the protagonist Elle Woods (Reese Witherspoon) having a confident comeback, even before she got accepted to Harvard Law School, showing her ex-boyfriend, Warner, and the viewers that she is a multifaceted and self-determining protagonist. *Courtesy of author.*

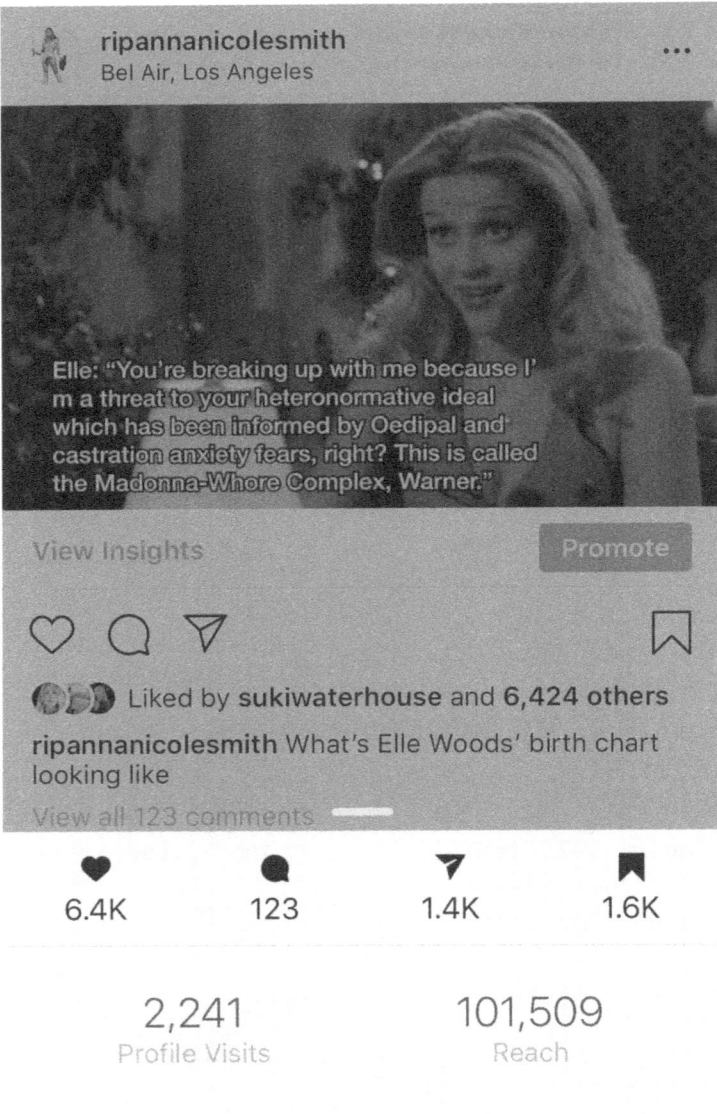

ripannanicolesmith
Bel Air, Los Angeles

Elle: "You're breaking up with me because I'm a threat to your heteronormative ideal which has been informed by Oedipal and castration anxiety fears, right? This is called the Madonna-Whore Complex, Warner."

View Insights   Promote

Liked by **sukiwaterhouse** and **6,424 others**

ripannanicolesmith What's Elle Woods' birth chart looking like

View all 123 comments

6.4K   123   1.4K   1.6K

2,241   101,509
Profile Visits   Reach

Figure 8.2. The statistics at the bottom show the number of times ripannanicolesmith's profile was viewed as well as the number of users who saw the meme (reach). *Courtesy of author.*

words, there is good reason to be concerned by the dispossession of feminist activism by digital neoliberal capitalism and, further still, the toxic onslaught of misogyny that these platforms have enabled through basic privacy breaches, trolls, and 4chan.[6] The vast digital gender divide has prevented women of all stripes from engineering large-scale platforms and thus designing spaces that reflect back their needs and priorities, political or otherwise (Noble 2018). Women, specifically digital feminists, have never been barred outright from tweeting or chatting, but rarely have they been imagined as potential constituents of networked sites. Women of color, Indigenous women, queer and trans women, disabled women, and intersections in between know all too keenly that this lack of imagination is symptomatic of a world from which they have been systematically excluded.[7]

That said, big money and mobilized, systemic misogyny are hardly new factors that Global North feminism in its "fourth wave" is only now charting. They are, after all, enduring features of patriarchal capitalism. What has changed both across successive "waves," and from "old media" to new, is navigating the lack of consensual boundaries around "connected life" (Turkle 2011, 168) and, by extension, the contours of everyday life. There are no limits to how much digital content we can consume and how much we can produce. What few mechanisms of self-discipline exist, including deleting accounts or app and website blockers, cannot stem the actual surfeit of information flows or our collective draw to its notifications and feeds. There are no buffers from the seduction of potential friends and followers—these are networked audiences whose promise of accumulation mirrors digital economic growth itself. "Online, your audience can keep expanding, and the performance never has to end," observes Jia Tolentino (2019, 15), writer and former editor of *Jezebel*. That lack of consent carries a particular cost for many female-identified users of the internet who, according to Tolentino, must work against the grain of social conditioning that encourages a continuous (nonconsensual) performance of self. Reflecting on trolling as a form of online abuse that disproportionately harms women, she notes that "the rise of trolling, and its ethos of disrespect and anonymity, has been so forceful in part because the internet's insistence on consistent, approval-worthy identity is so strong. It's the self-calibration that I learned as a girl, as a woman, that has helped me capitalize on 'having' to be online" (16). Tolentino goes on to note that her "only experience of the world has been one in which personal appeal is paramount and self-exposure is encouraged; this legitimately unfortunate paradigm, inhabited first by women and now generalized to the entire internet, is what trolls loathe and actively repudiate" (16). Tolentino identifies an overlap that Marxist feminists such as Silvia Federici (2004) and others have long circled around, which is that women's very bodies have historically been indivisible from supporting how capitalism is structured and how it daily reproduces its power over people and the uses of the earth. What Tolentino "learned as a girl" is not distinct from the design of the internet in late capitalism, but essential to how it generates profit, since without unremitting access to female bodies, not only would the internet's largest privately owned industry, pornography, collapse, but equally explicit practices like trolling, which unfold with impunity on publicly traded entities like Twitter, would also wither, since they rely on terrorizing women to shore up their power.[8]

Tolentino's citational community is eclectic and, interestingly, in the same essay, "The I in the Internet," she includes an extended engagement with sociologist Erving Goffman, whose 1959 text, *The Presentation of Self in Everyday Life*, remains formative to the anthropological branch of performance studies. Adapting Goffman's classifications of "front stage" and "back stage" to the context of mediated connectivity, Tolentino analyzes how the internet has eroded the "back stage," the space of interiority, an observation that is part of a larger school of thought about the nullification of the self through networked practices.[9] Interiority is the space where subjects can not only take a respite from their social roles but also assume contradictory versions of themselves and force a break with consistency altogether, a heterogeneity rarely afforded by "front-stage" scenarios. We too are interested in the erasure of the "back stage" and the demands this places on digital feminists like Cochrane and other creatives to engage in a "front-stage" consistency that revolves around "self-exposure," raw confessionality, attentiveness to followers, and bespoke intimacy with users and subscribers. For example, Cochrane describes how a week without posting on Instagram will be noticed by followers, fans, and readers: "Usually, the responses to some Instagram silence will constitute messages of relief, where followers write and say they are glad I am posting more consistently again." The toll of "'having' to be online" is real—burnout, brain fog, inattention—but just as real are the tactics that digital feminists use to manage these performances, which range in scope from strategic platform use to fashioning avatars and authoring ironic memes.

In "Constructing the Platform-Specific Self-Brand: The Labor of Social Media Production," coauthors Scolere, Pruchniewska, and Duffy (2018) interviewed fifty-two content creators, including designers, writers, and marketing consultants. The researchers sought to examine the ways in which cultural workers represent themselves on several user-generated sites resulting in what they call "platform-specific self-branding" (4). Cultural workers make use of multiple platforms, and are consistently present on those platforms, because of the assumption that each social media site, each "front stage" variant, affords different audiences different features for self-presentation and self-promotion, and different "digital impression[s]" (4). The coauthors articulate these benefits in terms of "imagined affordances": "Those in our sample routinely made decisions about the platforms on which to create and

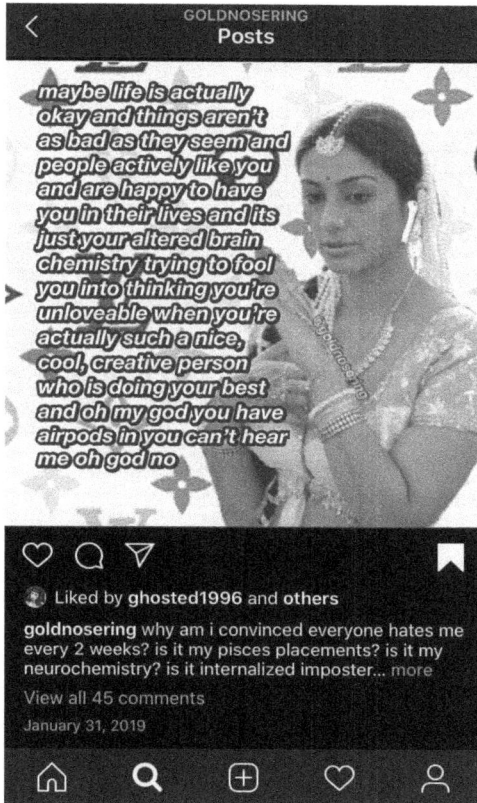

Figure 8.3. A screenshot of a post by goldnosering (January 31, 2019). The memer has comically Photoshopped AirPods onto a woman adorned in bangles, neck, and head jewelry and combined the image with razor wire stream-of-consciousness block text. The combination of self-deprecation and laughter connects this meme to other textual traditions of humor writing and stand-up that prioritize emotional transparency. *Courtesy of author.*

share content based upon considerations of each site's material and design features ('low-level affordances'), the site's perceived culture ('high-level affordances'), and the interaction of these elements within the wider social media environment" (4).

For Cochrane, who considers herself better at Instagram than at Twitter, the findings on affordances resonated with her own experience of producing content. She thinks in images, often in the film scenes or cinematic situations she recalls when authoring memes. Her own success—at monetizing her Instagram account and receiving work offers from people she has met through Instagram—is due to the digital ecosystem that has taken root through the flow of images shared and posted on the site. In 2019, Cochrane began to make strategic use of a "back stage" technical feature on Instagram, the Close Friends list. This feature was introduced in November 2018, allowing users to select which followers can view the temporary Instagram stories on an exclusive list. Cochrane was inspired by Gabi Abrão, known as sighswoon on Instagram, who added a Patreon tier that would allow followers access to her Close Friends list and decided to do the same.[10] While Cochrane has a desire to be candid and open with her followers, posting content that makes her feel vulnerable, whether it be bawdy humor that takes the form of a still-image meme or the antithesis of ironic content, say, a more personal message about her health, she feels more "free" to post what she wants on the Close Friends list. Since launching her Patreon account in December 2018, she has noticed that subscribers are less likely to hurl abusive or rude messages, the type of "front stage" heckling that can be common to Instagram followers. Many "patrons" comment positively upon candid videos of Cochrane's hijinks with family, or solo traveling on a shoestring budget with friends who live on vintage sailboats along the west coast of Canada. She describes this output as akin to a small-scale transmedia reality show for "back stage" audiences. (Transmedia is Henry Jenkins' term to describe cultural workers who are the writers, directors, editors, and producers of their own content.) Media scholar Anne Jerslev (2016) notes that "performances of a private authentic self are the most valuable commodity in social media celebrification" (5240). This commodity only heightens in value as it circulates among "close friends" and on exclusive lists.

While content creators search for ways to make money off their products and performances of self, they do not control the means of production and so live with constant insecurity and algorithmic mystery. This was most recently instanced in shadowbanning, the flipside of the Close Friends feature, which became a source of concern among users in 2019. This is when the platform blocks your content without your knowledge unless someone searches for you in their "following" list. The repercussions of effectively becoming invisible marks a potential loss of income, and spins into doubt any assurances that influencers will even appear onstage. Scolere, Pruchniewska, and Duffy (2018) note that these algorithmic vulnerabilities are most felt when platforms introduce new modifications and features, often with little advance notice:

> Algorithms are, of course, concealed to users—the oft-used "black box" metaphor is an evocation of Gaver's (1991) concept of "hidden affordances"; however, these were rendered perceptible to our interviewees at moments of change. That is, shifts in the display or ordering of content led creative producers to infer updates to the platform's algorithm. (4)

Ultimately, the use of the Close Friends list to generate potential income and limitedly reserve control over who is watching—not to mention provide a

Figure 8.4. A screen capture of dyingbutfine (posted February 19, 2020). This call for crowdsourced funds lays bare the ways in which work, survival, and creative imprint are knotted into one another. While Instagram is a "formal" billion-dollar business, the creatives who maintain it through their posts work within a more informal economy of small-dollar donations and subscriptions. What are the implications of crowdsourcing a living wage, or simply a wage that covers the rent? How do these appeals overlap with both donating to a charity and paying for entertainment? And do those users who pay feel an entitlement over the creative in terms of boundaryless access and availability? *Courtesy of author.*

sense of intimacy for subscribers tuning in—enables a certain kind of "micro-celebrity" to flourish online.

Cochrane often uses what she calls celebrity *avatars* to express herself on her Instagram account. These avatars range from Hollywood celebrities to characters in 1990s chick flicks to canonical French theorists. Her thumbnail profile picture for ripannanicolesmith rotates on a regular basis and, in as many weeks, might feature a blond female warrior in too-tight medieval armor holding a shield in one hand and sword in the other, Puerto Rican reggaeton musician Nicky Jam posing with his long acrylic nail tips, or Paris Hilton smiling impassively in pigtails. Given that "microcelebrity"[11] on the internet often manifests as lifestyle videos, blogs, or photos by and for cisgender young women—this is by no means the only type of content in circulation, but in the realm of microcelebrity it tends to be the "most watched" (Jerslev 2016, 5233)—the use of celebrity avatars seems apt. In place of an unbroken stream of selfies on Instagram, ripannanicolesmith and digital feminists such as Kristel Jax (dyingbutfine) and the anonymous account goldnosering all make varied use of stock celebrity imagery, or in the case of Jax and anonymous, vintage Barbie dolls and the animated character Lisa Simpson. These avatars do not diminish the authenticity of the *actual* women blogging on these accounts, since the content of so many of the posts themselves roast mainstream celebrity culture, fashion and beauty, "life and style." These influencers are available to their followers, but their "to be looked at ness" is not what is on display; rather, it is other signifiers of far more famous people who orbit from their privileged position of being groomed by stylists, handled by publicists, and filtered down to followers through sponsored content.

Here, it is worth pausing to note the genealogy of "microcelebrity." Media theorist Theresa M. Senft (2013) used this term to describe the subjects in her fieldwork, which, like Cochrane today, was informed by her auto-ethnographic experiences of life and work online. In the early aughts, Senft (2013) first was and then turned to study "cam girls," or "young women who were broadcasting their lives on the internet" by means of "still image, video, [and] blogging" (346). The "cam girl" phenomenon was a precursor to the kind of female-identified microcelebrity that has become germane to platforms such as YouTube and Instagram, and in the 2020s, the rise of video

Figure 8.5. A screen capture of a meme by ripannanicolesmith (posted February 18, 2020). The meme includes a film still from *She's All That* (1999). It's a classic close-up that frames the faces of the romantic leads Zach Siler (Freddie Prinze Jr.) and Laney Boggs (Rachel Leigh Cook), in profile, staring into each other's eyes, bringing the film to its *Pygmalion*-style conclusion. Ripannanicolesmith has inserted a block of yellow text in the bottom left corner and imagines Laney speaking in full voice to Zach. In the comment section, the imagined Laney cites, in a single breath, performance studies scholar José Esteban Muñoz and psychologist Nancy Van Dyken, reimagining *She's All That* as a queer dynamic between equals that negates heteronormative mating rituals of palatable conquest. *Courtesy of author.*

sharing apps such as TikTok. Microcelebrities are unlikely to have the kind of stylist and public relations machinery described above to produce content across multiple platforms or endorse particular brands, and nowhere near the exclusive status of a star, which Jerslev (2016) notes is the quintessence of what it means to be a mainstream icon of red carpets and glossy magazines (5236). What's more, they may not be interested in explicitly resourcing or branding themselves for profit. Sheft (2018), in a prologue to a collection on microcelebrity a decade after coining the term, notes the distinction: "Today, I speak of micro-celebrity as a practice, rather than a person: it's the presentation of one's online self as a branded good, with the expectation others are doing the same. When this presentation involves an intention to monetize, I call that person an influencer" (16).[12] Whether microcelebrity or influencer, regular contact and immediate reach are valued over exclusivity and distance. This is the very gist of social media platforms. Facebook, Twitter, Instagram, Snapchat, and TikTok will not work unless the users on them "act" in order to maintain an "internet presence." What we wish to emphasize is that microcelebrity as a neologism *and* as internet phenomenon is gendered in its origins and its daily practice. The imperative to always act, to always be onstage, is the imperative of mimesis or reproductivity. It is what leads Cochrane to ask herself: "When do you know that you have completed enough work? What do you perceive as work, or which tasks, as someone who uses social media as a creative and critical platform, elicit feelings of accomplishment rather than guilt over 'nothing getting done'?" Her self-doubts are relevant to digital labor and domestic labor (its own never-ending yardstick), which continues to be cast as "women's work," and discounted from what writer and broadcaster Sandi Toksvig (2018) calls the "formal economy."

It is no small coincidence that male-identified microcelebrities tend to dominate an altogether different type of internet presence through competitive gaming platforms such as Fortnite and Amazon-owned Twitch in which their work is measured through performance indicators and their metrics are known to other players and fans. Given the dangers of generalization, we wonder, if it is within the realm of the sayable to suggest that when it comes to matters of microcelebrity men must play and women must perform? We're painfully aware that such statements reinforce essentialist divides even through the very naming of them here, but we court generalization because we're interested in how digital feminists might buffer themselves against being reduced to the "approval-worthy" actor. Digital feminists, rather than negate spectacle, openly play with its signifiers. This is networked communication as ironic encounter. Paris Hilton in pigtails and other avatars are not just a source of droll laughter, they protect the digital feminist from being the "bearer of the look" (Mulvey 1975, 11). They establish a boundary between the content creators and her followers.

For Cochrane, celebrity avatars are but one tactic. She also plays with the core tenets of microcelebrity, including that of round-the-clock availability, shifting the geotagged location of ripannanicolesmith from luxury districts such as Bel Air to progressive haunts like Berkeley. This play on locations is itself a commentary on "trending locations," on centers and peripheries, but also a speculative ode to blonde bombshell Anna Nicole Smith (1967–2007), who met an untimely death by prescription overdose, posthumously leaving a litigious trail that went all the way to the US Supreme Court.[13] Derided in the press for marrying octogenarian oil magnate J. Howard Marshall (1905–1995), who died but one year after they married, it is not hard to imagine Smith once luxuriating poolside (in her dirty-old-man-wealth) in a gated Bel Air mansion. While taken as a real possibility, what is taken as a radical impossibility is the notion that this or any pinup model might grace the campus town of Berkeley. We can't picture it. So Cochrane pictures it for us, summoning counternarratives through her recombinant image and text.

Cochrane and many of her Millennial peers first took their cue from Dre, a Montreal-based Colombian Canadian Instagrammer who goes by gothshakira.[14] Dre politicized the nascent Instagram meme imaginary by combining images of celebrity Latinx women in the American diaspora with lengthy, flowery block text above them. She explicitly countered the shortened text of apolitical memes that typically begin with "tfw." Slang for "that feel or face when . . . " or "when you . . . " tfw is followed by a shared feeling, often one that is personal and meant to signal recognition by users. In the process of reformatting memes, gothshakira spawned a widely used block text aesthetic that ranges from critique to polemic to irony.[15] Another user, California-based Binny, who goes by scariestbugever, is affiliated with gothshakira through online friendship.[16] Scariestbugever posted non sequitur images of sad animals and original memes, discussing her depression, mania, and issues with alcohol. This emotional transparency unfolds in the context of a real time audience who follow you and who digital feminists follow and track back through metrics.

Cochrane began sourcing images of female celebrities that had taken up real estate in her teenage psyche such as Paris Hilton and Kim Kardashian. As noted above, these women function as frequent avatars in her memes. She has publicly fantasized about Hilton and the Kardashian sisters reading critical theory and frequently used her meme text as a window into the "back stage," crafting first-person observations about their role as hyperfeminine objects in the networked circuits of late capitalism. This fantasy often takes the form of a digital avatar in a single frame. The stock figures of feminine conformity are outfitted with new, anti-conformist scripts that recast them with an emotional life and a life of the mind. They reappear on her feed as formidable intellects. As viewers, we may laugh because what is highlighted

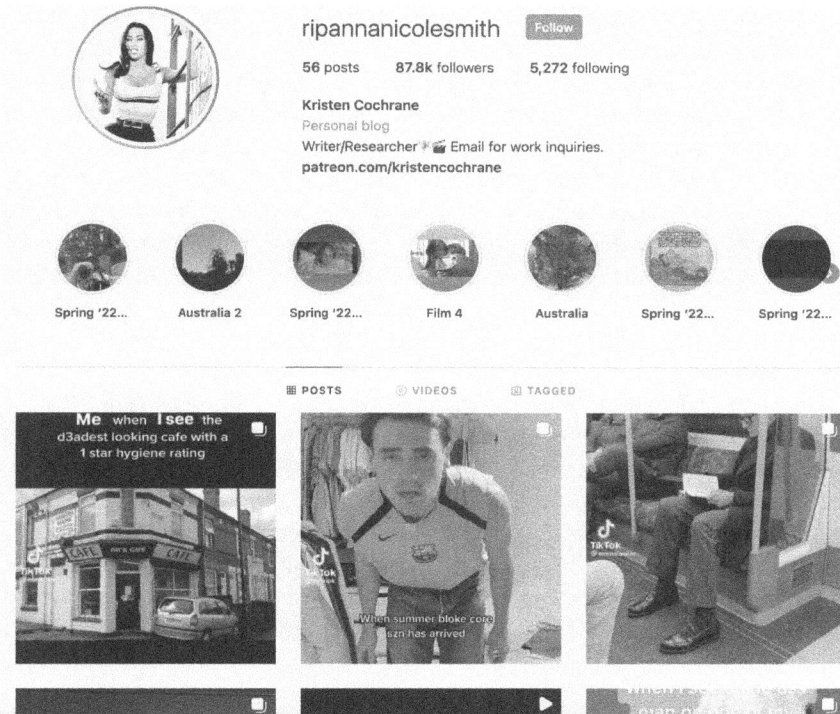

Figure 8.6. A screenshot of the profile picture, description, and snippet of stories of ripannanicolesmith (April 26, 2022) with links to Cochrane's Patreon page. Unless you select particular stories, images of Cochrane do not dominate her feed. The visual aesthetic is largely made up of celebrities and TikTok videos. Of all the images listed in this chapter, this is among the most recent screenshot. ripannanicolesmith has gone through multiple iterations in the more than two years since this piece was first coauthored reflecting the shift in cultural production toward TikTok. Cochrane has also radically edited her posts down to a svelte fifty-six where once she had more than two thousand and counting. She uses the Instagram stories as a personal travelogue and archive of TikTok material and memes from across the Internet. Her former bio line, "meme dispensary," has now been replaced with the description, "personal blog" and the workman's shingle, "writer/researcher." *Courtesy of the author.*

is the impossibility that Barbie or the Kardashians could ever, for example, contemplate Foucault's imbricated conceptions of knowledge and power. After all, that is how we first came to know "her," as a performing object so consumed by quicksilver surfaces that she could never entertain the possibility of structural thought. And perhaps life was better before Foucault, because at least "she" (Paris or Kim or Anna or Barbie) was satisfied that her choice of lipstick and bright pink halter top was hers and hers alone. Now, she must contend with the fact that she is an assemblage of signs; a performer who rents out signifiers without ever fully owning them. Except that she doesn't buy it. She always felt herself to be a subject.

How do we contend with the reality that, for many women who embody the aesthetic choices of Kim Kardashian or Anna Nicole Smith, they are not taken seriously in the workplace or outside of "obscene" or pornographic contexts? The memes of this genre have highlighted urgent questions relating to aesthetic and sartorial agency, and how this intersects with one's ability to be respected and treated with dignity. Does the ease with which audiences across media both laugh at and with the subjects depicted in the memes reveal the source of that laughter to be hyper femme women—devoid of the ability to be interested in topics outside of cosmetic consumerism or a heteronormative marriage?[7]

For many, the triumph of films such as *Legally Blonde* (Dir. Robert Luketic, 2001, US), and reality television shows such as *Keeping Up With the Kardashians* and *The Real Housewives* franchise, is that the women in these media texts are not only celebrated for their gloriously excessive personal styles, which flirt with the gaudy, but that they are also astute professionals in fields like law, business, psychology, and medicine. Moreover, the emotional intelligence and labor that often goes invisible is recognized and celebrated by viewers. These patterns of recognition continue onto social media, whether users are engaging with the Instagram posts of a cast member from a reality television series or liking and commenting upon the posts of ripannanicolesmith, who fashions fan fiction narratives using devices such as editing and adding fictional text to screenshots.

Digital feminist interventions regularly embrace paradox through comic contradiction—this ironic trait is often manifested in memes, which through viral image and text not only capture the constraints of heteronormativity but dismantle its discursive logic. But these performances of irony are also susceptible to paranoid and conspiratorial readings. In her 2002 essay "Paranoid Reading and Reparative Reading, Or, You're So Paranoid, You Probably Think This Essay Is About You," Eve Kosofsky Sedgwick advocated for a mode of reception that could offer more generosity to its texts, rather than the suspicious hermeneutics and interpretive strategies that had dominated queer theory and antihomophobic scholarship in the 1980s and 1990s. Her intervention contains echoes of the tensions between agency and co-option that have occurred in twenty-first century American pop culture, from the 2000s to our current moment, but also the barbed comments that can fill the sidebars of Instagram.

In the comment sections of feminist meme accounts, users will often engage in critiques of the memes that regularly fall under what is colloquially known as "reaching," wherein the meme author or curator is given a paranoid reading—the allegation being that they have uttered something sexist,

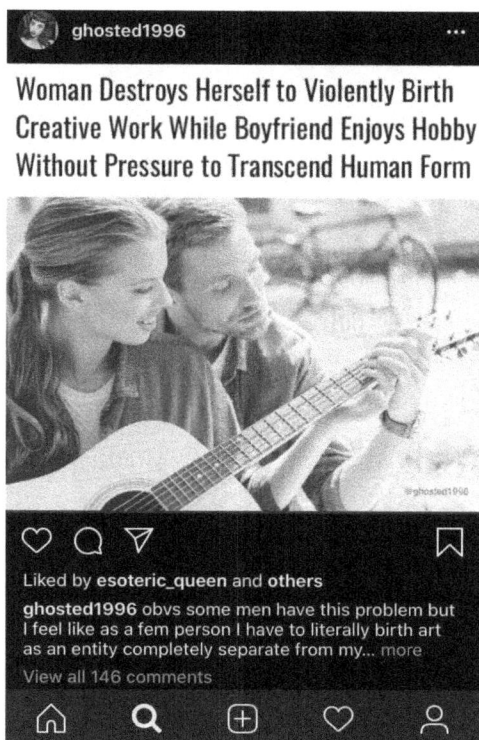

Figure 8.7. While not a celebrity meme, this post by ghosted1996 (February 13, 2020) by California-based visual artist Haley Byam is indicative of how irony and sincerity can overlap through the pastiche of image and text, an observation made by Cochrane in the crafting of her own memes. *Courtesy of the author.*

homophobic, transphobic, or racist. While some users will send a direct message to discuss the perceived grievance with the meme, others will write hostile comments that can seem to negate a desire for the compassion that one would assume to undergird a progressive political value system. In these circles, it is devastating to be characterized as something which would suggest the meme author or curator is not progressive, and users wield this tool prolifically. It also begs the questions: Who gains from policing the content of digital feminists through hostile acts of "reaching"? In other words, who benefits from these rituals of humiliation and silencing? These comments in the paranoid style have been circulating on leftist and feminist adjacent platforms since the rise of the #MeToo, undermining this fourth wave movement through lateral violence. If paranoia becomes the dominant mode, then depoliticization will follow, and so too will the neoliberal postfeminism

Figure 8.8. The meme pictured above by Decolonial.Meme.Queens (March 4, 2022) shows two stock images drawn in the Noble Savage tradition: a bare chested Plains Indian in a headdress riding a horse in the overexposed sunset. It is the type of romanticized imagery of Native American and First Nations from the Plains and Prairies that was popularized by settler photographer and proto-anthropologist Edward S. Curtis (1868–1952) but is as old as the discourse of First Contact. The top caption of the meme, "trying to prove your intelligence to white people" (all lowercase) is paired with a silhouetted image of both the rider and horse hunched over in apparent defeat. The bottom caption and image of the meme, "bad english on purpose" (again, all lowercase) shows the Plains Indian astride the horse, body outstretched to the sky in a kind of ecstasy. The meme uses irony to overturn classic Noble Savage imagery by captioning the images with an internal monologue that is at odds with an Indian "everyman" stripped of any identifying features. If, previously, you assumed that the sublime state of the Plains Indian was because of his "pure" relationship to nature, the meme offers an altogether different (and very funny) interpretation of a man free from the mental load of white expectations. *Courtesy of the author.*

chronicled by Angela McRobbie, Ariel Levy, and others in the early years of the millennium.[18]

In light of the paranoia surrounding the use of irony, a pause for reflection on irony's redemption is needed. Whether this use is seen in goldnosering's stream-of-consciousness humor, ghosted1996's sincerity and self-doubt, or decolonial.meme.queens' sharp demonstration of the mental load of whiteness on Indigenous People, the examples embedded in this chapter, alongside that of ripannanicolesmith, show irony to be a necessary tool. These feminist creatives mirror the short-order timing of a stand-up who must fight for the full attention of her scrolling audience and a shrink who uses comic distance to alert her patients to the work involved in undoing dominant cultural representations of gender.

Through shared practices such as irony and strategic platform use, the feminist memers in this chapter have found ways to persist online. While functions such as a Close Friends list can potentially be used to improve a content creator's cash flow (and reduce instances of online abuse), tactical irony can potentially be used to draw a line, to mark a boundary in the boundaryless terrain between influencers and their followers. And perhaps most importantly, irony is pure pleasure. In Cochrane's words: "It's also fun to mock each other's beliefs, it keeps us humble, it's campy, it echoes the history of queer witticisms." Importantly, irony forges spaces of solidarity and coalitional affinities. It interrupts and disrupts what has been called the toxic positivity of certain affective mores, which, alongside the corporate co-optation of feminisms, has become part of hegemonic feminist affects. We thus return to a kind of feminist killjoy (vis-à-vis Sara Ahmed) within fourth-wave feminist movements and networks, but a killjoy who incorporates the necessary and urgent critique of late capitalism owned by technology monopolies.

REFERENCES

Banet-Weiser, Sarah. 2018. *Empowered: Popular Feminism and Popular Misogyny.* Duke University Press.

Dean, Jodi. 2010. *Blog Theory: Feedback and Capture in the Circuits of Drive.* Polity Press, 2010.

Ellcessor, Elizabeth. 2014. "Constructing Social Media's Indie Auteurs: Management of the Celebrity Self in the Case of Felicia Day." In *Making Media Work: Cultures of Management in the Entertainment Industries*, edited by Derek Johnson, Derek Kompare, and Avi Santo, 188–209. New York University Press.

Federici, Silvia. 2004. *Caliban and the Witch: Women, The Body, and Primitive Accumulation.* Autonomedia.

Jerslev, Anne. 2016. "In the Time of the Microcelebrity: Celebrification and the YouTuber Zoella." *International Journal of Communication* 10: 5233–51.

Kavenna, Joanna. 2019. Interview: "Shoshana Zuboff: 'Surveillence capitalism is an assault on human autonomy.'" *The Guardian*, October 4, 2019.

Kosofsky Sedgwick, Eve. 2002. "Paranoid Reading and Reparative Reading, Or, You're So Paranoid, You Probably Think This Essay Is About You." In *Touching Feeling: Affect, Pedagogy, Performativity*. Duke University Press.

Levy, Ariel. 2005. *Female Chauvinist Pigs: Women and the Rise of Raunch Culture*. Free Press.

Mulvey, Laura. 1975. "Visual Pleasure and Narrative Cinema." *Screen* 16 (3): 6–18.

Noble, Safiya Umoja. 2018. *Algorithms of Oppression: How Search Engines Reinforce Racism*. NYU Press.

Rottenberg, Catherine. 2018. *The Rise of Neoliberal Feminism*. Oxford University Press.

Scolere, Leah, Urszula Pruchniewska, and Brooke Erin Duffy. 2018. "Constructing the Platform-Specific Self-Brand: The Labor of Social Media Promotion." *Social Media + Society* (July 2018).

Senft, Theresa M. 2013. "Microcelebrity and the Branded Self." In *A Companion to New Media Dynamics*, edited by John Hartley, Jean Burgess, and Axel Bruns. Wiley-Blackwell.

———. 2018. "Fame, Shame, Remorse, Authenticity: A Prologue." In *Microcelebrity Around the Globe: Approaches to Cultures of Internet Fame*, edited by Crystal Abidin and Megan Lindsay Brown. Emerald Publishing Limited.

Tolentino, Jia. 2019. *Trick Mirror: Reflections on Self-Delusion*. Random House.

Toksvig, Sandi. 2018. "The Gender Pay Gap Isn't the Half of It: Our Economy Runs on Women's Unpaid Work." *The Guardian*. April 9, 2018.

Tortorici, Dayna. 2020. "Infinite Scroll: Life under Instagram." *The Guardian*, January 31, 2020.

Turkle, Sherry. 2011. *Alone Together: Why We Expect More from Technology and Less from Each Other*. Basic Books.

Zuboff, Shoshana. 2019. *The Age of Surveillance Capitalism: The Fight for a Human Future at the New Frontier of Power*. Public Affairs.

NOTES

1. We borrow this expression from Shoshana Zuboff. In her book, *The Age of Surveillance Capitalism* (2020), she argues (as many have done before her, including Jodi Dean) that social media platforms such as Facebook have relativized information flows by refusing to differentiate between, for instance, evidence-based research and high-voltage disinformation, journalism, and opinion or editorial rant, fostering an environment of "radical indifference" (505).

2. There is precedent for this type of collaborative (analyst/participant) writing in the realm of microcelebrity. See, for example, Jonathan Mavroudis and Esther Milne,

"Researching Microcelebrity: Methods, Access and Labour," *First Monday* 21, no. 7 (2016). doi.org/10.5210/fm.v21i7.6401.

3. This follower count was documented in April 2022.

4. In an interview and profile by Joanna Kavenna for *The Guardian*, Shoshana Zuboff describes the early-2000s rise of Google and Facebook and the technological innovations they ushered in as "a rogue mutation of capitalism marked by concentrations of wealth, knowledge and power unprecedented in human history." Kavenna summarizes the reaches and breaches of these tech titans: "Gmail was launched in 2004; Google subsequently admitted that it has scanned private correspondence for personal information. In the same year, Facebook was founded, its business model also based on the capture of and access to personal information." Kavenna then quotes Zuboff directly: "The metaphor Zuboff uses is one of conquest: 'With so little left that could be commodified, the last virgin territory was private human experience.' In 1986, 1% of the world's information was digitized. In 2013, it was 98%."

5. See also Dayna Tortorici (2020), "Infinite Scroll: Life under Instagram," in which she summarizes the impact of Facebook and its subsidiary Instagram (acquired in 2012), including how the former utilizes the latter to collect data and develop its capacity for surveillance.

6. There are many resources on this topic; a good place to start is the writing of broadcaster Emily Chang and her opinion piece for the *New York Times*, "What Women Know About the Internet," April 10, 2019. There has also been scholarly analysis of the continued fallout of Gamergate (2014), an incident that involved the vicious online harassment, including death threats, against game designer Zoë Quinn. See, for example, Michael Salter's "From Geek Masculinity to Gamergate: The Technological Rationality of Online Abuse," *Crime, Media, Culture* 14, no. 2 (August 2018): 247–64.

7. Media critics such as Hiba Ali would argue that this observation does not go far enough, because "exclusion" does not account for the fact that low-wage, nonunionized Black and brown laborers are essential to the running of corporations such as Amazon, which rely on the exploitation of these workers to service their distribution centers and courier routes. See Hiba Ali, "Amazon's Surveillance System Is a Global Risk to People of Color." *Zora*, September 25, 2019. zora.medium.com/amazons-surveillance-system-is-a-global-risk-to-people-of-color-a5030a19d5e1.

8. See also Noble's (2018) analysis of the pornography industry in *Algorithms of Oppression*; she demonstrates how the industry has been at the forefront of the monetization and technological innovation of the internet.

9. This includes the wide-ranging work of Turkle, Zuboff, Jonathon Crary's *24/7: Late Capitalism and the Ends of Sleep*, and many others.

10. A description of Gabi Abrão's use of the Close Friends list opens an article by Kaitlyn Tiffany in *The Atlantic*, "'Close Friends,' for a Monthly Fee,'" September 17, 2019. www.theatlantic.com/technology/archive/2019/09/close-friends-instagram-subscription-charge-influencers/598171/.

11. This term was first coined by Theresa M. Senft in her 2008 book *Camgirls: Celebrity and Community in the Age of Social Networks* (New York: Lang).

12. In this prologue, Sheft hyphenates the word micro-celebrity.

13. See Katarinna McBride. "The Anna Nicole Smith Case: An Opera in Five Acts: The Fascinating Battle over Anna Nicole Smith's Husband's Estate Is Over, and the Late Anna Nicole Lost Everything. Or Is It? And Did She?" *Illinois Bar Journal* (May 2010) 266–67.

14. While Dre produces online content connected to her life, she wishes to maintain her privacy. Goth Shakira seems to have retired from meme-making, though she still uses social media.

15. See Barbara Calderón piece for *Remezcla*, "Don't Blame Independent Creators for 'Selling Out' When It's Their Only Option." Published online 5 Apr. 2017.

16. See their coauthored article for *Vice*, "How Feminist Memes Hit the Mainstream." Published online 3 Jan. 2017.

17. While this predates the Hilton generation, we might think of the scene from *The Seven Year Itch* (Dir. Billy Wilder, 1955, US) in which Marilyn Monroe stands above a subway grate, her white, pleated cocktail dress flying thigh-high every time a train rumbled by, as a laughing at and with the star. Monroe makes herself an object of pleasure on the street, and her sense of glee mixes with her desire to be sensual, to have an erotic encounter with herself in public.

18. See McRobbie's *The Aftermath of Feminism: Gender, Culture, and Social Change*. Sage, 2008. See also Levy's *Female Chauvinist Pigs*. Levy and McRobbie chronicle the rise of "postfeminism" and, in the extended quote below, Levy describes the inverted logic of "frat bro" culture:

> Only thirty years (my lifetime) ago, our mothers were "burning their bras" and picketing Playboy, and suddenly we were getting implants and wearing the bunny logo as supposed symbols of our liberation. How had the culture shifted so drastically in such a short period of time? What was almost more surprising than the change itself were the responses I got when I started interviewing the men and—often—women who edit magazines like *Maxim* and make programs like *The Man Show* and *Girls Gone Wild*. This new raunch culture didn't mark the death of feminism, they told me; it was evidence that the feminist project had already been achieved. We'd earned the right to look at Playboy; we were empowered enough to get Brazilian bikini waxes. Women had come so far, I learned, we no longer needed to worry about objectification or misogyny. Instead, it was time for us to join the frat party of pop culture, where men had been enjoying themselves all along. If Male Chauvinist Pigs were men who regarded women as pieces of meat, we would outdo them and be Female Chauvinist Pigs: women who make sex objects of other women and of ourselves. (3)

Chapter 9

Queering Digital Activisms

The Collective Rhetoric of Edit-a-Thons

Micki Burdick

In an article in the *New York Times*, Justine Cassell (2011) described the gendered nature of the "editing wars" currently unfolding within the online space of Wikipedia: "A woman who wishes to collaboratively construct knowledge and share it with others might not choose to do so as part of a forum where engaging in debate and deleting others' words is key." In response, Art+Feminism is a campaign devoted to fighting back by intervening within the "editing wars," and creating spaces for "cis and trans women, the arts, and feminism" within the popular online platform of Wikipedia ("Art+Feminism" 2018). The goal is to not only create and edit articles based in feminist thought, but to also diversify the intellectual labor behind the (re)crafting of Wikipedia. Individuals often associate forms of digital activisms such as hacking with male-dominated and "masculine" forms of communication. Activists attempt to correct this by arguing that more "feminine" voices must be heard. However, the Art+Feminism campaign attempts to queer dominant notions of digital activisms through purposeful collectivity and an emphasis on embodiment when engaging with the textual layers of Wikipedia.

Using the framework of collective rhetoric, in this chapter I unveil compelling aspects of the edit-a-thon that prompt the queering of digital activisms and the stories that unfold. Collective rhetoric is a set of consciousness-raising practices and "validation of worldviews through the articulation, or the strategic linking, of individual experiences" (Dubriwny 2005, 396). The individual experience within the collective transforms the audience into participants of an event. What happens when collective feminist tactics mix with digital forms of activism that are often relegated to the neoliberal discourses of productivity and individuality? Within literature on feminist DIY

activism, the focus stagnates on the subversion of norms through performativity outside of dominant systems as well as within new ways of existing
in a space. However, these discourses often adhere to binaries that separate
masculine-feminine ways of interacting and modes of activism.

I contend that the focus on individual actions editing (Wikipedia) should
be traded in for those of the collective through an engagement with activist
bodies and their "queering" practices in the physical editing space. I define
queering as "crafting alternate identity constructions," following work within
rhetorical studies and queer theory by Alyssa Samek (2015, 393). The spaces
where digital activisms take place such as Wikipedia are often not inclusive
of people of all identities, which becomes the exigence for not only editing but also "queering" the online archive of knowledge (Rosner and Fox
2016). The Art+Feminism campaign works inside rather than outside of the
masculine-dominated canon of Wikipedia to transform digital activisms and
their gendered baggage. These practices of editing craft new stories and ways
of living in the world outside of gendered binaries, revealing new constructions of identity and embodiment within feminist activisms (Samek 2015).
Coming together within a physical space to embody editing becomes a means
of articulating community as well as new ways of thinking represented within
Wikipedia, which are normally centered on the masculine-feminine speech
binary. Overall, this chapter expands collective rhetoric that argues for collectivity as a way to subvert neoliberal, postfeminist discourses, which privilege
individual choice based in the false belief that progress has been fully made
for women (McRobbie 2009).

In this chapter, I first lay the groundwork for conversations surrounding the
use of practices such as hacktivism and DIY activism. Next, I explore theories
of collective rhetoric and the intersection of feminist and decolonial thought.
I outline my contribution to collective feminist rhetoric as a praxis for representation while also performing the subversion of neoliberal discourses.
The importance of Wikipedia as a digital space is contextualized within the
particular intertextual nature of the canon and its importance for those in the
Art+Feminism campaign. I subsequently analyze the Art+Feminism guides,
including connecting the tactics of the edit-a-thon to a collective rhetoric
through the texts as well as the queering of digital activisms more broadly.
Collectivity becomes a way to orient digital activisms away from the emphasis on "masculinity versus femininity" and toward an inclusive space of
popular knowledge and processes used to get there. Edit-a-thons attempt to
queer digital spaces through the visibility of those who identify as women,
trans women, and nonbinary people similarly to the ways that such groups
have queered physical spaces through visibility (Rand 2013). However, the
Art+Feminism edit-a-thon goes a step further by also queering the way the
individual engages in embodied practices of editing. I contend that the focus

on the individual actions should be traded in for those of the collective and the processes of queering they engage in through their bodies within the editing space.

THE EDIT-A-THON AS COLLECTIVE/ FEMINIST RHETORIC

Art+Feminism is a campaign created to "improve the coverage of cis and transgender women, non-binary folks, feminism and the arts on Wikipedia" ("Art+Feminism" 2018). The campaign labels itself as a "do-it-yourself" and "do-it-with-others" project through collective editing of the online, open-access database Wikipedia. In order for Wikipedia, a widely used online source for people around the world, to be more inclusive in regard to gender and sexuality, the campaign encourages what they call edit-a-thons. Art+Feminism's website states that only 10 percent of editors on Wikipedia are people who do not identify as cis men. This lack of representation in editors is translated into the cause of gaps in the knowledge of Wikipedia and historical narratives it provides ("Art+Feminism" 2018). Edit-a-thons step in as possible remedies to these gaps in knowledge by bringing a diverse group of individuals together to physically edit in person while challenging the online space to be more inclusive.

Wikipedia is one of the largest open-source, general reference websites in the world. It is web-based, free-content, multilingual, and "anyone with Internet access can write and make changes to Wikipedia articles" ("Wikipedia: About" 2019). The only expressed limits to editing are a set of community guidelines that demand articles to be "impartial" and "factual," which are policed by a set of volunteer editors who keep track of new or edited entries. Because of the wide reach of Wikipedia and its domineering masculinity, an effort to change the platform's content through feminist hacking has rhetorical implications for broader distribution of knowledge to the public. The Art+Feminism campaign was started in 2014 by four artist friends in response to the lack of diverse representation on Wikipedia. It is a collective that aims "to create meaningful changes to the body of knowledge available about feminism and the arts on Wikipedia" and is now a global phenomenon (Mitesser 2017). Every March, members recruit for over 280 events on six continents to create and edit thousands of Wikipedia articles in the form of what they describe as edit-a-thons. Although people are encouraged on a specific day to edit together, there is an open invitation to create an editing event any time of the year. Also, while there are many Wikipedia editing campaigns, for example AfroCrowd, a group seeking to increase the number of people of African descent in the Wikipedia community, Art+Feminism is specifically worth exploring because of its claim to thousands of collective edits and a worldwide reach (Mitesser 2017).

One important facet of the edit-a-thon guides is the conceptualization of the gender gap as the exigence for editing in the first place. The Gender Gap is a metaphor used to explain the statistical discrepancies in the identity of the editors and content of Wikipedia. The Gender Gap guide accessed through the edit-a-thon website uses the term along with links to statistics about women in the arts ("Closing the Gender Gap on Wikipedia" 2018, 8). According to the campaign's guides, this gap is created by a paucity of women and queer people telling their own stories in popular digital spaces. The authors of the campaign believe that "without representation from cis and trans women in the preservation of their own stories, we get skewed content that misses the mark on the value and existence of their impact on history" ("Quick Guide for Editors" 2018, 2). Therefore, the focus of the campaign is representation broadly, but includes an additional collective, performative element; everyone must commune in a physical space to make concrete change in visibility of certain groups within the extensive online canon of Wikipedia.

DIY FEMINIST ACTIVISM

The Art+Feminism edit-a-thon stems from a lineage of DIY feminist practices that work to subvert dominant modes of community building and visibility, specifically, the history of DIY independent feminist publishing. One of the earliest publications in this lineage include Margaret Sanger's newspaper *Woman Rebel* published in 1914, in which she illegally offered information regarding contraception and sexuality (Piepmeier 2004, 34). Others, in a lineage of often-forgotten histories of Black feminist publishing, are Amy Ashwood-Garvey's founding of the *Negro World* in 1914 and Ida B. Wells-Barnett's publications on lynching in the late nineteenth century (Martin 2000; Wells-Barnett 2014). Because of innovations in technology, like the creation of the mimeograph machine, many feminist publications were printed in the 1970s (Piepmeier 2004, 36). Some of the most popular publications at the time included "Anne Koedt's 'The Myth of the Vaginal Orgasm' and the Boston Women's Health Book Collective's *Our Bodies, Ourselves*" (Piepmeier 2004, 36). Publications like these influenced the feminist activism of the time.

Feminist DIY activism is studied in its various published forms, including the distribution of publications called zines, made popular by the group Riot Grrrl (Demo 2000). Riot Grrrl was a musical movement of feminists in the 1990s that centered around the creation of zines, distributed personal magazines, and the reclaiming and retooling of the term "girl" for youth-based political change (Piepmeier 2004; Demo 2000). Zines enable a unique type of activism because of their creative, personal content and their unconventional distribution, therefore subverting capitalist norms of production. Mostly, however, DIY feminist activisms are used to challenge dominant stereotypes through a visibility politic. Within the lineage of DIY independent feminist publishing, there exist histories of radical feminist activism that specifically emphasize visibility politics (Siegel 2007). These include "second wave feminist manifestos, such as the 1968 'Principles' of the New York Radical Women, the Redstockings' 'Manifesto' of 1969, and the 1970 'Woman-Identified Woman' statement of the Radicalesbians" (Piepmeier 2004, 40). Later, in the 1990s, the Lesbian Avengers attempted to also render legible their particular identities through the use of public tactics that played into the narrative of "lesbian chic," embodying sexuality to subvert dominant stereotypes of lesbians at the time through comics (Rand 2013).

While DIY activisms have historically centered visibility, for this same reason they sometimes fall prey to co-optation by postfeminist culture. For example, Riot Grrrl was appropriated by dominant discourses of "Girl Power"' in the 1990s that actively disavowed feminism, including popular music groups like the Spice Girls (Zeisler 2017). By giving in to patriarchal and capitalist fetishizing in order to make their sexual identities "acceptable" within society, a visibility politic can only go so far when managing the dominant, neoliberal, appealing forms of acceptable activism and identity. I describe neoliberal activisms as those that emphasize individual choice and personal representation, mistaking structural inequalities for issues of personal choice (Asen 2017, 331). Postfeminism is directly connected to neoliberalism as it is based in the belief that feminism has been completed and, therefore, individual choice is possible within the current overarching power structures. Angela McRobbie (2009) explains that postfeminism also emphasizes freedom and choice as tropes that make feminism "decisively aged and made to seem redundant" (11). While this sounds like a future not yet possible, postfeminism argues that women are able to currently achieve these aims through personal perseverance and making the "right" choices under capitalism. For example, while the Lesbian Avengers focus on identity was commendable at the time, they also tied lesbian identity explicitly to sexualized bodies which was then able to be co-opted by dominant logics surrounding sexual orientation and stereotypes surrounding promiscuity (Rand 2013). Therefore, along with identity, the ease in which representations are co-opted through neoliberal frameworks from subversive visibility politics must be taken into account.

A politics of visibility and the practice of complicating postfeminist neoliberalism thus shape the politics of feminist hacktivism, which is the creative use of computer technology that specifically works against networks of global capital. David Gunkel (2005) describes hacktivism as drawing on "the creative use of computer technology for the purposes of facilitating online protests, performing civil disobedience in cyberspace and disrupting the flow of information by deliberately intervening in the networks of global capital" (595). Typically seen as a masculinist form of activism, some feminist groups have decided to subvert these norms through their own collective hacking practices (Rosner and Fox 2016). For example, a group of new mothers in California who call themselves Mothership HackerMoms use the term as way to claim the identity while caretaking in order to refigure the masculine notions of "progress" and "innovation" (Rosner and Fox 2016). Consistent across these lineages, DIY feminist activism reframes the expected. As gendered norms and expectations are traversed, these activists craft spaces of belonging for groups such as mothers, lesbians, and community amongst women. But, as Demo (2000) argues, "Since the 1848 Seneca Falls women's rights convention, activists advocating for gender equality have often been denied conventional forums for bringing their message to the people" (154). Thus, the Art+Feminism campaign works in these "unconventional" ways by performing inclusion in the collective forum of Wikipedia, paying specific attention to who gets to edit the canon.

COLLECTIVE RHETORIC

A theory of collective rhetoric examines the messages created and distributed under the name of a group and the consequences for these messages on the public (Simons 1982; Miller 1999). Collective rhetoric is a significant site of analysis for rhetorical theorists in social movements and organizing. Theories of collective rhetoric are fundamentally shaped by Black feminist thought, decoloniality, and critical race scholarship more broadly (Hill Collins 2009; Lorde 2007; hooks 2015; Rand 2014; Sowards 2019; Sowards 2010; Sowards and Renegar 2004; Enck-Wanzer 2012). Much of this work explicitly critiques neoliberal activisms. Scholars of collective rhetoric place the emphasis not on an individual speaking ideologically for a group but, instead, forward "a turn to the exploration of persuasive engagements that are truly collaborative in form, rhetorics that are generated through the interaction of many voices" (Dubriwny 2005, 397). Therefore, a theory of collective rhetoric has three defining dimensions: it transforms audiences into active participants, validates the experiences of the oppressed or marginalized, and allows these individuals to tell their own stories within the collective (Dubriwny 2005). I argue that the importance of a collective rhetoric lies in its capacity to account for the complicated mitigation between personal/political and private/public that often underscores conflicts within feminist thought. In particular, a theory of collective rhetoric reveals the flaws within rhetorics of individual choice in a capitalist society.

Feminist scholars such as Dubriwny (2005), hooks (2015), Lorde (2007), and Rand (2014) have underscored the "personal as political" dimension of collective rhetoric. For example, in the case of the Redstockings' abortion speak-out, women used the practice of consciousness-raising to shift dominant cultural assumptions regarding legal abortion. By making the personal political, individual experiences were given social and, therefore, political capital (Dubriwny 2005, 401). The tactic of consciousness-raising through narrating experience and expertise is used in order to center the stories and bodies of those who are marginalized, allowing them to be heard. In doing so, it interpellates the audience as participants, while private experience is rendered public and used as grounds for fomenting identification. Theories of decoloniality also clarify how embodiment and anti-Western notions of "human" are critical dimensions of collective rhetoric. For example, Darrel Wanzer-Serrano (2012) interrogates the Young Lords' rhetoric of "the people" through a decolonial perspective, arguing that their collective rhetoric delinks their discourse from hegemonic, Western traditions in a "radical, decolonial challenge to the modern social imaginary" (3). Others in this tradition, such as Stacy Sowards (2019), explain how living within marginalized groups and spaces, in this case the border, can lead to different versions of collective imaginary and resistance outside Western, American, white, norms called "differential consciousness" (2019). I extend this body of literature by thinking about the collective's direct impact on digital feminist practices as well as thinking through the gender binaries and labeled gendered practices that often accompany certain types of collective activism.

Taking Art+Feminism as a rhetoric of inquiry activist project, I underscore the importance of decoloniality through a collective rhetoric, de-linking speech from masculine versus feminine forms. Instead, Art+Feminism allows for bodies to edit text in a canon with others in order to identify where these "gaps" in knowledge can be filled, all the while knowing that there is never an end to the practice of embodied knowledge. Indeed, the edit-a-thon provides a powerful pushback to neoliberal investments in individual agency, emphasizing embodied, collective practices through collaborative editing in shared physical space and deprioritizing white men within the canon of Wikipedia. Collective rhetoric can be seen as an overarching framing device for the rethinking and queering of digital activisms in these ways.

ART+FEMINISM AS A SITE OF
COLLECTIVE RHETORIC

The Art+Feminism campaign utilizes collectivity to change the visibility politics of Wikipedia while turning its audience into active, editing participants. In line with Sowards and Renegar (2004), I argue that transcending the gender binary while thinking through collective rhetoric is imperative for inclusive and performative knowledge-making. In order to collectivize the campaign, participants use digital practices such as Quick Guides and editable forms as well as tactics that include physical editing, organization, and coming together in community spaces that often hold special meaning for participants.

From the Art+Feminism campaign, I analyzed a series of "how-to" guides for people to create and execute their own edit-a-thons: "Closing the Gender Gap on Wikipedia," "Quick Guide for Editors," and "Quick Guide for Organizers." These guides collectively answer questions of who has access to reform a popular archive of knowledge, how Art+Feminism believes this is best practiced through their edit-a-thons, and the role of how-to guides in DIY feminist activism. Some of the main tenets of the campaign found within the guides include the belief in art and open access resources, feminism as a lens, representation, and the experiences of all types of women as important and overlooked aspects in the encyclopedia of knowledge ("Quick Guide for Editors" 2018). The editor guide specifically includes a checklist for the leader of the extended campaign, a sample Facebook event invitation, a press release to explain what the campaign is doing and why it matters, a sample email for local media to cover the event, as well as handouts for participants in your new campaign group to find resources in learning how to edit Wikipedia pages and feminist resources to explain why their participation in this activism matters.

Because the materials on the website and the guide itself hold Creative Commons licensing through the campaign, fellow activists are encouraged to translate the guide or to even alter it in ways they see fit for their own group without prior permission. The event itself throughout the guide is described in detail according to basic guidelines, but even the form of the event itself is encouraged to be changed based on the needs of the other organizers. The main goal is to center particular narratives on a platform that often does not include them, which can be done in a variety of forms. The guides encourage people to come in with a specific topic in mind to edit in order to fill the gaps in knowledge on Wikipedia ("Closing the Gender Gap" 2018). For example, the text recommends holding the edit-a-thon in an art space so you can use the art around you as a point of departure for creativity in editing. Participants can feel connected to what they are editing and may want to edit those articles having to do with the space or those related closely to their own identities. Therefore, I use both the guides and the edit-a-thons themselves as my points of departure for analysis, focusing on the ways they craft subjectivity, interpellate their audiences and participants as activists, and rely on collective space to queer the archive.

CRAFTING SUBJECTIVITY

Within the Art+Feminism Quick Guides, subjectivity is created through a collective intertextual format, where the textual arena of Wikipedia in fragmented pieces crafts the ideal subject. Because "only 10% of Wikipedia's editors identify as cis or trans women," the amount of information and recorded experiences of these groups is less than ideal ("Closing the Gender Gap" 2018, 2). The ideal is, instead, seen in the cis, heterosexual male subject that is crafted through the pieces of the texts and the texts throughout history that frame this person as the optimal subject. In this way, the guides and campaign are attempting to craft a new subject through the anonymous editing of the multifaceted text of Wikipedia. The creators in their educational tools on the "gender gap" guide argue that women in general have historically been left out of the art world and that only by making editors a more diverse group of individuals can we attempt to close the gap ("Gender Gap" 2018). The campaign attempts to explain and enact the importance of making sure these prior texts to draw from are inclusive, diverse, and that people have histories of women, trans women, and nonbinary people to learn from in these contexts. Therefore, "Art+Feminism mobilizes, trains and supports a growing global community that collectively creates and updates articles on Wikipedia, adds images to Wikimedia Commons, expands WikiData entries, and more" (Art+Feminism 2020).

A collective rhetoric uses consciousness-raising to uphold the stories of those from the marginalized into a collection of stories that achieve political impact (Dubriwny 2005). The campaign leaders argue that when they and others like them are "not represented in the writing and editing of the stories and records of people like us, the content gets messed up. The stories get mistold. We lose out on the real history. That's why we're here: to change it" ("Quick Guide for Organizers" 2018, 3). Because of Wikipedia's broad scope and reach, it is an easy text to draw upon for brief and wide information. Creating a "respectable and reliable" canon is an important goal if you agree with the leaders of the campaign that, when you edit Wikipedia, "you contribute to one of the largest canons of information on the internet" and that representation within this canon matters ("Quick Guide for Editors 2018,

3). Therefore, the Art+Feminism campaign aims to craft a new ideal subject that is inclusive of almost all genders and gender performances within the context of Wikipedia as well as within the diversity of those editing. The exigence comes from studies that conclude "Wikipedia has fewer and less extensive articles on women" and "have shown gender biases in biographical articles" (Art+Feminism 2020). The crafting of new views of subjectivity are central to the decolonial underpinnings of collective rhetoric. In the case of an edit-a-thon guide, the actual visibility of diverse bodies in the room and experiences narrated in Wikipedia were and still are important for the organization's goal to edit "10,000 pages of women, people of color and LGBTQ communities by the end of 2018" ("Quick Guide for Editors" 2018). However, like decolonial framings of collective rhetoric, the Art+Feminism edit-a-thon as an event goes further to detach subjectivity and visibility from neoliberal underpinnings through creating an audience of immediate, accessible activists in a collective space.

AUDIENCE AS ACTIVISTS

In crafting subjectivity through their online and in-person campaigns the collective rhetoric of Art+Feminism transforms the audiences of their materials (website, tutorials, and guides) into active participants (Dubriwny 2005). In the Quick Guide for Editors PDF, each page of the document comes with a double-sided page; the right side has a picture of a diverse group of people collectively editing on most pages and the left side has a bolded phrase or question for the reader. One page exclaims "WHAT IF YOU HAD THE POWER TO EDIT 2018?" and on the next page "EDITOR=YOU" ("Quick Guide for Editors" 2018). Art+Feminism attempts to deconstruct the assumption of a singular agentic being in a situation through its efforts that focus specifically on change through collective action, specifically by calling all of those reading the document "editors." Collectivity for the campaign is a process of acting in new ways and creating knowledge outside of the text itself—editors perform what Wikipedia does but make these performances inclusive through their own forgotten bodies. These actions in collective spaces are ways to shift individuals away from a theoretical orientation to texts as isolated and able to solely affect and be changed by singular agents.

As an "intersectional feminist non-profit organization that directly addresses the information gap about gender, feminism, and the arts on the internet," the organizers and editors of Art+Feminism edit-a-thons know that this large gap cannot be understood and solved within individual actions alone—turning the audience into activists is what grounds this mission statement's credibility (Art+Feminism 2020). The Art+Feminism guides aim to focus the concept of subjectivity on a larger scale, making everyone responsible for noninclusive histories and texts to draw upon and the need to change them. Agency is articulated to community as the center of knowledge production because, through the process of editing, knowledge is never seen as a static thing and neither is community. "SPREAD THE WORD" and "JOIN THE COMMUNITY" are printed on the last two pages of the guide, showing the importance of sharing the campaign through the guide—the only way to allow others to have the proper materials to join ("Quick Guide for Editors" 2018). The audience of the edit-a-thon become active participants through the collective space, physically coming together with others, as well as through a focus on new ways of interpellating new members into the campaign.

There are many attempts to collectivize the campaign and practice of editing overall, transforming audiences into activists. Positioning the digital PDF guides as grassroots, vernacular publications explains the collectivity of this activity and the end goal of editing through their form. The form of the documents as "Quick Guides" and pamphlets, easy to hand out or send to others, show that the collective effort to come together and edit pieces of texts is an important facet of the campaign extending even further than the canon of Wikipedia. The Quick Guide for Organizers is a nine-page PDF that is directly downloadable from the Art+Feminism home website. Most of the pages in the Quick Guide PDF include templates for press-related tasks that can be edited for personalized content: "Here's another sample of copy can use to articulate what the Art+Feminism edit-a-thon does and why it matters. Feel free to edit the copy as you like. Make it your own" ("Quick Guide for Organizers" 2018, 6). There are example invitations/emails/press releases/ social media posts given for the audience of the guide to distribute the spirit of the campaign to other constructed audiences. These new audiences include possible attendees of your (the audience member/participant's) event, various media outlets, and friends on social media; any of these people and others can host these events. As soon as the DIY guide is opened, the authors construct an audience member as having "joined" the campaign and ready to host their own event ("Quick Guide for Organizers" 2018, 2). The Quick Guide, much like a feminist zine, uses a model of interpellating its audience directly into the agenda of the campaign when picked up (in this case, downloaded). These examples construct audiences that become participants and are able to collect a broader audience and more participants through the reconfiguration and distribution of the guide.

COLLECTIVE SPACE

The campaign describes an edit-a-thon as a community organized event that aims to teach folks how to edit, update, and add articles on Wikipedia. These events take place year-round at "museums, coffee shops, colleges, and community centers" ("What is an Edit-a-Thon?" 2019). The purpose of editing Wikipedia is to come together with others who will also do the same. Editing is an action that can take place in private, but the campaign wants people to gather in spaces that inspire creativity and brainstorming with other editors in the collective. They talk about the actual space of edit-a-thon events in ways that center physical collectivity: "Edit-a-thons are interesting communities when the content being edited is about the community. . . . If you are at an art space, could you use the current exhibitions as a point of departure?" ("Quick Guide for Organizers" 2018, 3). This focus on digital and physical community brings the collective to the center of the campaign while reconstructing the cultural fragments of Wikipedia to become more inclusive of the experiences of those gathered. The performance of editing becomes public in a community-oriented space. Performing this editing outside of individual, private, male-dominated spaces also shifts assumptions of who is able to participate in digital activisms and how. The collective space allows the campaign to ensure that everyone's edits are kept on Wikipedia, since the Edit Guide states that the cis and trans women who do edit Wikipedia are "more likely than men to have their edits reversed" and continuously give the statistic that only 10 percent of editors on Wikipedia identify as women ("Closing the Gender Gap" 2018, 2). There is a list of guidelines for editing and adding information on Wikipedia in ways that will not lead to these posts being flagged and possibly deleted. The campaign explains that these guidelines are to protect editors because they "want to be clear that just because Wikipedia's rules say something or someone isn't notable, does not mean it's not notable" ("Quick Guide for Editors" 2018, 4). Because editing is monitored by volunteers through Wikipedia, the campaign does its best to aid in a higher chance of stories being told and kept on the online canon through collectivity and support.

An article in *The New Yorker* documented this collectivity within an edit-a-thon visit: A woman in the space "told me that she couldn't imagine herself sitting alone at home editing Wikipedia. 'But here, it's addictive'" (Lavin 2016). The process of being within the collective allows and encourages sharing of experiences as well as creating new ones with those who contribute similar or varied narratives to the collective consciousness-raising. The Edit Guide also asks people to "Share your stories and experiences with us online because you know we are family" a common metaphor used within queer communities and discourses of kinship ("Quick Guide for Editors" 2018, 5). The Quick Guide states that the campaign will explicitly donate funds to those who would like to host edit-a-thons for refreshments and childcare during editing times ("Quick Guide for Organizers" 2018, 3). The collective nature of these spaces, as well as the ways in which audiences are automatically treated as participants, utilizes a collective rhetoric that assumes intertextuality to make the personal political.

QUEERING DIGITAL ACTIVISMS
THROUGH COLLECTIVITY

Hacking and editing are gendered practices. In attempting to resist this, I argue that Art+Feminism queers these practices by challenging gendered socialization and stereotypes. However, more generally, there exists an over-all gendered nature to feminist and digital spaces when thinking about digital forms of activism based in concepts such as "hacking" or "editing." Many authors who are writing and blogging about the edit-a-thon want to gender the reasons why women are not editing in a certain way. One blogger, who is also an editor on Wikipedia, created a post entitled "Nine Reasons Why Women Don't Edit Wikipedia (In Their Own Words)" (Gardner 2011). The author, a woman editor herself, states that "Some women don't edit Wikipedia because they aren't sufficiently self-confident, and editing Wikipedia requires a lot of self-confidence," as well as "Some women don't edit Wikipedia because they are conflict-averse and don't like Wikipedia's sometimes-fighty culture" (Gardner 2011). She argues that "There is lots of evidence to suggest this is true" and states that if these are the experiences of women and the narratives they have told her, then they must be valid and taken seriously (Gardner 2011). While these are the true feelings of women within these spaces and should be taken seriously, the framing of this as a "choice" that women "opt out of" because of gender socialization ignores the structural issues in favor of convenient narratives that individualize and depoliticize blame.

These assumptions feed into the gendered expectations of those who are not cis men, their experiences, and where they are placed in certain roles in society. People hope to explain away the gap in editing with gendered categories, expectations, and statistics. However, one of the founders of the edit-a-thon conveyed the issues surrounding these gendered, neoliberal norms well when they said: 'We really resent the outcomes-focused, neo-liberal drive in all things. . . . How do you quantify community?" (Lavin 2016). The feminism of the Art+Feminism campaign brings together a variety of bod-ies, genders, and sexualities to queer spaces of popular knowledge and the practices used to get there. Therefore, queering is descriptive of the campaign itself in its changes to the online canon of Wikipedia as well as the action of coming together and encouraging people of all genders to perform queering of the canon and digital activisms. A postfeminist worldview is subverted through the never-ending canon of Wikipedia, offering the idea that there is always more work to be done within this gendered sphere.

However, there also exists a tension between the "queering" of Wikipedia and excluding trans men from representation in the canon. The radical possibility posed by Art+Feminism in challenging and transforming the gender politics of Wikipedia is undermined by its cumbersome and exclusionary trans politics. In a space wherein alliances between cis/trans women and trans men and nonbinary people could be amplified, transmasculine folks are invited to edit, but their history is lost in the canon and not specifically hoped to be recovered through the campaign. By not explicitly taking a stand for their history to also be represented in the online canon of Wikipedia, the Art+Feminism campaign still has work to do within a true queering of digital activisms as well as creating a true collective rhetorical form of feminist activism. Anyone can edit the information on Wikipedia in general, and this is an aspect of the open-source platform that extends to the campaign itself: "We welcome anyone and everyone interested in learning more about editing Wikipedia to attend, regardless of experience, gender, or background" ("The Gender Gap" 2018, 6). Through these discourses, the attempt to make everyone a part of collective activist efforts for representation allows for the personal to become political in a way that emphasizes the importance of collective involvement.

Instead of focusing on visibility alone, Art+Feminism furthers their activism to queer the way individuals engage in the embodied practices of editing: collective processes engaged through bodies within the editing space. Many scholars "link hacking with masculine narratives of rebellion, pointing to a degree of boyish revolt associated with electronics tinkering and disassembly" (Rosner and Fox 2016). Women-operated hackerspaces have opened an alternate view: "enlivening connections between hacking and histories of women's craftwork rooted in a feminist politics of fracture" (Rosner and Fox 2016, 560). While the Art+Feminism campaign centers the work of those who identify as women and nonbinary people, it does not gender their editing or hacking processes. Unlike those who argue that the role of DIY feminist activisms is to open spaces for not only women but "feminized" practices, the edit-a-thon complicates the gender binary and acceptable modes of behavior for "masculine" versus "feminine" forms of living and contributing. The Art+Feminism campaign subverts a postfeminist worldview through the emphasis on continual progress for all genders and performances through collective action. The leaders of the campaign had a goal to edit ten thousand pages by the end of 2018, which they eventually accomplished, but noted throughout that the gender gap is a space that can never be completely closed under the current system ("Quick Guide for Editors" 2018, 2). This statement is in line with their critique of the current system's sex and gender binary system, which is upheld through the metaphor of the "gap" between two binary entities (male, female). While they believe in the power of their collective activity to tackle the gender gap, they argue that "it takes more than one event a year to close the information gap. Keep learning" ("Quick Guide for Editors 2018, 6). The queering of digital activisms to subvert gender norms, stereotypes, as well as the individualistic nature of online activist practices ultimately culminates in an edit-a-thon's use of collective rhetoric. Therefore, collective rhetoric can be utilized in ways that go past simply consciousness-raising and can be forged for feminists to subvert postfeminist thought and neoliberal uses of digital activisms.

CONCLUSION: COLLECTIVE EMBODIED (H)ACTIVISM

Art+Feminism edit-a-thons are unique DIY feminist activisms generating alternative modalities for creativity, archival practices, and knowledge production as they subvert neoliberal discourses that focus on productivity and individuality. The focus on the representation of editors rather than on the content of the articles (although, representation within articles is part of the original exigence for their mission) allows for the queering of activisms through embodied collectivities. Through the lens of a collective rhetoric, I have argued that the Art+Feminism edit-a-thon creates representation through embodied editing practices as well as tools to edit content on Wikipedia. Art+Feminism edit-a-thons offer an example of how collective digital feminist-based practices of editing/hacktivism can queer digital activisms often based in neoliberal discourses. This queering of digital activisms also critiques a postfeminist worldview, demonstrating how the gender gap, much like Wikipedia, is an ongoing process of collective editing and struggle. Art+Feminism edit-a-thons convey the importance of taking up collective rhetoric in current feminist thought. With a renewal of collective rhetoric comes the chance to view other forms of contemporary activism within and even beyond the digital age to make the personal political for all gendered bodies. Connecting collective rhetorics based in feminist and decolonial theory to embodied DIY projects of visibility, feminist activists and scholars are able to continue to critique the popular neoliberal-based feminism that ground individual, consumer-based activism. Edit-a-thons explore the possibilities of community, embodied gathering that has been lost in DIY independent feminist publishing and that conveys new ways of writing together and creating community around feminist issues, from large political struggles to something as seemingly "simple" as new entries on Wikipedia.

REFERENCES

Art+Feminism. 2019. "Art+Feminism." www.artandfeminism.org/.
———. 2018a. "Art+Feminism." www.artandfeminism.org/.
———. 2018b. "Closing the Gender Gap on Wikipedia."
———. 2018c. "Quick Guide for Editors."
———. 2018d. "Quick Guide for Organizers."
———. 2018e."What is an Edit-a-Thon?." www.artandfeminism.org/find-an-event/.
Asen, Robert. 2017. "Neoliberalism, the Public Sphere, and a Public Good." *Quarterly Journal of Speech* 103 (4): 329–49.
Cassell, Justine. 2011. "A Culture of Editing Wars." *New York Times.* February 4, 2011.
Collins, Patricia Hill. 2009. *Black Feminist Thought: Knowledge, Consciousness, and the Politics of Empowerment.* 2nd ed. Routledge.
Demo, Anne Teresa. 2000. "The Guerrilla Girls' Comic Politics of Subversion." *Women's Studies in Communication* 23 (2): 133–56.
Dubriwny, Tasha N. 2005. "Consciousness-Raising as Collective Rhetoric: The Articulation of Experience in the Redstockings' Abortion Speak-Out of 1969." *Quarterly Journal of Speech* 91 (4): 395–422.
Enck-Wanzer, Darrel. 2012. "Decolonizing Imaginaries: Rethinking 'the People' in the Young Lords' Church Offensive." *Quarterly Journal of Speech* 98 (1): 1–23.
Gardner, Sue. 2011. "Nine Reasons Women Don't Edit Wikipedia (in their own words)." *Sue Gardner's Blog.* February 19, 2011.
Gunkel, David J. 2005. "Editorial: Introduction to Hacking and Hacktivism." *New Media & Society* 7 (5): 595–97.
hooks, bell. 2015. *Feminism Is for Everybody: Passionate Politics.* Second edition. New York: Routledge.
Lavin, Talia. 2016. "A Feminist Edit-A-Thon Seeks to Reshape Wikipedia." *New Yorker.* March 11, 2016.
Lorde, Audre. 2007. *Sister Outsider: Essays and Speeches.* Crossing Press.
Martin, Tony. 2007. *Amy Ashwood Garvey: Pan-Africanist, Feminist, and Mrs. Marcus Garvey Wife No. 1.* The New Marcus Garvey Library, no. 4. Majority Press.
McRobbie, Angela. 2009. *The Aftermath of Feminism: Gender, Culture and Social Change.* Sage.
Miller, Diane Helene. 1999. "'From One Voice A Chorus': Elizabeth Cady Stanton's 1860 Address to the New York State Legislature." *Women's Studies in Communication* 22(2): 152–89.
Mitesser, Steph. 2017. "This is What Happens at a Feminist Edit-a-Thon for Wikipedia." *Magenta.* March 17, 2017.
Piepmeier, Alison. 2009. *Girl Zines: Making Media, Doing Feminism.* New York University Press.

Rand, Erin J. 2013. "An Appetite for Activism: The Lesbian Avengers and the Queer Politics of Visibility." *Women's Studies in Communication* 36 (2): 121–41.

———. 2014. "'What One Voice Can Do': Civic Pedagogy and Choric Collectivity at Camp Courage." *Text and Performance Quarterly* 34 (1): 28–51.

Rosner, Daniela K., and Sarah E. Fox. 2016. "Legacies of Craft and the Centrality of Failure in a Mother-Operated Hackerspace." *New Media & Society* 18 (4): 558–80.

Samek, Alyssa A. 2015. "Pivoting Between Identity Politics and Coalitional Relationships: Lesbian-Feminist Resistance to the Woman-Identified Woman." *Women's Studies in Communication* 38 (4): 393–420.

Siegel, Deborah. 2007. *Sisterhood, Interrupted: From Radical Women to Grrls Gone Wild*. New York: Palgrave Macmillan, 2007.

Simons, Herbert W. 1982. "Genres, Rules, and Collective Rhetorics: Applying the Requirements-Problems-Strategies Approach." *Communication Quarterly* 30 (3): 181–88.

Sowards, Stacey. 2010. "Rhetorical Agency as *Haciendo Caras* and Differential Consciousness Through Lens of Gender, Race, Ethnicity, and Class: An Examination of Dolores Huerta's Rhetoric." *Communication Theory* 20 (2): 223–47.

———. 2019. "Bordering Through Place/s, Difference/s, and Language/s: Intersections of Border and Feminist Theories." *Women's Studies in Communication* 42 (2): 120–24.

Sowards, Stacey, and Valerie Renegar. 2004. "The Rhetorical Functions of Consciousness-Raising in Third Wave Feminism." *Communication Studies* 55 (4): 535–52.

Wells-Barnett, Ida B. 2014. *On Lynchings*. Dover.

"Wikipedia: About," 2019. Wikipedia. en.wikipedia.org/wiki/Wikipedia:About.

Zeisler, Andi. 2016. *We Were Feminists Once: From Riot Grrrl to CoverGirl®, the Buying and Selling of a Political Movement*. New York: Public Affairs.

Chapter 10

Pushing Back

How Blogs and Podcasts are
Empowering Birthing Bodies Online

Shaylynn Lynch Lesinski, Tammy Rae
Matthews, and Kelly J. Drumright

In 1986, the Center for Disease Control (CDC) began monitoring maternal mortality rates (MMR) in the United States. Since then, MMR has risen steadily from 7.2 per 100,000 live births in 1987 to 17.4 in 2018 (National Center for Health Statistics). The mortality rates for Black birthing bodies are significantly higher, with non-Hispanic Black mortality rates at 37.1 per 100,000 live births in 2018. Infant mortality rates in the United States also reflect this significant disparity between white and Black birthing bodies: "The 2018 infant mortality rate for infants of non-Hispanic black women (10.75) was more than twice as high as that for infants of non-Hispanic white (4.63), non-Hispanic Asian (3.63), and Hispanic women (4.86)" (Ely and Driscoll 2020). The situation is similarly dire for Indigenous women, who "are approximately three times as likely as non-Hispanic (white) women to die of pregnancy-associated causes" (Kozhimannil, Interrante, Tofte, and Admon 2020). The current state of birth in the United States reveals that the history of anti-Black racism in obstetrics and gynecology has not been addressed on a systemic level. Indeed, we could say that these statistics of obstetric and gynecological care for non-white birthing bodies constitute severe "intersectional failures" (Crenshaw 2016).

Birth blogs and podcasts spread the word about firsthand experiences that the statistics alone cannot communicate. Experiences of violence and vulnerability, yes, but also of empowerment and joy. As Poonam Sharma Mathis, host and creator of *Pregnant in a Pandemic*, shares, "as a second-time mother in the middle of this pandemic, waiting for this baby to arrive any minute now, I felt I needed to do something . . . to at least virtually bring women like myself together. . . . I think we can help each other by talking it through and sharing whatever we feel, and whatever we know, which is why I've launched this podcast." The practice of sharing birth stories online—specifically through birth blogs and the podcast medium—expands the cultural conversation about birth beyond the limits of medical spaces and discourses. We argue that sharing birth stories online privileges the experiential knowledge of birthing bodies themselves, thereby disrupting the hierarchy of knowledge in so-called Western medicine that positions birthing bodies' lived experience last. Our specific interest in the practice of sharing birth stories online is how it connects birthing bodies to one another as well as to their own embodied knowledge, especially within the current context of an ongoing COVID-19 pandemic where online platforms are increasingly crucial for seeking connection and mutual support.

To that end, this chapter discusses the ways birth blogs and podcasts function as networked feminist coalitions with a twofold goal: to provide a pedagogical vehicle for information and to empower people giving birth. Because of this, we quote birthing blogs and podcasts at length to maintain the agency of those that speak from their birthing experiences. Our textual analysis reveals three distinct functions of birth blogs and podcasts: First, these media allow birthing bodies to push back against biocertified understandings of birth in medicalized spaces where the voices of birthing bodies are often ignored or silenced. The second function is to make visible options outside of the medical model of birth and labor. Thirdly, sharing birth stories online validates and reinforces the spectrum of "normal" sensations and emotions of labor, which empowers people to give birth through the recognition and celebration of their bodily capabilities. When viewed collectively, virtually sharing these stories creates an ever-expanding archive of birthing experiences that increases the visibility of non-cisgender, heterosexual, and/ or white experiences of birth and exposes rampant racism and anti-trans oppression in obstetric medicine.

In our view, engaging with birth through contemporary formulations of both intersectionality and biopolitics is necessary because of the history of enacting different biopolitical control mechanisms on people with uteruses depending on features such as race, ethnicity, gender, and sexuality. Biopower "highlights the way in which the biopolitical state is fundamentally reactive in relation to life," with biopolitics referring to how bodies are defined and categorized by governing laws, rules, societal norms, and organizations (Mills 2013, 75). These systems produce regulations for the entire populace of related bodies based on gender, sex, body function, body appearance, or any other defining and/or marginalizing feature.

We also find the intersectional-biopolitical theoretical culture jam necessary because of the central role experience and community play in our analysis of birth blogs and podcasts. Both experience and community "have been fundamental to Black feminist praxis, and Black feminist thought provides an important perspective on how these ideas work within resistant knowledge projects" (Collins 2019, 158). Moreover, queer, trans, and/or BIPOC theorists have demonstrated how studying biopower (power over bodies) and biopolitics (politics governing bodies) reveals how structures sort bodies to support governance according to oppressive Western power structures (Puar 2007). We echo Patricia Hill Collins (2019) when she affirms that, "as a work in progress, intersectionality is a critical social theory in the making, one that may already be doing substantial theoretical work without being recognized as such" (23). Indeed, proposals such as those made by Kramer, Strahan, Preslar, Davis, Goodman, and Callaghan (2019) show that intersectionality is already informing medical practitioners' and institutions' responses.

RACISM, CIS-SEXISM, AND SETTLER COLONIALISM: THE HISTORICAL AND CULTURAL CONTEXT OF BIRTH IN THE UNITED STATES

As Deirdre Cooper Owens (2018) notes in her book *Medical Bondage: Race, Gender, and the Origins of American Gynecology,* the gynecological field is founded on nonconsensual experimentation on enslaved Black women by white, male doctors, and scientists. Throughout the nineteenth century, Black women's bodies and organs "were used as clinical matter that was displayed for observation and dissection so that white women's pathologies and sick bodies could be cured" (Cooper Owens 2018, 21). Cooper Owens also notes that monitoring and increasing the reproductive capacity of Black bodies became more important to gynecological practitioners after Congress banned the trafficking of peoples from Africa in 1808 (15). In addition to policing Black peoples' reproduction, the United States' settler-colonial project had (and continues to have) a vested interest in controlling the reproductive and birthing practices of Indigenous peoples. In addition to being considered "pathologically unhealthy" by a racist medical system, "the practice of forcing Native women to travel to hospitals because their traditional ways of caring for pregnant people were outlawed contributes to an endless cycle of poor outcomes" (Pember 2018). Moreover, many Indigenous folx are "cut off from traditional diets, support networks, and community midwives due to colonization and assimilation," and as a result "many Native mothers have chronic health conditions that means giving birth is a high-risk activity" (Pember 2018).

We maintain that the violence experienced by many birthing bodies in the United States today can be traced back to the imposition of racist, cis-sexist, and settler colonialist obstetric and gynecological practices. In the early twentieth century, "the male medical profession managed to convince middle-class women . . . to abandon the social model of care as practiced by midwives and seek their services in hospitals under the promise of safer, less painful births" (Luce et al. 2016, 5). As birth transitioned into hospitals, it became medically mediated in new ways. Most notably, the hospital setting places birthing bodies alongside the general "sick" that needed healing, thereby situating the birthing process squarely within a pathologizing medical discourse. As Walker (2012) argues, "the language and mentality of new standard procedures of birth functions as ways to represent the body as mechanical, inefficient, failing and diseased" (16). Birth began losing its previous status as a natural, biological process; it began to be viewed as an unnatural state that should be contained, controlled, and medicated.

The shift toward giving birth in hospitals also foregrounded the sensations of pain, which in turn validates the need for a hospital setting and medical intervention. Emphasizing pain to validate the medicalization of birth then informed popular media representations of the process, perpetuating fear and eradicating the concept of normal birth: "In the U.S., non-medicalized representations of pregnancy and birth [on television] would be largely absent and marginalized when they were presented, thereby being hidden from, or distorted in public discourse" (Luce et al. 2016, 8). The medicalization of birth also prioritizes authoritative medical knowledge that undermines the capabilities of the birthing body. Therefore, the birthing body within a medical space is viewed as inferior and birth is "performed" on a birthing body rather than something a birthing body "performs" (Luce et al. 2016). The fearful rhetoric surrounding birth simultaneously disempowers birthing bodies and reinforces the need for modern medical intervention.

From a general standpoint, the structure of the medical industry in the United States is contingent upon a precarious relationship between the patient and the care provider. A capitalist medical market within a neoliberal system means that the patient is also a customer and handles the burden of payment regardless of the circumstances. Obstetrics is a pillar of this system, especially considering that many birthing bodies cannot choose the conditions of their labor and delivery. In fact, "childbirth is one of the most expensive payouts for insurance companies and more than 300,000 American individuals give birth every month. . . . Since insurance companies make money by taking in more than they pay out, the customers often have to shoulder some—or a lot—of the financial burden" (Miller 2015). Here, unmedicated births, informed consumer-clients, and a growing prevalence of home births can disrupt the traditional relationship between the patient-as-consumer and the medical industry to avoid the bloated insurance payouts associated with a hospital birth that results in extensive medical interventions. Media depictions of birth also contribute considerably to the perception of birth that validates medical intervention and undermines the birthing body. In addition to centering the experiences of overwhelmingly white and cisgender women in heterosexual relationships, representations of birth in the media are highly manipulative and constructed.

Unsurprisingly, the medical model of birth became the dominant depiction found in film and television given the wider transition to hospital births that took place during the mid-twentieth century which, uncoincidentally, happened around the same time as television sets were entering an increasing number of US homes. In their study of depictions of birth on television, Luce et al. (2016) highlight three distinct themes: first, the "medicalization of childbirth, which includes birth [is] depicted as risky and dangerous and hence something to fear"; second, "media becomes the dominant way for women to learn about childbirth, despite the representations being mostly negative"; and third, "birth [is] missing as a normal 'everyday' life event" (3). For instance, reality television shows such as *A Baby Story* and *Birth Day* place a strong emphasis on the obstetricians' ability to "save" the baby or the birthing person from a dangerous birth scenario. These birthing people are often told what will be done to them or the baby, rather than participating in the process of making informed decisions after learning about available options—a common feature of hospital births. More specifically, the reality television genre has a vested interest in focusing on the drama of the birth process, as programs privilege entertainment and profits over education. Despite the "constructed and partly fictional" status of reality television, "such portrayal [of birth] whets our desire for the authentic" (Luce et al. 2016, 5). We might then understand the proliferation of sharing birth stories online as a response to such authentic desires. Birth blogs and podcasts are essential educational tools that expose and validate options outside of the medical model of birth. Sharing birth stories virtually gives birthing bodies the information and resources to navigate persistent, expensive medical intervention, as well as the ability to reframe their approach towards care providers.

CHALLENGING BIOCERTIFICATION AND AUTHORITATIVE KNOWLEDGE THROUGH BIRTH BLOGS AND PODCASTS

We suggest that birth blogs and podcasts constitute "challenges to biocertification" (Samuels 2014, 140) by exposing the practices within the medical institution that uphold these systems of punishment against birthing bodies.

We maintain that the birthing body is historically pathologized within Western patriarchal systems of power, resulting in the mediation and control of these bodies. The impact of biopower and biopolitics on birthing bodies is even more pronounced for marginalized identities, such as women of color and transgender bodies, which leaves these bodies susceptible to specific structural oppressions that manifest in medicalization of birthing bodies. Birth blogs and podcasts expose these structural oppressions, and they also provide visibility and resources for birthing bodies to push back against systems that inherently wish to control, contain, and mediate their birthing experiences. Brigitte Jordan's (1980) theory of authoritative knowledge helps examine how birth blogs and podcasts resist biocertified conceptions of birth. Jordan defines authoritative knowledge as the notion that certain types of knowledge are valued over other forms of social and political knowing. In medicalized spaces (i.e., hospitals), authoritative knowledge works to diminish the birthing body's achievements and establish a power dynamic that leaves the laboring person with minimized agency.

In this section, we explore how blogs and podcasts allow birthing bodies to gain the tools and knowledge necessary to question and even challenge authoritative knowledge and to negotiate persistent cultural norms and assumptions about birth. While many of the blogs and podcasts we have surveyed support a critique of the medical model of birth, the overarching function of birth blogs and podcasts remains to document the birth experience. We see this evidence through blogs and podcasts that feature hospital transfers and hospital births, such as *The Birth Hours* (episodes 483–485), all of which focus on positive hospital birth experiences. In this chapter, we focus specifically on the documentation of birthing bodies whose experiences expose the racial and heteronormative biases. These biases reveal the systemic inequities that place marginalized birthing bodies at significant disadvantages, and even in danger within the medical system. We look at how birthing bodies share their stories to speak out in these virtual spaces and trace how they operate as sources of solidarity and empowerment against the sense of inconsequentiality in the face of powerful institutions, such as the American Medical Association.

First, authoritative knowledge presents the doctors' opportunity to manipulate birthing people into procedures that augment the birth process to monitor and control the length and progression of labor within a hospital setting, in which multiple bodies are birthing simultaneously. These procedures, called intrapartum interventions, include "bed rest/recumbent position, electronic fetal monitoring (EFM), limited oral intake during labor, frequent vaginal exams, inductions/augmentations, amniotomy, regional anesthesia, catheterization, ineffective pushing, episiotomy, instrumental vaginal birth and cesarean surgery" (Jansen et al. 2013, 84). Intrapartum interventions have become so common that birthing people are often forced into these interventions through a variety of tactics that underscore the function of authoritative knowledge in medical spaces; some of the tactics are "medical treatment without informed consent, omission of information, overriding one's refusal of a treatment and misrepresentation of medical situations and the need for interventions" (Hodges 2009, 9). For example, this mother describes her experience of receiving a procedure without consenting, providing not only a firsthand account of the practice but the emotions and sensations resulting from unelected intervention:

> To make matters even worse, during a push I heard the metallic snip of scissors and I immediately knew she had cut an episiotomy on me. I was shocked. My heart sank and my strength was totally sapped. We were so close and then BOOM one more big thing on the list of "I don't wants" to throw on top of that burning heap. I was so disheartened and upset she didn't ask for informed consent or even warn me. (McFall 2014)

Maintaining authoritative knowledge and the resulting unchallenged doctor–patient hierarchical dynamic is essential to holding and controlling birthing bodies during labor and birth. Research has also revealed that these interventions occur in a cascading effect, meaning that once intervention begins it is often needed throughout the laboring process, fortifying the need for medical technologies and medical knowledge (Cooper Owens 2018; Hodges 2009; Jansen et al. 2013).

Secondly, authoritative knowledge does not allow for the recognition of individual experience or the body's ability to birth. This injustice results in conditioning birthing people to believe their bodies' biological instincts and responses to labor are unworthy of their personal and their obstetricians' attention. Black birthing bodies are further eroded due to racialized assumptions and stereotypes about Black bodies. In her blog about her birth experience featured on *One of Many,* Tasha Chambers, a self-identified Black mother, describes being ignored when alerting her nurse and her physician to her pain: "The pain from the nurse pushing on my stomach was so bad that I felt like I had jumped out of my body. I grabbed her hand and pleaded with her to stop. My OB-GYN tried next and I did the same with him. I questioned why they would keep pressing on my stomach when I alerted them that I was in excruciating pain. I nearly blacked out from the pain" (Chambers 2012). By sharing their experiences online, birthing bodies can express the collective disenchantment, disappointment, and dissatisfaction with the current medical model of birth that silences birthing bodies, especially racialized ones.

Outside of exposing the function of authoritative knowledge in medical spaces, another primary function of birth blogs and podcasts is to provide access to a wide range of information. Many focus on so-called natural birth, definitions of which shift depending on the birthing individual. These media grant a central space for birthing bodies to get information about hospitals, cesareans, doulas, midwives, birth classes, and circumcision as well as information about how birth looks, sounds, and feels. Accessing such information is essential to empowering birthing bodies and expanding the cultural definitions and perceptions of birth and labor. Birth blogs and podcasts create an archive of birth experiences in which birthing bodies can educate themselves on the processes of childbirth. While each birth is unique, the physiological process of vaginal delivery is similar across identities, even if meanings and symbolism change across cultures. We recognize some of these similarities across multiple birthing stories. Specifically, individual birth stories can help identify the emotions and sensations that are a normal part of the birth process, including feelings of fear and inconsequentiality:

> Wave after wave of overwhelming, squeezing sensations and deep pain came over me. It seemed like I had no break in-between and I felt so tired. . . . I wanted to control my situation and, as any woman who has been in natural labor knows, you cannot control labor," one mother shares. "You must give into it and roll along with it," she continues. "If you don't, fear can take over and can cause it to feel more painful. I got a bit nauseous at this point as well. Hot, cold, continual contractions, nausea . . . all good signs of transition and yet, I still felt like I wasn't going to be able to 'do this'—which actually is another sign of labor being almost over. ("Rueger's Birth" 2016)

Descriptions such as this one from the blog *Birth Without Fear* encompass the gamut of birth sensations and emotions. The detailed descriptions of sensations of waters breaking, contractions, transition, and pushing have the most authenticity and authority when coming from individuals who have given birth. Birth stories offer a space that prioritizes the birthing person's voice and amplifies it as a source of information for other birthing people, facilitating accurate, if not personal, expectations. They also reestablish the value of what birthing bodies are feeling during birth, which is essential to combating authoritative knowledge and the policing of birthing bodies. In these spaces, experiential learning is validated as expertise. The following excerpt, also from *Birth Without Fear*, illustrates the power of having information and expresses empowerment in asking for what you want during birth:

> They put those awful elastic straps on me to monitor the baby. I asked the doctor if I could get them off and sit in the tub. THEY PUT ME IN A ROOM WITH A TUB!!! Oh, it was wonderful. Dr. Lady told me I could. I waddled my way to the tub, and my doula showed up and turned some incense on and my husband

massaged my shoulders. The nurse brought me a Sprite. It was nice. My contractions were strong and steady. (Parrilla 2016)

Here, Krista Parrilla recalls that the process of placing a birthing body on immobilizing monitors as soon as one is checked into a room is routine and is thus normalized. However, rather than accepting this as part of her birth, she asks to detach herself from constant monitoring in favor of intermittent fetal monitoring. Parrilla's account of advocating for her desired birth within the rigid hospital birth structure may provide an example for people who may not have known about the available options.

Despite the apparent ease with which Parilla seems to ask for alternatives to the routine birthing process, the emotional and physical damage of being pressured into unnecessary medical intervention during birth cannot be understated. In another post, a white mother shares that such an experience motivated her to find her voice and her ability to maintain a sense of control in an environment in which she previously felt entirely ineffectual. "Since my first [birth] had ended in an unnecessary third-degree episiotomy against my written and verbal consent, staying on my hands and knees made me feel grounded and less vulnerable. I did not want any coaching on how and when to push and I think everyone instinctually [sic] knew that" ("Quinlan's Birth Story" 2016). Stories like this one about the struggle to gain a sense of control and authority during labor reveal the consequences of biocertified, medical discourses.

Normalizing Loss

The loss of "normal birth" in US culture also means a loss in the spectrum of regular occurrences of birth, including miscarriage, stillbirth, and infant mortality. These difficult scenarios can be naturally occurring instances of birth in all forms of biological birth processes. However, the medical model of birth views these as a failure of medical intervention. Therefore, discussions and visibility of these occurrences must be minimized if not entirely omitted from the medical model of birth, which silences the voices of families who have experienced loss. It is yet another space of recognition and empowerment that is provided by birth blogs. Birth blogs and podcasts create spaces to acknowledge loss as a tragic yet sometimes unavoidable part of birth and provide venues to connect about shared experiences of loss.

The language used in these spaces also reinforces the normalcy of loss in birth. Babies born in the wake of loss are often referred to as a "rainbow baby," a reference to the rainbow that comes after a storm. The rainbow-and-storm imagery both normalizes the loss and gives individuals who have experienced such loss the language to start conversations in place of traditional silence and isolated grief. Within these online spaces, parents are given sovereignty to fully embrace and acknowledge their loss as well as the hopeful promise of new life. Many blogs have specific topic threads on loss. *Birth Without Fear,* for example, offers a series of posts that begin with the words, "I am strong because . . . " followed by personal stories of what fuels this strength. The following excerpt from parent Logan Kinney comments on the lack of conversation about infant death, explaining how strength is still derived from this story: "I am strong because I will tell his story. Our story. He will be known for the beautiful boy that he is, not a baby forgotten or never spoken about." The post then positions the reader as also strong: "You are strong for opening your heart and reading this. You are strong for listening to a story about a baby who doesn't make it, which is an unthinkable tragedy." The post continues, speaking to readers who may identify with the loss of a child or with reimagining a future for a child: "If you have had a high-risk pregnancy, or a child whose genetic blueprints are different . . . you are a warrior. If you have had to consider a life for your child so different from what you imagined, you amaze me. If you have had to face your child's death, you are an incredible force of maternal nature and I see you" (Kinney 2015). The post's language and tone assume that an audience is available and, importantly, that a need to share such stories exists. Kinney's words here recognize the community of birthing people dealing specifically with loss.

Documenting Non-white, Non-cisgender Birth Experiences

Non-white, non-cisgender birthing bodies are exceptionally vulnerable to the effects of biopolitics. Unlike blogs and podcasts by white, cisgender women, discursive accounts of experiences of birth and labor shared by individuals at multiple intersections of marginalization expose the inequities of care and implicit biases that permeate the medical system in the United States. Therefore, documenting marginalized individuals' experiences is essential to pushing back against biocertified notions of birth that reassert homophobia, transphobia, and racism.

Grover Wehman-Brown, who identifies as a transmasculine butch and has given birth, created the podcast *Masculine Birth Ritual* as an attempt "to fill the void of stories, imagery and collective imagination about what it feels and looks like for masculine of center people to conceive, carry, birth and nurture humans" (Wehman-Brown 2018b, "Introduction to *Masculine Birth Ritual*"). Addressing a collective audience, Wehman-Brown argues that:

It's our work to unearth those stories and images if they exist and it's our work to make new stories and images for all the sea horse dads, butch mamas, pregnant babas, non-binary taties, and stud mommies that come after us. A masculine birth ritual. We can recover, we can design, and we can pass around the tools for our collective survival and dignified embodiment on this planet at this time. (September 2, 2018)

It is this call for new stories that fuels each episode of the podcast.

When trans, nonbinary, genderqueer, and gender nonconforming individuals share their birth stories, even as they share stories of empowerment they cite experiences of gender dysphoria, visibility, and invisibility, as well as struggles with finding and seeking postpartum care. In episode four of *Masculine Birth Ritual*, "People Didn't Know What to Do with Me" guest Ryan discusses his experience with gender dysphoria and postpartum birth care: "I think it's the first time that I've like really felt and I didn't have this language for it at the time but really felt really, like, intense dysphoria around my body. I just knew that I was having a really hard time dealing with my body post birth," Ryan shares. He continues:

The hardest parts for me around being a trans guy and giving birth have been . . . like, physically having changes in my body that probably I should seek medical support for, but, like, not wanting to use the language or go to the services that requires that, like, I would have to do to actually get that support, so just not doing it. . . . Like there are a ton of services for that and I don't want to access any of them. (October 16, 2018)

Here, we see how rampant cissexism, both ideologically speaking and in terms of the language that is used within the medical system, presents an additional challenge for these individuals navigating medicalized birth spaces, which can harm both the birthing parent and child (smith 2018). As a result, some trans, nonbinary, genderqueer, and gender nonconforming pregnant people choose not to disclose their status to providers, while others have friends or family members run interference with hospital staff to address misgendering. Ryan recalls his wife and friend having to intervene with staff on his behalf:

My partner did a lot of the leg work around emailing people around their comfort with gender and the language they use and we finally found someone who just talked about birth in really technical ways and talked about the people who were giving birth as "birth parents." . . . She ran just, like, a ton of interference . . . talking with the nurses anytime there was a shift change, just like pronouns, language—that's, like, all she did. (October 16, 2018)

The relative lack of documented birth experiences from gender nonconforming, trans, queer, and nonbinary individuals reveals that different identity positions are at different stages of recognition, struggle, and intervention.

As Wehman-Brown (2018b) observes in response to Ryan, "I live in a super, super queer area . . . and there was nothing for people in my position." This lack of visibility for trans and queer birthing bodies is not limited to medical spaces and medical communities; it expands into the social spaces of birth as well. Ryan discusses not only the lack of community for him due to the gendered characterization of birth in social spaces, but that even close family and friends did not hold space for his birth experience:

> I didn't read baby books, I didn't do . . . baby prep, I didn't go to . . . baby groups because I just couldn't do anything that was womanizing . . . and there wasn't anything that wasn't [womanizing]. . . . They didn't know how to treat a person who was pregnant who wasn't a woman. . . . People didn't treat me like I had just had a kid . . . people treated me like a non-gestational parent. . . . I couldn't go to mom groups because I was either misgendered or invisible. . . . I feel like the entire fact that I gave birth got erased, about a week after I did it. (October 16, 2018).

Ryan's birth experience reveals some of the stark inequities facing the gender nonconforming, trans, and nonbinary birthing community. Documenting these experiences for non-cisgender birthing people functions to push back against the social and institutional systems that disregard their experiences as marginal or even as entirely absent from the discourses of birth.

Perhaps due to varying positions of privilege—institutional medical privilege as well as (cis)gender and racial privilege—posts by white cisgender birthing bodies often focus primarily on the sensations and emotions of birth. Black birthing individuals, however, tend to document institutional racism expressed through the actions and assumptions of medical staff. Black birth blogs reveal a shared understanding of Black women's experiences of institutional racism during birth. This is expressed explicitly and intentionally in the titles of the birth blogs such as *One of Many*, *My Brown Baby*, *Sun Kissed Doulas*, and *Black Women Birthing Justice.* The blog titles suggest a shared experience as well as a distinctive community and audience for these birth stories. Indeed, posts on the aforementioned blogs document treatment and interactions with physicians and hospital staff that paint a composite picture of the crisis facing Black birthing bodies in US hospitals. In the following excerpt from the blog *My Brown Baby*, Tara Pringle Jefferson describes an unexpected visit from a social worker hours after giving birth to her daughter:

> "You know," [the social worker] said, scribbling some notes, "we've found that parents who live in smaller residences have higher incidences of child abuse." What was I supposed to say to that? I guess she took my silence as an answer. "Well, you watch out for that," she said. "It's not something we like to see." She flipped to the next page and continued. "So you'll be establishing paternity? Do

you need assistance with that? DNA testing, anything?" [. . .] It felt nasty and impersonal. Full of assumptions about who I was, what type of man I'd chosen to be the father of my child and what type of mother I'd turn out to be. (Pringle Jefferson 2013)

Here, rather than describing the sensations and emotions of her labor, Pringle Jefferson recounts the staff's assumptions and the interrogation to which she was subjected without reason or explanation, clearly demonstrating the emotional and psychological toll of invasive and racist hospital protocols.

In "One of Many," a guest blog by senior strategist Tasha Chambers on *Mission Partners*, Chambers describes her experiences of being both emotionally and physically violated during birth:

The anesthesiologist came in next. He whispered: "They authorized me to give you the cheap [medicine]. It wears off quickly. I'll give you something stronger." This was one of those moments I have never forgotten. Even as a Black woman with quality health insurance, my medical providers made decisions and assumptions for me. They assumed my pain could be tolerated. They made a decision that I couldn't afford to be comforted like others. My pain didn't matter. My birth plan didn't matter. My motherhood didn't matter. (Chambers 2016)

Chambers' account is strikingly similar to Jefferson's in that she is not aware of the reasons she is subjected to painful and invasive procedures. However, the focus here is on how the assumptions made by staff and physicians manifest in both her physical and emotional pain. She describes her medical team's apathy as decisions are made about her body, pain level, and insurance without Chambers' knowledge or consent. It is precisely this type of racism that is directly contributing to the mistreatment and deaths of Black birthing bodies in the United States.

Other stories completely distinguish a positive experience of the birthing process from the less-positive interactions with hospital staff and social workers. On the blog *Birthing while Black*, Denene Millner (2012) recounts the racial discrimination she suffered during her stay at a hospital that marketed an exclusive luxury birth experience. We include a good portion of this blog post to demonstrate the gravity of the situation.

Despite an incredible birthing experience facilitated by my personal angel/ob-gyn, from almost the moment my baby took her first breath, her mother was treated like a 14-year-old drug-addicted welfare queen, there to push out yet another daddy-less baby. Seriously. They tested my newborn for drugs (though I've never taken an illicit substance in my entire life) without my consent—something I later found out hospitals do at disproportionately higher rates with Black babies than white ones. Despite that I paid for the private room and meals, I was immediately put in a massive post-birth room with three other women and their newborns. I was moved only after I asked why I wasn't in a private room—a question that elicited scowls and foot-dragging from the nurse until she bothered to check my paperwork to see that, indeed, I'd paid for a private room. . . . Once in the private room, the nurses disappeared for nine hours! Seriously. *Nine.* I had no diapers. No idea how to breastfeed properly (and no bottle or milk to feed my baby if I chose to formula feed). No instructions on what to do to care for my post-birth body (was it okay to walk? Pee? Wash?). Nothing. I seriously thought I was being punished for asking (nicely) for what I'd paid for. . . . The nursing staff was genuinely surprised (!) that the guy by my side, Nick, was my husband—and actually said that stupid ish out loud.

Millner's descriptions show the staff's preoccupation with her economic status as well as assumptions about her lifestyle and relationship. These experiences illustrate that, despite her attempt to avoid a poor hospital experience by purchasing a (supposedly) exceptional labor and delivery package, Millner was still subjected to unnecessary procedures rooted in racial stereotypes and subpar care. These factors suggest that Millner's race was the definitive factor in her mistreatment by hospital staff and call for further intersectional and biopolitical examinations of how birth practices are represented in media and played out in real life.

While media depictions of birth are still heavily invested in representing a medical model of birth, some representations are beginning to broach the subject of Black maternal death in prime time—an area that continues to deserve greater attention and focus. On April 15, 2019, Fox aired an episode of the medical drama *The Resident* entitled "If Not Now, When?" that fictionalized the very real events of Kira Dixon Johnson's death at Cedars-Sinai hospital in Los Angeles three years earlier on April 13, 2016. Dixon died eleven hours after her son was born on April 12 via an elective C-section due to complications sustained during the procedure. Johnson's symptoms and pain were ignored, overlooked by hospital staff, causing extensive internal bleeding that ultimately resulted in her death. The episode reveals the harrowing statistics that Black people are four times more likely than white people to die from birth-related complications and that, as Roeder (2019) writes, US hospitals are one of the most dangerous places to give birth in the so-called "developed" world.

CONCLUSIONS

In the face of the racist, cis-sexist, and settler colonialist obstetric and gynecological practices that prevail in the United States to this day, birth blogs and podcasts are redistributing much-needed knowledge back into the hands of bodies with the capacity for pregnancy. Through such media, people can gain access to a range of authentic representations of birth and birth processes, when, otherwise, they may have only been exposed to the medicalization and cis-representation of birth, and the sometimes-adverse images that perpetuate fear and danger. Birth blogs and podcasts are placing value back into the experiences of birthing bodies and challenging authoritative knowledge by curating access to information and firsthand accounts of birth and labor experiences. These media also make visible alternative methods and models of birth that operate outside an institutional medical system engrained and invested in Western intervention during birth. These blogs and podcasts supply a democratic approach to birth education that is not beholden to a structural investment in controlling and policing bodies. Lastly, birth blogs and podcasts signal a necessary shift in the cultural rhetoric surrounding birth: by moving away from a discourse of pain, fear, and danger, sharing birth stories online enables birthing bodies to push back against oppressive patriarchal systems that benefit—in terms of material wealth and cultural capital—from convincing birthing bodies that they are insufficient, incapable, and powerless.

These alternative methods and models of birth have never been more apparent than during the COVID-19 pandemic. More people are considering home birth rather than risking exposure in overcrowded hospitals and are therefore seeking resources on birth blog websites and podcasts. These websites and podcasts have risen to this call by prioritizing COVID-19 information on their pages, offering extensive resources through their virtual channels. For example, *Evidence Based Birth*'s homepage features links to virtual birth education classes, a free "Birthing in the Time of Covid-19" video, and information on finding virtual doulas. Hospitals have incorporated virtual communication practices to facilitate minimal exposure to non-birth workers and family members during labor and in the days postpartum. Birth practices in general, both in and out of hospitals, have shifted rapidly during the COVID-19 pandemic to ensure safe, healthy labors. Importantly, these practices are being rigorously documented by people who have and will give birth, which contributes to the ever-growing virtual archive of birth stories that provide critical lived experience, knowledge, and support to birthing bodies everywhere. In light of this increase in documentation, there are also compelling opportunities for future research. It would be beneficial to the future of birth research and documentation to consider which bodies are visible within these contexts and why. Research focused on the structural hierarchies of visibility in the variety of mediums being employed to document birth would potentially yield crucial knowledge about the discourses of birth in media.

REFERENCES

Chambers, Tasha. 2019. "One of Many: A Black Woman's Birth Story." *Mission Partners.* April 16, 2019.

Collins, Patricia Hill. 2019. *Intersectionality as Critical Social Theory.* Duke University Press.

"Coronavirus COVID-19: Evidence Based Birth Resource Page." *Evidence Based Birth.* evidencebasedbirth.com/covid19/.

Ely, Danielle M., and Anne K. Driscoll. 2020. "Infant Mortality in the United States, 2018: Data from the Period Linked Birth/Infant Death File." *National Vital Statistics Report* 69 (7): 1–17. www.cdc.gov/nchs/data/nvsr/nvsr69/NVSR-69-7-508.pdf

Helm, Angela. 2019. "Fox's The Resident Partners With Activist to Shine Light on America's Maternal Mortality Crisis." *The Glow Up.* April 17, 2019.

Hodges, Susan. 2009. "Abuse in Hospital-Based Birth Settings?" *The Journal of Perinatal Education* 18 (4): 8–11.

Jansen, Lauren, et al. 2013. "First Do No Harm: Interventions During Childbirth." *The Journal of Perinatal Education* 22 (2): 83–92.

Jefferson, Tara Pringle. "The Social Worker Will See You Now: A Postpartum Experience This Black Mom Will Never Forget." *My Brown Baby.* August 27, 2013.

Jordan, Brigitte. 1980. *Birth in Four Cultures: A Crosscultural Investigation of Childbirth in Yucatan, Holland, Sweden and the United States.* 2nd ed. Eden Press Women's Publications.

King, Angela. 2004. "The Prisoner of Gender: Foucault and the Disciplining of the Female Body." *Journal of International Women's Studies* 5 (2): 29–39.

Kinney, Logan. Oct. 19, 2015. "I Am Strong—I Continued to Live." *Birth Without Fear.* birthwithoutfearblog.com/2015/10/19/i-am-strong-i-continued-to-live/.

Kozhimannil, Katy B., Julia D. Interrante, Alena N. Tofte and Lindsay K. Admon. 2020. "Severe Maternal Morbidity and Mortality Among Indigenous Women in the United States." *Obstet Gynecol* 135 (2): 294–300. www.ncbi.nlm.nih.gov/pmc/articles PMC7012336/.

Kramer, Michael A., Andrea E. Strahan, Jessica Preslar, Nicole L. Davis, David A. Goodman, and William M. Callaghan. 2019. "Changing the conversation: applying a health equity framework to maternal mortality reviews." *American Journal of Obstetrics and Gynecology* 221 (6). DOI: doi.org/10.1016/j.ajog.2019.08.057.

Luce, Ann, et al. 2016. "'Is It Realistic?' The Portrayal of Pregnancy and Childbirth in the Media." *BMC Pregnancy and Childbirth* 16 (1): 1–10.

MacDorman, Marian F., Eugene Declercq, Howard Cabral, and Christine Morton. 2016. "Is the United States Maternal Mortality Rate Increasing? Disentangling trends from measurement issues." *Obstet Gynecol* 128 (3): 447–55. www.ncbi.nlm.nih.gov/pmc/articles/PMC5001799/pdf/nihms810951.pdf.

"Maternal Mortality." 2019. *National Center for Health Statistics, Centers for Disease Control and Prevention.* November 20, 2019.

Mathis, Poonam Sharma. 2020. "Episode 2: Katherine the Doula Shares the Birth Worker's Perspective." *Pregnant in a Pandemic.* Podcast. March 16, 2020.

McFall, Darby. 2014. "Bring Forth Beckham." *Hall of McFall.* December 4, 2014.

Miller, Korin. 2015. "9 Women Share Exactly How Much It Cost Them to Give Birth." *Women's Health Magazine.* March 10, 2015.

Millner, Denene. 2012. "Birthing While Black: This African American Mom's Experience Was Anything But VIP." *My Brown Baby.* January 25, 2012.

Mills, Catherine. 2013. "Biopolitical Life." In *Foucault, Biopolitics and Governmentality*, Södertörn Philosophical Studies, 73–90.

Owens, Deirdre Cooper. 2018. *Medical Bondage: Race, Gender and the Origins of American Gynecology.* University of Georgia Press.

Parrilla, Krista. 2016. "Happy Hospital Birth." *Birth Without Fear.* March 4, 2016.

Pember, Mary Anette. 2018. "The Midwives' Resistance: How Native Women Are Reclaiming Birth on Their Terms." *Rewire.News.* January 5, 2018.

Puar, Jasbir K. 2007. *Terrorist Assemblages: Homonationalism in Queer Times.* Duke University Press.

"Quinlan's Birth Story." 2016. *Birth Without Fear.* February 1, 2016.

Rettberg, Jill Walker. 2014. *Blogging.* Polity.

Roeder, Amy. 2019. "America Is Failing Black Mothers." *Harvard Public Health.* Winter 2019.

"Rueger's Birth: Learning to Give into the Power of a Woman's Body." 2016. *Birth Without Fear.* January 6, 2016.

Samuels, Ellen. 2014. *Fantasies of Identification: Disability, Gender, Race.* New York University Press.

smith, s. e. 2018. "For Nonbinary Parents, Giving Birth Can Be Especially Fraught." *Rewire.News.* January 25, 2018.

Synan, Abbie. 2020. "Are Temporary Birth Centers the Answer to Alleviating Hospitals during the COVID-19 Outbreak?" *Rewire.News.* May 20, 2020.

Walker, Coral A. 2012. "Giving Birth to Misconceptions: Portrayal of Childbirth in Popular Visual Media." Master's thesis, Haverford College.

Wehman-Brown, Grover. 2018a. "Introduction to *Masculine Birth Ritual.*" *Masculine Birth Ritual. Podcast.* September 2, 2018.

———. 2018b. "People Didn't Know What to Do with Me." *Masculine Birth Ritual.* Podcast. October 15, 2018.

Chapter 11

Feminism and Networked Individual Activism

The Case of Susan Fowler

Minna Aslama Horowitz and Neil Feinstein

A FRAMEWORK FOR THE COMPLEXITIES OF
CONTEMPORARY FEMINIST ACTIVISM

In early 2017, Susan Fowler (later: Susan Rigetti[1]), a former Uber employee, wrote a blog post about her treatment at Uber, including descriptions of blatant sexual harassment. She recounts how, as a site reliability engineer, she was initially excited to innovate for the company but immediately started receiving a string of inappropriate messages from her manager. Her attempts to remedy the situation through official channels at the company had no effect. She decided to quit and publish her story on her blog.

Some three years later, the #DeleteUber and #MeToo hashtags have circulated widely on social and legacy media, Uber CEO Travis Kalanick and many other members of Uber management have resigned, Fowler has offered advice on how to address harassment cases (including at the Supreme Court and concerning the California Legislature), and she has been hired as the technology op-ed editor at the *New York Times*. Fowler has been named a Person of the Year by *Time*, the *Financial Times*, and the Webby Awards and has appeared on *Fortune*'s 40 under 40 list, *Vanity Fair*'s New Establishment List, *Marie Claire*'s New Guard List, the Bloomberg 50, the Upstart 50, and the Recode 100 lists. Fowler's memoir, *Whistleblower*, was published in March 2020, and there is a movie documenting Fowler's story, provisionally called *Disruptors*, in the works.[2] Reflecting on her experience to Leslie Hook from *The Financial Times* for her Person of the Year profile (2017),

195

Fowler notes: "Women have been speaking up for many, many years but were very rarely believed, and there were almost never any real consequences for offenders. This year, that completely changed."

Fowler's story is a tale of transforming workplace adversity into professional success and media visibility using social media as a megaphone. But is she correct when claiming in the interview for the *Financial Times* that something has shifted in the way gender discrimination is being heard and taken seriously? How can we understand and assess her case and others' cases as examples of networked feminist activism?

There is no denying that in the past decades, social media has significantly shaped the strategies and tactics of social activism, leading to terms such as "hashtag activism" (e.g., Cammaerts 2015; Castells 2012; Jackson, Bailey, and Foucault Welles 2020; Tufekci 2017). It has been argued that we are moving from organization-based activism to "cloud protesting" of networked individuals (Milan 2015). At the same time, we are witnessing the spectacular commercial success of personal branding online, often called influencer culture (Gorbatov, Khapova, and Lysova 2018), coupled with conventional advertisers and social media influencers adopting feminist themes ("#femvertising"—for example, Skey 2016), or, more broadly, the "marketplace feminism" of brand building and enhancing a company's bottom line (Zeisler 2016). Social media has dramatically changed the practice of social activism and how social movements gain traction. Perhaps the most oft-cited example is the Arab Spring (e.g., Cammaerts 2015; Castells 2012), but there are now hundreds of cases, ranging from the originally American #BlackLivesMatter to the global #Occupy movement (e.g., Gordon 2015). Social media is now being used by activists for several purposes—ranging from debating, recruitment, and organizing to the surveillance and documentation of protest (Cammaerts 2015). Because of consumer expectations, brands are taking public stands on social and political issues, leading to what is now known as brand activism (Sarkar and Kotler 2018, 219).

Commercial influencer culture and social justice activism, even if entirely different in their ultimate goals, are inextricably intertwined in today's media landscape. They share a quest for purposeful impact, and their tactics and tools on social media may be the same. For instance, both advertising and social justice use hashtags to take narrative stances and make them available to networked publics. For both, hashtags create the "electronic word-of-mouth" effect, especially on mobile social networks (e.g., Shin, Chae, and Ko 2016), but, crucial for social movements, they also enhance modes of "ecstatic sharing" that may solidify opinions and views or divide them (Giaxoglou 2018). All these trends have had and are having a significant impact on feminist activism and thus the way it should be understood from the perspectives of gender studies, feminist media studies, and feminist movements in general. These developments coincide with the reemergence of heated debates on gender-based discrimination in the public sphere. Perhaps the most famous and powerful is the widespread phenomenon of the #MeToo movement against sexual harassment. Defined by its iconic hashtag, the #MeToo movement has largely been driven by celebrities and social media influencers, but its goal is social and personal justice, not product promotion. These new, often complex, and even contradictory, representations and acts of feminism in and via the media have been labeled, in the words of the cultural scholar Sarah Banet-Weiser (2018), popular feminism.

Regardless of the contradictory characteristics of digital communication and activism, many activists claim that social media has opened a new frontier for women's rights organizing (see, e.g., Powel 2018) because it encourages solidarity and emphasizes shared experiences—as illustrated by the much-discussed, oft-cited, and widely researched #MeToo movement. Digital communication and platforms offer several benefits for feminism: first, they offer great potential for broadly disseminating feminist ideas; second, they may shape new modes of discourse about gender and sexism; third, they connect to different constituencies; and fourth, they allow creative modes of protest to emerge (Baer 2016, 18).

Yet the need for structural, systemic change appears to be too often overshadowed by both celebrity stories and individual, highly personal experiences, not to mention the lure of massive virality offered by hashtag activism, without any concrete actions necessarily following. But tools for digital activism are not built for feminists, and they do not protect against harassment; indeed, the online backlash especially against young women, women of color, queer women, and women in the Global South may be nothing short of brutal (e.g., Marwick 2019). Ultimately, the strengths and possibilities of feminism flourish online but, as so aptly phrased by the scholar of rhetoric Kristen Hoerl (2019) about #MeToo, "an intersectional awareness about sexual harassment and the #MeToo movement requires that we attend to the discourses that enable and sustain them while also thinking critically about how #MeToo's public articulation and circulation have served broader structures of inequality that have centered white, cisgendered [sic] women's experiences at the expense of people of color, LGBTQ+ individuals, and Indigenous communities" (263). Digital tools and platforms may broaden opportunities for activism, but not everyone is equal in digital visibility and reach.

How can digital feminist activism succeed and maximize its impact? In this chapter, we argue that a multidimensional approach is essential to understanding activism in the contemporary media ecosystem, including the current strands of individualized activism and popular feminism. Drawing from concepts and empirical analyses of social movement research, feminist media studies, and studies of digital promotional culture, this chapter first addresses an analytical framework that can help dissect the current conditions of feminism and networked individual activism: the tools (of digital networks), the actors (of networked activism), and the context (of today's feminist discourses and actions), which together constitute the contemporary complex activism landscape. The chapter then illustrates this framework with a specific case: the chain of events after Susan Fowler decided to openly discuss workplace sexual harassment at Uber on social media. From a blog author with only one hundred followers to viral activist influencer and editor at one of the most powerful legacy news outlets in the world, Fowler, through her case, highlights the capacities of a "networked individual activist" within #MeToo: her case points out the potential and fragility of digital feminist activism and suggests communicative strategies and tactics for influencer-driven social change.

TOOLS: DIGITALLY ENABLED (FEMINIST) ACTIVISM

"As most of you know, I left Uber in December and joined Stripe in January. I've gotten a lot of questions over the past couple of months about why I left and what my time at Uber was like. It's a strange, fascinating, and slightly horrifying story that deserves to be told while it is still fresh in my mind, so here we go," wrote Susan Fowler in a 2017 blog post titled "Reflecting on One Very, Very Strange Year at Uber." There is no question that digital communication as a tool has changed activism worldwide. For instance, Fowler's blog post and its viral aftermath on social media—it was shared over 22,000 times online in just a few days (Kuchler 2017)—is a nearly picture-perfect example of the new kind of viral digital democratic communication and powerful activism that technology platforms can enable. Fowler begins her message by saying, "As most of you know," indicating that she was informing her own social network about the events of the past year. McGarty et al. (2014) wrote that social media usage contributes to "an acceleration of processes that normally occur much more slowly." According to Jost et al. (2018), the self-mediated network of the poster creates a social environment where information is "pre-validated" and recipients are more likely to "like" and "share" (110), thus facilitating technology-enabled activism.

Much of the writing about the contemporary media environment addresses the extent that technology can facilitate a wider array and deeper forms of participation (Carpentier 2011). Media platforms are becoming increasingly interactive; it is often argued that the barriers to entry in new media contexts are dramatically lower than in traditional media and that opportunities to produce and distribute content are now much more widely available (Benkler 2007; Carpentier 2007; Hargittai and Walejko 2008; Napoli 2011). The platforms and applications of, first, the internet and then mobile media have been theorized as engines of democracy and community by a wide range of scholars in the fields of cultural studies, law, sociology, and political science (e.g., Benkler 2006; Ito et al. 2013; Pickard and Yang 2017; Rheingold 2002; Tufekci 2018). According to many cultural scholars (Jenkins 2006; Jenkins, Ford, and Green 2013; Shirky 2010), we are also spawning a culture of participation that creates public and civic value—sometimes mixing commercial and popular culture elements and social justice causes in new ways, as exemplified in fan activism and the like.

The traditional definition of a social movement is understood as a set of opinions among a population that represents the desire to change something in social structures (e.g., McCarthy and Zald 1977); cases like #MeToo and related actions by Fowler and others seem to fit the bill. Many scholars have mapped the ecosystem of how different technologies and platforms enable activism in different ways (e.g., Gordon 2015; Tufekci and Wilson 2012). But networked activism brings new dimensions to movements: the online world offers new, borderless opportunities for raising awareness, networking, recruiting, organizing, and deliberating within movements. However, although technology fosters strategies and tactics for social change in many ways, it also facilitates communicative practices in which ideological enemies can be surveilled and even attacked (Cammaerts 2015). Thus, the means of networked activism do not necessarily lead to more powerful activism.

While some scholars have contended that digital media might have created "Democracy's Fourth Wave" in contexts such as the Arab Spring (Castells 2012; Howard and Hussain 2013), others have noted that the relationship between democracy and mediated participation needs to be examined in a more nuanced way (Lunt et al. 2013). Participatory realities and opportunities are not identical all over the world (Carpentier, Dahlgren, and Pasquali 2014; Jenkins, Ford, and Green 2013). And—in general, as Sarah Banet-Weiser (2018, 2–3) posited—the "economy of visibility" of networked activism is not only about communicative strategies and tactics but also intertwined with how technology is devoted to the accumulation of likes and clicks, most often for commercial purposes.

For feminists, the internet and, later, social media have enabled a complex and contested platform for activism. Early on, many activists and scholars noted that the internet was male-dominated, men monopolize technology, and gendered power relations are deeply embedded within technoscience (Wajcman 2010). More optimistic thinkers saw the possibility that online environments would enable a world beyond gender binaries. Much has been written about possibilities to experience and reinvent gender online, including virtual worlds (e.g., Boellstorff 2008). In addition, the internet has been key to the formation of movements that focus on nonbinary gender identification (e.g., Shapiro 2004). Still, many have seen the online space as an opportunity for women and feminists to connect and organize in new ways. Social media, in particular, offer possibilities for the latter, and the visibility of feminism has increased due to online platforms (e.g., Carstensen 2014, 484–90). Plenty of antisexist activism has emerged, fueled by what the feminist media scholar Cynthia Carter (2014) called "collaborative anger for social change" (643). However, the online feminist culture is as heterogeneous as the feminist movement itself, and networked activism is equally diverse. Online platforms offer different opportunities, along with limitations and challenges, and users employ them in different ways (e.g., Carsten 2014, 491). As Banet-Weiser (2018) noted of #MeToo and other feminist campaigns, while hashtag activism has shown its power in stimulating public awareness due to the logic of an economy of visibility, it often stops with reposting or retweeting and does not translate into political action (141). Others, such as the legal scholar Tim Wu (2016) and the business professor Shoshana Zuboff (2019), have shown how social media and other platforms limit our choices to act even as they operate as "attention merchants" that capitalize on our data. Networks are neither free nor value-free tools of activism, and networked activism does not automatically boost the success of a movement.

One of the key scholars of hashtag activism, Zeynep Tufekci (2017), suggested that social movements can be assessed by four capacities. #MeToo as a broad phenomenon is a prime example of a massive, global *narrative capacity* (the ability to start public debates) and *disruptive capacity* (the ability to halt practices of harassment). However, sustained policy and legislative changes (*institutional/electoral capacity*) appear to be less readily achievable. Finally, *signaling capacity* (a movement's ability to display power to act) is constantly challenged due to individualized, celebrity-driven cases, the commercialization of feminism, and numerous counternarratives (189–222). Tufecki (2017) offers a sobering reminder about digital technology as a tool for activism: "Technology alters the landscape in which human social interaction takes place, shifts the power and the leverage between actors, and has many other ancillary effects. It is certainly not the only factor in any one situation, but ignoring it as a factor or assuming that a technology could be used to equally facilitate all outcomes obscures our understanding" (124).

ACTORS: NETWORKED INDIVIDUALS

On February 19, 2017, @erclairebaer tweeted: "Mind-blowingly inappropriate and unacceptable practices @Uber. Don't think I've ever deleted an app so quickly. #deleteuber https://twitter.com/susanthesquark/status /833415550638313472" (as quoted in Bhuiyan 2017 for *Vox*). The reactions, positive and negative, of ordinary netizens to Susan Fowler's blog were immediate, and so were their actions: "Don't think I've ever deleted an app so quickly." Suddenly, there were legacy media stories about the case with other bloggers joining in and, of course, a crisis response from Uber. But none of that might have happened had social media users not embraced the blog posts, shared them widely, and began boycotting Uber. Traditionally, sociologists have defined social movements by ideological opponents (here, Uber), informal structures (commenting on the blog, tweeting, sharing, etc.), and collective identities (e.g., Diani 1992). Could collective identities apply to Fowler's case? To be sure, her story appeared to touch many because they had experienced gender-based harassment in different fields and professions, and it moved others because they recognized the particularly masculine, if not misogynist, tech culture at play. But it is hard to see a specific feminist, or other, community forming around Fowler's actions. She shared her story on her blog for those in her immediate circle—not as an open letter, a public manifesto, or a viral hashtag. In her text, there was no call to action, no prompts for mobilization, and little reference to feminism as a movement.

This leads one to wonder: just because individuals unite over a shared belief or concern, does this establish an activist movement? Networked communications could define this activity as such, but that is tentative: there is no community or movement as we know them in the mass media era. While a message of resistance is directed at a clearly defined audience, causing the recipients to "think, question, and calculate" (Blee, 2012, 2), is this communication meant for creating collective action/movement, or is it directed to individuals?

The way networked communication positions activists is at stake in this kind of phenomenon of individuals coming together but not exactly forming a community or movement as we knew them in the mass media era. Activist-researcher Stephania Milan (2015) argues that we are moving from organizations to "networked individuals," which has resulted in something she calls "cloud protesting." She notes that social media has brought with it certain new mechanisms that social movements have embraced to gain visibility. Performance is central to activism. The attention of allies and opponents is gained with tagging and hashtags. One can join in the online action at any point, and a short-lived action, such as a social media post, can resurface and reignite action (Milan 2015).

The above traits of networked individuals, their actions, and their tactics are similar to those of social media influencers, who have used them to great effect. Given the visual economy that impacts activism, understanding activist actors as influencers is crucial. To date, most studies of influencers have come from the fields of advertising and cultural (celebrity) studies. Although the concept of influencers and personal branding originated in marketing, there are now a vast array of studies in different disciplines that examine the phenomenon in social media from a multitude of perspectives, ranging from self-promotion to fame and celebrity to reputation management (Gorbatov, Khapova, and Lysova 2018). Both studies and practices have identified some typologies of influencers, and existing research has explored their distinctive capabilities, which might, for example, be based on their individual and social capital (Wiedmann, Hennigs, and Langner 2010). Advertising industry research indicates that a majority of followers on social media believe social media influencers have as much or more than their real-life friends, and many even consider influencers to be within their circle of friends (see, e.g., O'Malley 2019). Influencer marketing, in general, has gendered characteristics: most social media influencers are women, and female influencers are becoming increasingly important for advertising, as they are thought to portray authenticity and inclusiveness (see, e.g., Nickalls 2018).Most of the studies have focused on how paid influencers may sway public opinion on behalf of the organization, but little research has examined influencers who advocate not for the company but for a grievance, an ideology, or a movement.

Many of the reasons why advertisers employ influencer marketing have parallels among networked individual activists. The "meaning" of the influencer—such as her connection to or expertise about the product, service, or cause she is promoting—impacts a follower's attitude about that product, service, or cause. When exploring customer attitudes, "meaning transfer" plays an important role (Lim et al. 2017), creating an "endorsement effect" that has a positive impact on consumer attitude (McCracken 1989). And the apparently seamless blend of consumerism and activism that is employed by many celebrities and influencers (e.g., Mukherjee and Banet-Weiser 2012; Van Den Bulck 2018) may further blur the borders of persuasive messaging and activist awareness-raising. From another angle, as the seminal work on connective (vs. collective) action by scholars Lance Bennett and Alexandra Segerberg (2012) has shown, personalization applies to both activism and those potentially interested in joining: in the digital age, few of us want to give up our personal beliefs and identities in exchange for more traditional collective organizing. That, too, has a parallel in the consumer culture that celebrates individual identity formation through consumption (e.g., Thompson and Loveland 2015). In Banet-Weisner's (2018) terminology, one could, in fact, argue that the economy of visibility offers networked activism the same tools as the consumer culture. Both use social media to attain similar goals and loyalties and ensuing activities to advance their cause; both may also battle for attention in the same fora.

CONTEXT: POPULAR FEMINISM

Maureen Dowd for the *New York Times*: You've deleted your Uber account.

Susan Fowler: Confirm!

MD: I should delete my Uber account.

SF: Oh, confirm.

MD: Emma Stone should play you in the movie.

SF: That's what I was thinking.

MD: Ashton Kutcher should play Travis [the former Uber CEO].

SF: Yes. He's one of the few people who defends Travis. (Dowd 2017)

Tools, the activists who use them, and the sociocultural context that envelops them are intricately intertwined, as indicated in the *New York Times* interview above. Clearly, the context of today's feminism is marked by opportunities provided by digital tools, related user-generated content, and overall democratization, but individualization, fragmentation, virality, and the hypercommercialization of communication also result in what Tufekci (2017, 30) calls the fragility of activism. She further notes that the media and public visibility constitute "oxygen" for a social movement. Banet-Weiser (2018) links this feature to her concept of economy of visibility, creating the current conditions of what she calls *popular feminism*. This entails visible and loud discourses and actions for gender equality in its many forms. At the same time, the economy of visibility feeds reactionary popular misogyny (Banet-Weiser 2018, 2–3).

Popular feminism clearly intersects with commercial consumer culture—often aligning itself with branding strategies rather than social change (e.g., Murray 2013), thus creating a conflicted context for contemporary feminism in its many forms. While acknowledging the empowering possibilities of popular culture, feminists have been at the forefront of critiquing popular gender representations of promotional culture for over half a century. A longitudinal overview of research over the past decade (Grau and Zotos 2016) emphasizes that the basic debate about the effects of representations of women and men in advertising still rages: Do portrayals reflect societal trends or create them? The same study also suggests that portrayals are becoming notably more diverse but mostly for men (767). In recent years, however, the so-called femvertising has become an everyday occurrence, exemplifying the uneasy alliance of consumerism and feminism. Or, as the *Guardian* put it: "Hashtag feminism has gone viral, with soap, shampoo, and even energy firms launching social media campaigns marketing feminism" (Iqbal 2015). To be sure, with today's digital tools and individualized activism, purchase intention is akin to activation or participation in a cause. This can happen on a small scale by simply liking a post or it can move on to sharing it, commenting, and actively creating and disseminating new user-generated content. In addition, services now list social media influencers by field—whether beauty, fashion, or media celebrity—whose reach may also indicate any activist, including those with feminist leanings (see, e.g., Influence.co 2020, "Empowering the Influence Generation").

Fowler's initial blog posts, her practical advice about how to address sexual harassment in organizations (both on her blog and in the *New York Times*), and her interactions with legislative bodies to support structural change do not initially appear to be connected to what could be called neoliberal popular feminism of the social media era. But her post benefited from the logic of the economy of visibility; it might never have gone viral had Uber not been the focus of a hashtag campaign for its predatory activities just a few weeks earlier. In January 2017, #DeleteUber was trending on Twitter as a reaction to accusations that the firm was profiting from the protest against President Trump's ban on refugees and immigrants to enter the United States by turning off surge pricing when New York City taxi drivers refused to pick up passengers at New York's Kennedy airport (Isaac 2017a). The rise of Fowler as an upstart figure challenging sexual harassment in Silicon Valley got most of its fuel from the massive #MeToo wave of revelations and debates about sexual harassment. But, as many have noted, the movement had already been created by activist Tarana Burke over a decade earlier and was now being made famous mostly by celebrities. #MeToo, in a way, exemplifies the challenge of popular feminism: it combines awareness of sexual harassment with the mainstream focus on public figures and has been expressed on platforms that are characterized by simplification and driven by the virality of attention. In addition, the movement has been commodified, with its branding featuring cookies and T-shirts (Banet-Weiser 2018, 16–17). Consider the fact that in the conversation between Maureen Dowd and Susan Fowler that begins this section, they joke about celebrities who might appear in the inevitable biopic about Fowler's case, let alone the fact that a movie is under development.

Banet-Weiser (2018) highlights yet another aspect of the current popular feminist context: the counterpoint that is provided by the "bro culture" and "geek masculinity." She notes that the particular context of technology industries evokes specific tensions between popular feminism and popular misogyny, as exemplified by the extreme online violence against female gamers and feminist game critics during #GamerGate. Banet-Weiser also links this phenomenon to the neoliberal commercial culture and observes that one prominent narrative positions geeks as having significant cultural and economic capital due to the rise of tech industries but as lacking in erotic capital (Banet-Weiser 2018, 134–35). Other authors have also highlighted the inherent contradiction between the platforms created by Silicon Valley geeks and the ideals of, and activists working for, feminism (Marwick 2019; Vickery and Everbach 2018). Not only online attacks against women in tech but also workplace culture reflect misogyny, regardless of what the official declarations might indicate. Symptomatically, it is the male activists in technology, such as Edward Snowden, who are called whistleblowers rather than influencers and have elicited substantial analysis in terms of their impact on policy, foreign relations, civil rights, and so on (Park and Jang 2017).

What do Susan Fowler's actions and their impact as feminist activism look like when examined through tools, actors, and the sociocultural context? The Google Trends graph below is an example of Fowler's "popularity" in the economy of visibility, showing its dramatic peak shortly after her initial blog post. A detailed look using tools, actors, and the sociocultural context paints a more nuanced picture of the takeaways of this case for feminist activism.

TOOLS AND IMPACT

Prior to February 19, 2017, when Susan Fowler published "Reflecting on One Very, Very Strange Year at Uber," her blog had a very modest following. Nevertheless, the likes of this particular post quickly rose to 15,000 and responses to 500, at which point the author decided to close commenting. The responses on the blog included the criticism of Uber for its unethical

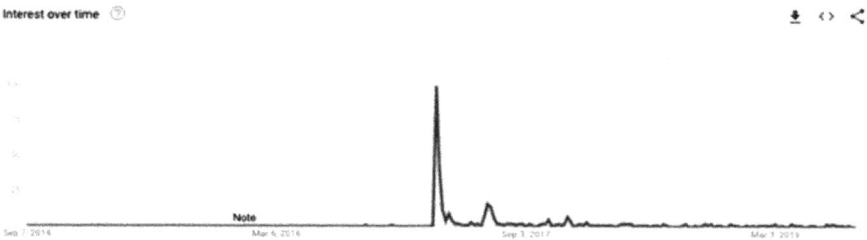

Figure 11.1. The impact of Susan Fowler's story revisited. Google Trends on web searches with the combined search terms "susan fowler uber" in the United States between September 1, 2014, and September 1, 2019. While this case is not solely about Uber, adding "uber" as a term in the search focuses the search results. *Note that there is another relatively popular author named Susan Fowler. A value of 100 indicates the peak popularity of a term; a value of 50 would mean that the term is half as popular: trends.google.com/trends/explore?date=today%205-y&geo=US&q=Susan%20 Fowler%20uber.

and exploitative practices in general and even of Fowler for working for such an unethical company. Most commentators, however, echoed this empathic and supportive comment that provides the context for Fowler's experience: "I have never worked in a single company in which HR was in any way different from what you describe here. It isn't just tech. It isn't just women. It's everywhere."

The accumulation of other texts—hundreds of thousands of tweets, hundreds of news stories, and other bloggers sharing their experiences online on their own platforms—clearly demonstrates the immense narrative capacity that a simple blog post may have. For instance, the post prompted the influential venture capitalist and Uber investor Freada Kapor Klein to pen an open letter admonishing Uber (see Shahani 2017). Until that point, the investment community was more concerned with Uber's $70 billion valuation (see Isaac 2017b) than with their bad-boy ethos.

The disruptive capacity that the post unleashed was also extraordinary. Uber CEO, Travis Kalanick, responded immediately with a statement (see Wagner 2017), and an additional response was quickly published by Uber board member Arianna Huffington (see Buhr and Dickey 2017), both promising a full investigation of what happened to Fowler. Later, on June 20, 2017, Uber investors pressured Kalanick to resign (Kent and Newcomb 2017). There were additional management changes as a result, with twenty people being fired or having left the company, and significant changes were made to the Uber board. The post ultimately brought with it opportunities for Fowler to have the capacity to help strengthen antiharassment actions institutionally through policy and lawmaking: she vocally lent her support to bill AB-3080, a California initiative that gives victims of sexual harassment and other workplace discrimination the ability to seek legal action (Russell and Loizos 2018). Certainly, the tools had to do with the signaling activist power to counter sexism as well: the #DeleteUber hashtag signaled and prompted (or extended) a concrete boycott of Uber's services. The same hashtag emerged yet again in 2019 in protest of Uber's initial public offering on the stock market (Siddiqui 2019).

However, just a few months after her viral story, Fowler's follow-up post—a normative five-point analysis of how companies could address sexual harassment—received only 240 likes (Fowler 2017b). In other words, in the economy of visibility, the tools of visibility do not guarantee impact; they are simply a starting point.

ACTORS AND IMPACT

It is noteworthy that #MeToo and other recent gender equality activist phenomena are often discussed as a movement, but in many ways, they are nothing like a traditional social movement. In Milan's (2015) words, individuals connect via networks. It is as if hashtags and other connectivity tools act as nodes that one can encounter, decide to attach to for a moment, and even perhaps return to. There is no specific center, no leader. Spontaneity and networks are typical of these kinds of movements; leadership is fluid, changing, popping up, and disappearing, and it is potentially within all individuals (Western 2014).

It seems Susan Fowler did not intend to start, let alone lead, a collective action. After the vast publicity, her role became that of an expert in sexual harassment, rather than an organizer or movement-builder. This kind of shift in public roles is illustrative of the ever-shifting cloud of protests around sexual harassment that *Time* awarded the Person of the Year to "The Silence Breakers"—women who had fought sexual harassment in 2017, justifying the decision as follows: "It became a hashtag, a movement, a reckoning. But it began, as great social change nearly always does, with individual acts of courage" (Felsenthal 2017). Similarly, the decision by the *New York Times* to hire Fowler was framed around her expertise (the primary source of her credibility, even more than her newfound identity of social justice warrior). Interestingly, the *New York Times* discussed Fowler's experiences and activism as individual traits of character, as literally her "brand": "She will bring her unique brand of courage, clarity of mind and moral purpose to our pages starting in September" (Bennet, Dao, and Kingsbury 2018).

CONTEXT AND IMPACT

Arguably, Susan Fowler is more than her brand; her case is part of something bigger. While she is an individual expert and not a self-proclaimed feminist activist, her personal story has, nevertheless, become political. She has prompted a chain reaction not only at Uber but also through other women sharing their stories. Her focus of change has been in one of the most publicly invisible contexts of misogyny: the tech industry. While Fowler has had to battle against that culture during and after Uber (for example, she had to temporarily shut down her Twitter account), she has fared extremely well in the economy of visibility and been widely and positively portrayed in mainstream media. As Banet-Weiser (2018) posited about popular feminism, feminism, at least a certain kind of feminism that fits the mold of the economy of visibility, is more visible than ever.

At the same time, the Google Trends search result highlights the very real challenge of Fowler's impact in today's attention economy. Her capacity to raise awareness and stir public conversations withered quickly, transforming her into a known influencer to her previous peers in the field of technology and to some readers of the *New York Times*. By contrast, a Pew Research Center study on activism in the social media age shows how #BlackLivesMatter, a hashtag connected to an organized movement originally started by Alicia Garza, Patrisse Cullors, and Opal Tometi, can repeatedly reignite the conversation, even more than #MeToo or any other hashtag linked to spontaneous cloud protesting (Anderson, Toor, Rainie, and Smith 2018).

Perhaps the most telling connection to popular feminism is, as the *New York Times* put it, Fowler's brand. She follows other "popular feminist memoirists," women successful enough that they can afford to write about gendered workplace inequalities (Banet-Weiser 2018, 94–96). The publicity for Fowler's memoir, titled *Whistleblower*, began nine months before its release: "The moving story of a woman's lifelong fight to do what she loves—despite repeatedly being told no or treated as less-than—*Whistleblower* is both a riveting read and a source of inspiration for anyone seeking to stand up against inequality in their own workplace" (Penguin Random House 2020).

These types of books commonly focus on self-worth and the related idea of confidence, knowing your worth and acting upon it. In memoirs of this kind, confidence most often becomes an insulated individual trait in the economy of visibility without any real connection to questions of gendered power imbalances, material histories, or structural inequalities that might impact one's possibilities for success (Banet-Weiser 2018, 95). Or, as Fowler herself put it in a May 2019 *New York Times* opinion piece: "Every standard that I hold myself to is a standard of my own making, one that is fully under my control. My self-worth doesn't depend on anyone else. Even if the world were to fall apart today, my sense of who I am and my place in this world wouldn't be destroyed. These days, power rarely crosses my mind" (Fowler 2019).

CONCLUSIONS: LESSONS FOR
DIGITAL FEMINIST ACTIVISM

Assessing Susan Fowler's role as a feminist whistleblower and her actions as networked activism is not easy. No one can deny women's voices that, before the digital era, would have remained silenced are now being heard in the mainstream, such as Malala Yousafzai's advocating for girls' education rights or Greta Thunberg's fight against climate change. At the same time, this type of incidental individual influencer carries several risks. An international comparative study on "The Silence Breakers" of #MeToo identified four main media frames through which these women have been portrayed (Starkey et al. 2019). Susan Fowler, the case for the United States, was found to have received the most diverse coverage and to embody all the frames: she was a courageous woman who spoke her truth, the stoic victim of an unjust system, the reluctant hero, and "the hysterical slut" (437). One could argue that a multitude of roles serve the economy of visibility and enable an adjustable frame for different moments and audiences. Given the continued relative invisibility of women and feminism in news media around the world (Global Media Monitoring Project 2015)—where at least, in theory, important political and social issues are discussed—these new forms, platforms, and actors have dramatically increased discussions on feminist issues and activism, including sexual harassment.

However, the context for the economy of visibility and related built-in mechanisms that thrive on a particular kind of attention may result in more of a celebrity than an activist or advocate frame in media coverage. And, while attention may be oxygen for a movement, it is sadly fleeting. The widely documented online harassment, misogyny, and even virtual violence against women is especially vicious for female and female-presenting public figures, and it seems to be ever more common and mainstream. (Marcotte 2019). The battle between popular feminism and popular misogyny is good business in a multimedia landscape that thrives on clickbait and conflict (Banet-Weiser 2018).

In the end, the lessons from the case of Susan Fowler are contradictory. After a few years at the *New York Times*, Fowler, later Rigetti, became a full-time author who has focused on her detective novel about an intern at the fashion magazine *ELLE* (Rigetti 2022), her newsletter on Substack,[3] and screenwriting.[4] It is not entirely surprising that an individual, accidental activist like Fowler/Rigetti wanted to move on from the #MeToo limelight. After all, she did not make a commitment to a movement. She wrote a personal complaint. Her visibility was due to the powerful, yet simultaneously fragile, momentum created by a hashtag with a larger movement behind it.

Milan (2015) reminds us that digital media may function as an organizing force where there is no community, collectivity, or movement that would naturally emerge, but she also notes that digital activism is, in many ways, at the mercy of the internal mechanisms, structures, and economies of social media platforms. Although many movements today shun hierarchies, as exemplified by the #Occupy movement, fully individualized activism bound by temporarily viral hashtags may not be the best answer. Finally, as Banet-Weiser (2018) notes of today's popular feminism, it says "I'm with her," not "We're with each other" (184). How can this be changed? Not everyone is or seeks to be an activist or advocate, but we must learn how to use and connect powerful stories such as Fowler's to form more coherent, more diverse, more collaborative, and sustainable conversations, networks, alliances, actions, and even movements. This may require us to give up, to a great extent, the idea of networks as offering the freedom to participate and understand them, as many thinkers currently do, more as neoliberal, market-driven, data-hungry, and attention-seeking. Studies on persuasive communication may help us in strategies, and feminist criticism will help us to question gendered power dynamics not only in terms of activist causes but also in activist networked practices. As Tufecki (2017) posits, the coevolution of power and protest is far from over, and social movements are far from static: "It is wrong to label movements that struggle as failures, just as it is wrong to conclude that a large protest, measured by the number of people on the street, is a sure sign of success" (274). Perhaps networked feminist activism needs entirely new ways of assessment.

REFERENCES

Anderson, Monica, Skye Toor, Lee Rainie, and Aaron Smith. 2018. "Activism in the Social Media Age." *Pew Research Center: Internet, Science & Tech.* July 11, 2018.

Baer, Hester. 2016. "Redoing Feminism: Digital Activism, Body Politics, and Neoliberalism." *Feminist Media Studies* 16 (1): 17–34.

Banet-Weiser, Sarah. 2018. *Empowered: Popular Feminism and Popular Misogyny.* Duke University Press.

Benkler, Yochai. 2006. *The Wealth of Networks: How Social Production Transforms Markets and Freedom.* Yale University Press.

Bennet, James, Jim Dao, and Katie Kingsbury. 2018. "Susan Fowler Rigetti to Join Opinion as Technology Editor." *New York Times.* December 7, 2018.

Bennet, Lance, and Alexandra Segerberg. 2012. *The Logic of Connective Action: Digital Media and the Personalization of Contentious Politics.* Cambridge University Press.

Bhuiyan, Johana. 2017. "A Former Uber Employee's Disturbing Claims of Workplace Sexism Reignite Calls to #DeleteUber." *Vox-Recode.* February 20, 2017.

Blee, Kathleen, and Amy McDowell. 2012. "Social Movement Audiences." *Sociological Forum* 27 (1): 1–20.

Boellstorff, Tom. 2008. *Coming of Age in Second Life: An Anthropologist Explores the Virtually Human.* Princeton University Press.

Buhr, Sarah, and Megan Rose Dickey. 2017. "Uber Board Member Arianna Huffington Releases Statement after Company All-Hands." *TechCrunch.* February 21, 2017.

Cammaerts, Bart. 2015. "Social Media and Activism." *The International Encyclopedia of Digital Communication and Society*, edited by Robin Mansell and Peng Hwa Ang, 1027–34. Wiley-Blackwell.

Carpentier, Nico. 2011. *Media and Participation: A Site of Ideological and Democratic Struggle*. Intellect.

———. 2007. "Participation and Interactivity: Changing Perspectives; the Construction of an Integrated Model on Access, Interaction and Participation." *New Media Worlds: Challenges for Convergence*, edited by Virginia Nightingale and Tim Dwyer, 214–30. Oxford University Press.

Carpentier, Nico, Peter Dahlgren, and Francesca Pasquali. 2014. "The Democratic (Media) Revolution: A Parallel Genealogy of Political and Media Participation." *Audience Transformations: Shifting Audience Positions in Late Modernity*, edited by Nico Carpentier, Kristian C. Schrøder, and Lawrie Hallett, 123–41. London: Routledge.

Carstensen, Tanja. 2014. "Gender and Social Media: Sexism, Empowerment, or the Irrelevance of Gender?" *The Routledge Companion to Media and Gender*, edited by Cynthia Carter, Linda Steiner, and Lisa McLaughlin, 483–92. Routledge.

Carter, Cynthia. 2014. "Online Popular Anti-Sexism Political Action in the UK and USA: The Importance of Collaborative Anger for Social Change." *The Routledge Companion to Media and Gender*, edited by Cynthia Carter, Linda Steiner, and Lisa McLaughlin, 643–53. Routledge.

Castells, Manuel. 2012. *Networks of Outrage and Hope: Social Movements in the Internet Age*. Polity Press.

Chang, Emily. 2018. *Brotopia: Breaking Up the Boys' Club of Silicon Valley*. Penguin.

Diani, Marco. 1992. "The Concept of a Social Movement." *The Sociological Review* 40 (1): 1–25.

Dowd, Maureen. 2017. "Confirm or Deny . . . Susan Fowler." *New York Times*. October 21, 2017.

Felsenthal, Edward. n.d. "Silence Breakers TIME Person of the Year 2017: How We Chose." *Time*. time.com/time-person-of-the-year-2017-silence-breakers-choice/.

Fowler, Susan. 2019. "Before I Could Change the World, I Had to Change Myself." *New York Times*. May 30, 2019.

———. 2017a. "Reflecting on One Very, Very Strange Year at Uber." *Susan Fowler*. February 19, 2017.

———. 2017b. "Five Things Tech Companies Can Do Better." *Susan Fowler*. May 21, 2017.

———. n.d.a "Susan Fowler." *Susan Fowler*. www.susanjfowler.com/.

———. n.d.b "Whistleblower by Susan Fowler: PenguinRandomHouse.com: Books." *Penguin Random House*. www.penguinrandomhouse.com/books/585732 /whistleblower-by-susan-fowler/9780525560128/.

Giaxoglou, Korina. 2018. "#JeSuisCharlie? Hashtags as Narrative Resources in Contexts of Ecstatic Sharing." *Discourse, Context, and Media* 22: 13–20.

Global Media Monitoring Project. 2015. *Who Makes the News?* The World Association for Christian Communication. cdn.agilitycms.com/who-makes-the-news/Imported/ reports_2015/global/gmmp_global_report_en.pdf.

Gorbatov, Sergey, Svetlana N. Khapova, and Evgenia I. Lysova. 2018. "Personal Branding: Interdisciplinary Systematic Review and Research Agenda." *Frontiers in Psychology* 9: 2238.

Gordon, Steven. 2015. "Fostering Social Movements with Social Media." *SSRN Electronic Journal*. DOI: https://doi.org/10.2139/ssrn.2708079.

Grau, Stacy, and Yorgos Zotos. 2016. "Gender Stereotypes in Advertising: A Review of Current Research." *International Journal of Advertising* 35 (5): 761–70.

Hargittai, Eszter, and Gina Walejko. 2008. "The Participation Divide: Content Creation and Sharing in the Digital Age." *Information, Communication & Society* 11 (2): 239–56.

Hoerl, Kristen. 2019. "Special Issue: The #MeToo Moment: A Rhetorical Zeitgeist." *Women's Studies in Communication* 42 (3): 263.

Hook, Leslie. 2017. "FT Person of the Year: Susan Fowler." *Financial Times*. December 12, 2017.

Howard, Philip N., and Muzammil M. Hussain. 2013. *Democracy's Fourth Wave? Digital Media and the Arab Spring*. Oxford University Press.

Influence.co. n.d. "Empowering the Influence Generation." influence.co/category/feminism.

Iqbal, Nosheen. 2015. "Femvertising: How Brands Are Selling #Empowerment to Women." *The Guardian*. October 12, 2015.

Isaac, Mike. 2017a. "What You Need to Know About #DeleteUber." *New York Times*, February 1, 2017.

———. 2017b. "Uber Fires 20 amid Investigation into Workplace Culture." *New York Times*, June 6, 2017.

Ito, Mizuko. 2013. *Hanging Out, Messing Around, and Geeking Out: Kids Living and Learning With New Media*. MIT Press.

Jackson, Sarah J., Moya Bailey, Brooke Foucault Welles. 2020. *#HashtagActivism: Networks of Race and Gender Justice*. MIT Press.

Jenkins, Henry. 2006. *Convergence Culture: Where Old and New Media Collide*. New York University Press.

Jenkins, Henry, Sam Ford, and Joshua Green. 2013. *Spreadable Media: Creating Value and Meaning in a Networked Culture*. New York University Press.

Jost, John T., Pablo Barberá, Richard Bonneau, Melanie Langer, Megan Metzger, Jonathan Nagler, Joanna Sterling, and Joshua A. Tucker. 2018. "How Social Media Facilitates Political Protest: Information, Motivation, and Social Networks." *Political Psychology* 39: 85–118.

Kent, Jo Ling, and Alyssa Newcomb. 2017. "Mass Firings at Uber After Harassment Investigation." NBC Universal, June 6, 2017.

Kuchler, Hannah. 2017. "Susan Fowler, the Techie Taking on Uber." *Financial Times*. February 24, 2017. www.ft.com/content/469fbaec-fa76-11e6-9516-2d969e0d3b65.

Lim, Xin Jean, Aifa Rozaini Bt Mohd Radzol, Jun-Hwa (Jacky) Cheah, and Mun Wai Wong. 2017. "The Impact of Social Media Influencers on Purchase Intention and the Mediation Effect of Customer Attitude." *Asian Journal of Business Research* 7 (2): 5.

Lunt, Peter, Anne Kaun, Pille Pruulman-Vengerfeldt, Birgit Stark, and Liesbet van Zoonen. 2013. "The Mediation of Civic Participation: Diverse Forms of Political Agency in a Multimedia Era." *Audience Transformations: Shifting Audience*

Positions in Late Modernity, edited by Nicl Carpentier, Kristian. C. Schrøder, and Lawrie Hallett, 142–56. London: Routledge.

Marcotte, Amanda. 2019. "Misogyny, Meet Hypocrisy: Climate Deniers Go after AOC, Greta Thunberg with Sexist Attacks." *Salon*. August 30, 2019.

Marwick, Alice. 2019. "None of This Is New (Media): Feminisms in the Social Media Age." *The Handbook of Contemporary Feminism*, edited by Andrea Press and Tasha Oren, 309–32. Routledge.

McCarthy, John, and Mayer Zald. 1977. "Resource Mobilization and Social Movements: A Partial Theory." *American Journal of Sociology* 82 (6): 1212–41.

McCracken, Grant. 1989. "Who Is the Celebrity Endorser? Cultural Foundations of the Endorsement Process." *Journal of Consumer Research* 16 (3): 310–21.

McGarty, Craig, Thimas, Emma, Laila Girish, Smith, Laura and Bliuc, Ana-Maria. 2014. "New Technologies, New Identities, and the Growth of Mass Opposition in the Arab Spring." *Political Psychology* 35 (6): 725–40.

Milan, Stefania. 2015. "When Algorithms Shape Collective Action: Social Media and the Dynamics of Cloud Protesting." *Social Media + Society* 1 (2): 1–10.

Mukherjee, Roopali, and Sarah Banet-Weiser, eds. 2012. *Commodity Activism: Cultural Resistance in Neoliberal Times*. New York University Press.

Murray, Dara. 2013. "Branding 'Real' Social Change in Dove's Campaign for Real Beauty." *Feminist Media Studies* 13 (1): 83–101.

Nickalls, Sammy. 2018. "Infographic: Influencers Are Bigger than Ever, and They're Just Getting Started." *Adweek*. June 4, 2018.

O'Malley, Gavin. 2019. "Many Followers Trust Influencers' Opinions More Than Friends.'" *Media Post*, August 21, 2019.

Park, Yong Jin, and S. Mo Jang. 2017. "View of Public Attention, Social Media, and the Edward Snowden Saga: First Monday." *First Monday* 22 (8). DOI: doi.org/10.5210/fm.v22i8.7818.

Pickard, Victor, and Guobin Yang, eds. 2017. *Media Activism in the Digital Age*. Routledge.

Powell, Catherine. "How Social Media Has Reshaped Feminism." *Council on Foreign Relations*, June 18, 2018. https://www.cfr.org/blog/how-social-media-has-reshaped-feminism.

Rheingold, Howard. 2002. *Smart Mobs: The Next Social Revolution*. New York: Basic Books.

Rigetti, Susan. 2022. *Cover Story*. New York: Harper Collins.

Russell, Jon, and Connie Loizos. "Uber Whistleblower Susan Fowler Backs California Legislation to End Forced Arbitration." *TechCrunch*, April 18, 2018. techcrunch.com/2018/04/18/uber-whistleblower-susan-fowler-backs-california-legislation-to-end-forced-arbitration/.

Sarkar, Christian, and Philip Kotler. 2018. *Brand Activism: From Purpose to Action*. Idea Bite Press.

Shahani, Aarti. "The Investor Who Took on Uber, and Silicon Valley." NPR. June 15, 2017.

Shapiro, Eve. 2004. "'Trans' Cending Barriers: Transgender Organizing on the Internet." *Journal of Gay & Lesbian Social Services* 16 (3–4): 165–79.

Shin, Jiye, Heeju Chae, and Eunju Ko. 2018. "The Power of e-WOM Using the Hashtag: Focusing on SNS Advertising of SPA Brands." *International Journal of Advertising* 37 (1): 1–15.

Shirky, Clay. 2010. *Cognitive Surplus: How Technology Makes Consumers into Collaborators.* Penguin.

Siddiqui, Faiz. 2019. "Internal Data Shows Uber's Reputation Hasn't Changed Much since #DeleteUber." *Washington Post.* August 29, 2019.

Skey, Samantha. 2016. "#Femvertising: A New Kind of Relationship between Influencers and Brands." *She Media.* April 16, 2016.

Starkey, Jesse C., Amy Koerber, Miglena Sternadori, and Bethany Pitchford. 2019. "#MeToo Goes Global: Media Framing of Silence Breakers in Four National Settings." *Journal of Communication Inquiry* 43 (4): 437–61.

Thompson, Scott A., and James M. Loveland. 2015. "Integrating Identity and Consumption: An Identity Investment Theory." *Journal of Marketing Theory and Practice* 23 (3): 235–53.

Tufekci, Zeynep. 2017. *Twitter and Teargas: The Power and Fragility of Networked Protest.* Yale University Press.

Tufekci, Zeynep, and Christopher Wilson. 2012. "Social Media and the Decision to Participate in Political Protest: Observations from Tahrir Square." *Journal of Communication* 62 (2): 363–79.

Van Den Bulck, Hilde. 2018. *Celebrity Philanthropy and Activism: Mediated Interventions in the Global Public Sphere.* Routledge.

Vickery, Jacqueline R., and Tracy Everbach, eds. 2018. *Mediating Misogyny: Gender, Technology, and Harassment.* Palgrave Macmillan.

Wagner, Kurt. 2017. "Uber's CEO Promises an 'Urgent Investigation' into a Former Employee's Sexual Harassment Claims." *Vox.* February 20, 2017.

Wajcman, Judy. 2010. "Feminist Theories of Technology." *Cambridge Journal of Economics* 34 (1): 143–52.

Western, Simon. 2014. "Autonomist Leadership in Leaderless Movements: Anarchists Leading the Way." *Ephemera: Theory & Politics of Organization* 14 (4): 673–98.

Wiedmann, Klaus-Peter, Nadine Hennigs, and Sascha Langner. 2010. "Spreading the Word of Fashion: Identifying Social Influencers in Fashion Marketing." *Journal of Global Fashion Marketing* 1 (3): 142–53.

Wu, Tim. 2016. *The Epic Scramble to Get Inside Our Heads.* New York: Penguin.

Zeiler, Andi. 2016. *We Were Feminists Once: From Riot Grrrl to CoverGirl®, the Buying and Selling of a Political Movement.* Public Affairs/Perseus.

Zuboff, Shoshana. 2019. *The Age of Surveillance Capitalism: The Fight for a Human Future at the New Frontier of Power.* Hachette Books.

NOTES

1. In this chapter, we call Susan Rigetti with the name associated with her activism, Susan Fowler; see, e.g., www.susanrigetti.com/.

2. www.penguinrandomhouse.com/authors/2169682/susan-fowler/.
3. See, susanrigetti.substack.com/.
4. See, www.imdb.com/name/nm9387946/.

Chapter 12

"I Want Us to Own the Goddamned Servers"

The Feminist Principles of Archive of Our Own

Sid Heeg

It's 2007. LiveJournal staff begin to remove content that violates their policies, deleting discussion boards, posts, and, in some cases, entire blogs. This is done without warning, leaving many users wondering where to post their content, or where their content has gone. While the content purge sought to respond to concerns of inappropriate material hosted on LiveJournal, fan communities and fan users—those who use the site to connect over similar interests in television, film, literature, music, and/or sports—were also caught. The content purge, now known as Strikethrough, isn't the only time when fans will come to question their legitimacy as a community and as deserving of a safe space. Later in 2007, the organization FanLib raised questions of fan exploitation for profit and monetization on LiveJournal, casting further shadows of doubt on the platform's ability to cultivate communities. As fan fiction and fanworks are often women and LGBTQ+ dominated activities, the purges affected the creative spaces of women and queer fans, marginalizing them for their online activities and innovative storytelling responses to more mainstream media. In many ways, these fans were targeted for their online behaviors and punished because these behaviors deviated from the norm and were found to be unacceptable. This chapter is an examination of this censorship, consent, fan labor, and how the foundation of An Archive of Our Own (AO3) can be interpreted through an explicitly feminist digital space lens in terms of both its design and user interface. Why? Because, like one Fanlore user writes, "I want us to own the goddamned servers, ok?"[1]

In this chapter, I focus on the movements Strikethrough and FanLib in relation to the creation of the Organization of Transformative Works (OTW) and AO3. The OTW is a nonprofit organization that works to preserve fanworks and fan culture. It is the governing body of AO3 and several other fan culture projects[2] and was founded by several users who had been affected by Strikethrough. I argue that AO3 not only provides a functional space for a wide variety of fan fiction, but it provides functional space in a way that other fan fiction websites do not through the ways that the foundation values the privacy and safety of fans first, ensuring their content and their communities are protected. AO3 is the direct result of the rise of social media networks in the early 2000s and their troubled relationships with fan communities and fanworks and, as such, the policies governing AO3's practices and values reflect the desires and wishes fans had before AO3 was created. These early years are punctuated by such movements as Strikethrough, Boldthrough, and other fanwork purges across sites like LiveJournal and FanFiction.net (FFN). Because of this, I look at the conversations that fans had with each other, focusing on their frustrations and discontents with how they were being treated and portrayed by those outside of fandom, and I come to examine AO3 both as a reader and a writer on the site.

As a queer fan, I discovered AO3 in 2013 when it first announced that its millionth work had been posted to the site. The user interface appealed to me more than other sites like FFN because I found this site easier to navigate and find fan works that appealed to my interests. Moreover, there is an agency that AO3 offers that other sides do not: AO3 also allows fan authors to abandon or "orphan" their stories. If I were to delete my account on FFN, all my stories would then be removed. But with AO3, I can orphan a story, meaning that my username is removed from the piece, but keep the work available in the archive for others to read. This functions to allow me to remove content from my username, enabling me to engage in other fandoms and switch my interests when needed.

The way in which I view fans and fan communities stems from Henry Jenkins' *Textual Poachers* (1992). Fandom here is described as participatory culture where the consumption of media turns into the production of new content (46). In contrast to the participatory fan is the casual fan, someone who consumes the media but goes no further in participating with its content. Participatory communities are where the discussions during Strikethrough and FanLib occur, and while the communities are open to all forms of fanworks, my focus is on how fan fiction communities came together to protect their content. Fan fictions (also called "fanfic" or "fanfics") are fictional stories written about an existing piece of media and produced by participatory fans. While AO3 enables fans to post any sort of fanwork, fan fiction is the dominant form of content on the platform and have been the focus of the content purges and other controversies during Strikethrough and FanLib.

In what follows, I consider three moments in the mid-2000s within online fandom circles that pushed fans together to claim AO3 as their own website. The first centers on content purges at FFN, the largest fan archive on the Internet with over 10 million posted works. FFN had two significant content purges in 2002 and 2012 where it removed content that was deemed not user friendly or considered taboo, including real person fiction (RPF)—fan fiction that depicts a real person in a work of fiction like an actor or a music band member. The second moment is Strikethrough from May 2007 that occurred on the then-prominent blogging website LiveJournal. This movement included blog purges and user profile terminations by LiveJournal staff due to content violating LiveJournal's policies. The third moment is the launch and subsequent closure of a short-lived website named FanLib and the dialogue and controversy it stirred up on the matter of whether fans can and should make money based on their fan creations. As we move through these events, I tell this story as a narrative recollection. These are stories and discussions I have read and shared during my time in fandom, so it is important to understand not only why we are here, at this moment of claiming AO3, but how we got here—why it matters that the OTW and AO3 began in the first place.

WEB 2.0 AND FANDOM

Many have noted the multitude of ways in which Web 2.0 and the emergence of social media websites have made it easier for fan communities to connect with one another and the content creators they are fans of (Chin 2018; Hellekson 2018; Linden and Linden 2017). Fandom has flourished with sites like LiveJournal and FFN, both launched in the late 1990s; Yahoo! Geocities from the early 2000s; and Twitter and Tumblr following in 2006 and 2007 respectively. These social networks have enabled fans to connect with each other and share a variety of content. Organizations like these offer an important avenue for fans to find and connect with others based on similar interests. The ability to categorize one's activities online made LiveJournal an appealing site for fans, and it became one of the dominant sites in the early and mid-2000s fandom. This eventually changed with the emergence of Tumblr in 2007 with its ability to share and create multimedia posts in contrast to LiveJournal's text only options (Hellekson 2018, 71). Importantly, Web 2.0 highlights two main things that are of value to fans: connectivity and versatility. The ability to share content with ease among other fans, and a wide variety of content that extends beyond fan fiction, including fanvids (assembled video clips), podfics (audio recordings of fanfics), fanart, and more, allowed fans to demonstrate their appreciation in whatever format they choose.

Launched in 1998, FFN was developed by Xing Li, a fan of the series *X-Files*, with the intent of making FFN a multifandom archive ("FanFiction. Net" n.d.). FFN is not the first fan fiction archive to emerge with Web 2.0, but it is one that became highly popular and highly successful in allowing a broad range of fans of different fandoms to come together and post content. Likewise, LiveJournal, launched in 1999 as a blogging platform, immediately appealed to fans for its threaded comments and friends lists, and how it allowed users to post whatever text they were working on. This contrasted with how traditional mailing lists worked for other fandoms. In an oral history project conducted by Lisa Cronin with Rachael Sabotini in 2012, Sabotini laid out the changes in fandom from her own personal experience with fan culture dating back to the early 1980s. She highlights the migration away from popular communication methods between fans like mailing lists to the embrace of social media and the emergence of Web 2.0. Sabotini suggests that mailing lists die because "people stop posting. Either because [of] no new blood, the conversations have happened so many times before, no new ideas, attention spans, drifting apart." She goes on to say that as "chat rooms became more common, then people got, you know, real time chatting about their fandoms and what they liked. That's when I think mailing lists started to cool off a bit. And then in 2002 . . . we were migrating over to LJ [LiveJournal] and that was really the end of the mailing list era" (Cronin 2012, 1:41:34). When a new platform comes along and it's more user friendly and engaging, it is understandable to see why fans would flock from one method to the next. LiveJournal would just be the next fan space to come along that was the most popular at the time.

Web 2.0 allows fans to communicate immediately and enables fans to broaden their interests via participation in various corners of the Internet. As Sabotini suggests in her interview with Cronin (2012), mailing lists could be strict in what they did and did not allow in terms of content. Fans found participation to be hard, so when LiveJournal and FFN emerged in the late 1990s, suddenly forms of fan participation began to change. Hellekson (2018) refers to fans as the "quintessential early adopters" with the emergence of the Internet in the early 1990s and social media platforms of the late 1990s. As Hellekson notes, LiveJournal enabled fans to not only blog and create content, but to create fan archives and index the variety of content they made for other fans to find with ease (71). Because of this, LiveJournal and FFN's popularity ushered in a new wave of fan participation, but the centrality of social media, bringing everyone together on one network platform rather than through scattered mailing lists, brought with it new issues that fans had to address, such as censorship and different sociopolitical stances and how they affect the ways in which fans interact with fan fiction. This is an issue that's common among any social media site and that can turn into what are colloquially known as "Internet mobs." If enough people are riled up about the same issue, they gather en masse and target their frustration and anger against others. So, where Web 2.0 enabled fans to connect more broadly and instantaneously than mailing lists, Internet mobs could just as easily target fans more directly, harassing them through the instantaneous nature of social media and anonymity. They could protect themselves from any potential blowback of the hate they gave, putting all the risk on the fans for sharing their content.

STRIKETHROUGH AND THE FFN PURGES: CENSORSHIP, MOB MENTALITY, AND FANDOM

It's largely recognized that early fandom communities were comprised of women (Jenkins 2018, 19; Meggers 2012, 58). These women "were consciously producing their stories for the entertaining of other women, often reworking genre conventions to foreground their common experiences as women in a patriarchal society or reimagining masculine characters to rethink how romance might operate on the basis of greater equality" (Jenkins 2018, 19). Fandom is also a space for members of the LGBTQ+ community. A majority of fanworks often feature queer subject matter and queer characters, many fans choosing to read certain characters as queer and demonstrating this through their fan created content. This is what Diana Anselmo refers to as queer cryptography, which "signifies the marriage of pre-internet queer reception practices (such as subtextual scanning, slashing, and simultaneous translation) and traditional female occupations (handcrafts and care work) with new digital technologies (including GIF making, blog posting, and vidding)" (85). Fan communities that I speak of here are similarly women and queer dominated spaces.

Exploring questions of sexuality and romance in fan fiction is a common form of writing in fandom, since fan fiction can be used to explore what mass media can't or isn't willing to show to the audience. In this way, "some stories use graphic sexual language and describe, in detail, sexual interactions between characters, while others employ classic 'fade to black' scenarios, in which less graphic language might be used to describe or even imply a sexual encounter" (Meggers 2012, 58). The graphic nature of many fan fiction stories and other forms of fan work and fan labor have often been used in other fan communities by nonfans (Chin 2018, 252). It is this othering and the practice of painting fans as deviant for their explicit fan fiction by nonfans that began to cause problems that may have started with Strikethrough and Boldthrough, but certainly does not end with it. One of the first big purges of fan content since fan archives emerged and gained traction occurred on FFN. In 2002, FFN announced it would no longer allow certain types of content, focusing on real person fiction. Any fan fiction involved in the RPF fandom was removed this same year, but this also coincided with the purge of many sexually explicit stories. Stories on FFN must be rated by their authors based on the graphic nature of their story. K is the most generic rating on the site, deeming the work safe for readers of all ages. M is the most explicit rating a story can have, carrying equal weight to an NC-17 rated film. During this purge, "the highest concentration of [sexually explicit stories] are growing in areas with subjects targeted to younger readers and with increasingly controversial subject matters. However, not all NC-17 based stories fall into the description but as result of their increasing volume a decision has been made to resolve this problem. Innocent writers will be affected but this has to be done considering the non-filtering scheme of the site" ("FanFiction. Net - September 12th, 2002 - Announcement" n.d.). This type of purge would happen again in 2012 for the same reasons.

Notably, sexually explicit fan fiction is quite common and is considered desirable in fandom. In their study of how men and women use and create sexually explicit material online, Yvonne Anisimowic and Lucia F. O'Sullivan (2017) conclude that sexually explicit fan fiction does make up a substantial minority among all sexually explicit content made and consumed online (831). But, the reality, as seen with the FFN purges, is that sexually explicit material can be considered taboo. And, depending on the fan and the fandom, sexually explicit material can cause fans to turn against the fan creator for their interpretation of characters or the type of content portrayed. This is what happens in Strikethrough and Boldthrough.

Like the FFN purges, LiveJournal admins started to remove content and users (taking it a step further than FFN) in May of 2007. Fans would see usernames on their friends' lists with a strike through them, giving the movement its name. Boldthrough occurred a few months later in the same fashion, only this time usernames appeared in bold if their accounts were suspended. Strikethrough began with LiveJournal staff removing journals based on a user's interest lists, including child pornography, incest, pedophilia, rape, domestic violence, BDSM, and sex work related content. It should be noted that the content removed was largely related to sexual crimes ("Strikethrough" n.d.). While the purge was, of course, well-intended, meant to remove illegal and violent materials that should not exist in these archives, content for survivors of rape, discussions of books that handled sensitive material, and some fan archives were also removed.

Mixing fan works with illegal content is to make the assumption that the fan fiction in question resembles child pornography or rape, which we know to be outright violent and exploitative abuses. However, in one key example, one of the largest fan archives on LiveJournal removed in Strikethrough was Pornish Pixies, a sexually explicit fan archive for the Harry Potter fandom, riffing off the series' cornish pixies. Sexually explicit fan content is created by consenting adults for consenting adults. The age gates and age restrictions are there for a reason, so as sexually explicit fan content got caught up in LiveJournal's illegal content purge, fans began to discuss among themselves their feelings on the matter of having their works be banned for simply being explicit.

LiveJournal user Stewardess explains their feelings of paranoia at the time of Strikethrough and the sense of a "witch hunt" that followed them and their online activities, saying anyone who isn't an outright ally to a fan creator could potentially be an enemy (Stewardess 2007, par. 8). Fans were being targeted for creating sexually explicit works, created and consumed consensually. As outsiders to fan communities, the actions LiveJournal took made fans feel all the more targeted and isolated. The rest of Stewardess' 2007 post continues to highlight sentiments of frustration of being attacked: "So when you write an essay urging fan fiction writers to be good, as measured by whatever moral yardstick you use, don't be surprised if . . . fans come down on you like a ton of bricks. No matter what reassurances you offer, you smell an awful lot like torch-bearing townsfolk coming for our pointy incest-themed BDSM rapefic hats. Worst case? Fandom will become even more splintered, with all vids, fan fiction, manips, icons, and even the fucking screencap posts—You illegally reproduced copyrighted images you thief!—locked up. The good news is that no one will be offended. The bad news is that no one will be here . . . except for the 100% legal and the sanctimonious. Which leaves me out" (Stewardess 2007, pars. 13–17). The "you" Stewardess is referring to was the online advocacy group Warriors for Innocence (WfI), which appears throughout posts related to Strikethrough as one of the perpetrators instigating the movement to purge LiveJournal of questionable and immoral material, fan fiction included. In a later edit to their original post, Stewardess adds a time line of their involvement in fandom, their movement to LiveJournal, beginning from 2003 and following Strikethrough intensely. They state that in April of 2007, the "small hate group" WfI started harassing SixApart/LiveJournal that the site is "harboring pedophiles" (Stewardess 2007, par. 23). Another argument for WfI used to target certain material on the site is that advertisers don't know what they're supporting—and what they're supporting is harmful to minors.

The end of Stewardess' original post brings up the sentiment that groups like WfI want to leave fan spaces sanitized of certain genres of content. This behavior of who has the moral high ground in fan spaces is often gendered. Laresen and Zuberins (2012) note that "shame, and a concomitant desire for secrecy, persists among female fans, particularly when any expression of sexuality is added to the mix. The shame is especially intense around the most 'othered; fan practices, such as slash and hurt/comfort. Even within fandom, and certainly from outside, the idea of women writing slash continues to elicit reactions of confusion, shock or even horror, while men indulging in the analogous genre—lesbian porn— is mainstream enough to be the focal point for a tour de force of ribald humor" (9). The actions taken by groups like WfI, SixApart, and LiveJournal make it clear that Strikethrough is an attempt to control the online activities of fans, many of whom are women- and queer-identified who use fan fiction to express themselves and their interests in safe spaces. It is an attempt to curb and control the desires of female and queer fans to ensure that they are seen as appropriate under the male gaze rather than explicit according to gendered norms.

But, as Meggers (2012) writes, "[in] addition to being a source for female-oriented erotica, fandom is a community in which discussions concerning sex and gender occur frequently outside the realm of fan fiction, an activity that provides additional opportunities for sex education and information seeking" (58). So, Strikethrough can be interpreted as a means to curb female sexual desire, sex education, and information on a variety of erotic content. LiveJournal's actions in removing content from fan spaces send a message to fandom: there are appropriate and inappropriate behaviors and they will be enforced. It makes LiveJournal suddenly an unsafe space to explore these issues and spurs on what user Stewardess felt to be a time of paranoia, a witch hunt. Without a place to safely explore what fans like, it is inevitable that the fans would leave LiveJournal and search for other areas that would accept their behaviors. And, as this is going on in one corner of the Internet, another movement begins a new debate on fan activities: profit.

FANLIB: FAN LABOR AND MONETIZATION

Shortly before the events of Strikethrough, FanLib was launched in open beta from March to April of 2007 before opening to the public in May of 2007. It was a short-lived period where a website and its owners were trying to help fans capitalize off their fan fiction and have their work recognized by the content creators they followed. FanLib was only live until 2008 before the company was bought out by Disney, but the conversations FanLib sparked among fans have much to do with the legal gray space within which fan fiction exists, how fans can monetize their work, and how fan labor can be another form of women's unpaid labor.

FanLib's purpose was to deliver "People Powered Entertainment™ in the form of online storytelling and fun, online events for entertainment fans" ("FanLib.Com - About Us - Introduction" n.d.). Their intent was to be mediators between fans and mainstream content creators (media companies, publishers, etc.) by hosting fan fiction contests where fans could submit their content and the winner could have their story written or reused in canon. Of course, the fan would no longer retain rights to their story should they submit, but winners could receive some form of compensation.

Two issues arise from this: first, the issue of who owns what; and second, receiving compensation for fan labor, often seen as a hobby. As LiveJournal user topaz_eyes put it, "They perpetuate the myth that something is worth doing only if you get paid for it" ("Fandom-for-profit, or why FanLib is IMHO not part of fandom by topaz_eyes" n.d.). As stated earlier, fan fiction exists in a legal gray space. Fans can show their appreciation through any medium of fanwork, but if they are being paid or are receiving some other form of compensation, then it becomes an issue because they are profiting off characters, worlds, and stories that belong to someone else. The concept of profiting off fan works is nothing new to fandom. "The fannish moral economy is a set of ethical guidelines, observed within fan communities. Such policing can involve a sense of what constitutes 'good' or 'appropriate' fan behavior. For example, a fannish moral economy may freely permit the use of characters in fan fiction, but prohibit or censure making money from the fan object as an intellectual property" (Hills, Matt 2012, 23). More often than not, fans are aware of the gray space they exist in when creating content. Some mainstream content creators have had issues with fans posting fan fiction, like George Lucas and the late Anne Rice, both of whom are known to have sent Cease and Desist letters to fans who have written fan fiction based on their content. FFN also has a list of authors whose content they will not allow to have fan fiction posted about ("FanFiction.Net" n.d.). But the common understanding among fan culture is that if a fan isn't making money or profiting from their work, then it should be allowed. When FanLib came in with the promise of profit and visibility, it took these unspoken and accepted rules of fandom and purposefully circumvented them for profit.

Many fans feel like FanLib exploited fans for profit while leaving all the risks of writing fan fiction (aka: the copyright side of it) to the fans themselves. Linden and Linden (2017) outline this issue: "FanLib scouted the Net and invited selected writers to publish on their site, but writers who agreed to do so were subject to a clause where FanLib owned everything the writers posted, but leaving the writers libel for all legal actions that production companies might take against them for infringing on intellectual property rights—leaving all the profits to the website, and all the risks on the individual writer" (102). Fans were left with all the risk but very little of the reward when they interacted with FanLib. On her LiveJournal account, user cupidsbow wrote an essay exploring issues of feminism and female activities in her post titled, "How Fanfiction Makes Us Poor." Her two guiding questions for this essay were: "is the non-capitalist aspect of fanfiction actually a method of silencing the artistic voices of women? And does it take away what should be legitimate opportunities for us to earn an income from what we create?" (cupidsbow 2007, par. 4). Should it be right for fans to make money off their fan fiction especially since fan fiction is seen as a women's craft and goes unpaid as so many other women's labor does? Or is this a question we should be regarding? cupidsbow has no answers: "I still think that the fanfiction community is the most amazing women's art culture I've ever experienced, and quite possibly the most amazing there has ever been, just in terms of sheer numbers and output. And perhaps that is enough; perhaps one of the foundation-stones of the fanfiction community is that it doesn't have to engage directly with capitalist imperatives, and messing with that ethos might unbalance everything" (cupidsbow 2007, par. 39). But, what angers cupidsbow about this debate of fan fiction's worth is the ways that outsiders often deride and mock fan fiction for being nothing more than derivative porn, despite it being an avenue for creative output and pushing the bounds of gender and sexuality in mainstream media stories.

The question of gender comes up often in the debate between fans and FanLib, with the most common critique being that the two creators of FanLib are men while fandom is a space largely dominated by women and queer people. Many fans see this as just another form of men exploiting marginalized genders and their work for profit, which is particularly egregious given that, for fans, even the idea of FanLib finding a way to profit off fan fiction goes against the idea of fandom being known as gift culture, where fans understand that no money is to be made off of their fan work and that the things they do create are best seen and understood as exchanges or gifts (Hellekson 2018, 71). But gifts are freely given with no expectation of a return value. When FanLib provides fans with the opportunity of being compensated for their work, they are deliberately going against the idea of fandom as gift culture and the freedom that comes with it. Like cupidsbow, it is hard to determine if fan labor and its close ties with women's labor should be compensated or not. Since then, FanLib largely came to be regarded as a time where men exploited women for their love and affection of media and the creative pursuits taken as a result.

ASTOLAT'S CALL TO ACTION: THE FORMATION OF THE ORGANIZATION FOR TRANSFORMATIVE WORKS

In the minds of fans, the actions taken by LiveJournal and FanLib solidified that no safe space exists for them unless they are the ones in control of the space they inhabit. On her LiveJournal account, user astolat made a post that is largely regarded as the first conception of AO3 and served as a guideline and foundation for AO3's services and principles. She opens the post by deriding FanLib and its services before suggesting that fan fiction needs a central archive, like animemusicvideos.org does, and compiles a list of the necessary features for such an archive. Most important of all, astolat says, it should be "run BY fanfic readers FOR fanfic readers" (astolat 2007). The post garnered much attention and many comments from the community, and it was ultimately out of this discussion that the Organization of Transformative Works was founded and registered as a nonprofit organization in September of 2007 ("Organization for Transformative Works" n.d.). This marked the beginning of fans taking their content and their desires for a space of their own into control. At the same time as the OTW was being formed, work on AO3 began with domain registration and recruited users who were familiar with Ruby on Rails as the web application framework for AO3. In October 2008, AO3 opened for a closed beta where the public was able to view the future site and recommend changes, but were unable to make accounts. In November of 2009, the site finally entered open beta and the public could request an invitation from the AO3 team to make an account. AO3 was designed to be a central archive for any and all fandoms in the same way FFN was. But, where FFN excluded certain genres of fan content and allowed only text format, AO3 enabled users to post whatever content they created, so long as it doesn't violate their Terms of Services. RPF, sexually explicit material, and material by authors who've had an issue with fan fiction (like Anne Rice and her Vampire Chronicles series) were all allowed, and AO3 mandated that it strives to be inclusive and safe for fans to use.

Fiesler, Morrison, and Bruckman (2016) suggest that AO3 embodies feminist human-computer interaction dynamics and community values in its design, making the website so responsive and making the archive one of the most popular for fan fiction among fans (2574). As previously mentioned, one of the common criticisms with FanLib was that it is primarily managed by heterosexual men, where fan fiction and fan communities are often dominated by women and queer people. With such a disconnect from the reality of how fan communities are composed, many fans have felt time and time again as if they were being exploited for their work by a group of men. These concerns about the encroachment of the outside into fan spaces factor into the design and management of AO3: "AO3 was designed and built with a great deal of input from the community. Moreover, it was designed and built by members of the community. This was an important early priority: rather than bringing in outside software developers, they searched for programming and design talent from members of the fan fiction community. When they needed more, they prioritized training them" (Fiesler, Morrison, and Bruckman 2016, 2578). Important lessons were learned in the decades of fan culture preceding

AO3. If other web developers and websites were not going to value what fan communities produce, then the fans would make their own site to control and moderate. In their research and interviews with AO3 users, Fielser, Morrison, and Bruckman found that "one user told [them] that she sees the existence of AO3 as being advocacy in itself. Advocacy in this sense is critical to the feminist commitment to empowerment, which is the core of AO3's mission and design" (2581).

The case to control fans' sexual desires, and in many cases the desires of both women and queer people, have made it so that fans created their own alternative site to host their content, since Strikethrough was not the only attempt to censor non-patriarchal forms of fan interaction. In the May 2019 Newsletter AO3 published to its site, the first item mentioned that "Recently, the Archive of Our Own has received an influx of new Chinese users, a result of tightening content restrictions on other platforms" (May 2019 Newsletter, volume 135). This announcement was made in reference to how the Chinese government was cracking down on what they consider to be problematic material on the Internet, targeting "slash writers." Slash fan fiction is the derivative name given to male/male romantic relationships using the slash symbol (/) between the names representing the romantic nature of it. The result of the Chinese government's actions led to many popular fan fiction archives either shutting down entirely or purging their catalogs of anything that could leave people open to investigation and possible arrest (Romano 2014). In the face of this erasure and censorship, AO3 became a safe haven for Chinese fan fiction that did not fit the government's societal expectations, making it so that AO3 can continue to grow and develop as an international archive that services many other languages beyond English.

In her book *Rogue Archives*, Abigail De Kosnik (2016) argues that AO3 as a fan-built fan fiction archive functions as a women's community archive. As she writes, projects like AO3 "are motivated not only by a fear of losing content to digital ephemerality, but also by a need to reinforce a sense of collectivity among the women and LGBTQ-identifying people who populate fan fiction fandoms. Fan archiving is driven by a political longing: a longing to protect and sustain female and queer communities and cultures" (34). To support fans' desires to explore sexuality and relationships, the team behind AO3 had to ensure they did not repeat the mistakes of past fandom spaces. They had to ensure inclusivity was one of their core values to prevent stories from being removed and fan authors from being targeted for the things they write. In astolat's (2007) post, she affirms this desire to let anything be published: "[allow] ANYTHING . . . with a registration process for reading adult-rated stories where once you register, you don't have to keep clicking through warnings every time you want to read" (par. 5). This marks a conscious choice to recognize that underage users do exist in fan spaces and that there must be a firm line between adult rated content and non-adult content. This comment makes clear that warnings need to exist, and that consent is an important part of participating in fandom.

Fiesler, Morrison, and Bruckman (2016) also highlight the warnings and tag function of AO3 to provide ample warning to readers, so they know what the stories are about before they interact with them (2580). These warnings are important because they reinforce the importance of consent that a reader must give in order to navigate their way on the site and if they wish to interact with a mature rated story. The tags, warnings, and ratings all provide readers with ample opportunity to ignore a story that doesn't appeal to them or that may harm them. If not a registered user on AO3, the first page a user comes to when going to AO3 is to agree to the Terms of Service before they use the site. This statement informs the user of the purpose of AO3, including what information will be available should they make a post and to whom it will be available, warnings about sharing personal information, and where users can find more detailed information about AO3's Terms of Service and Privacy Policy. The user then must check a box stating that they "have read & understood the new Terms of Service and Privacy Policy" before clicking a button that says they agree/content to its terms. Another important facet of the rating system for non-registered users is that if they click on any story that is rated M or above, they are given the warning that "this work could have adult content. If you proceed you have agreed that you are willing to see such content."

As seen, AO3 has been developed to provide ample warnings for users to know about the content of the story before entering the webpage to read it. It is, of course, up to the author's discretion to properly tag and label their story before being posted, but beyond that it is the users' responsibility to know what they are getting into when they interact with the content on the site. Now, if any fan fiction or user behavior is found to violate AO3's Terms of Service (TOS), users have the ability to report a story or user that is found to be violating the TOS. Users must give details as to why the fan fiction or user in question abuses the TOS. From there the case is reviewed by AO3's Abuse Team where the fan fiction and/or user may or may not be removed depending on what it is being violated.

Based on the issues that plagued past fandom (mob mentalities and targeted harassment and abuse) clause G, titled "Harassment," informs users that harassment is "any behavior that produces a generally hostile environment for its target. This includes activities such as bullying and hazing by groups of people as well as personal attacks by individuals. Not everyone agrees about what is offensive and unacceptable. Individual users are encouraged to try to resolve problems on their own before contacting the Policy & Abuse team" ("TOS Home" n.d.). One highlight is that users are responsible for the actions they take when interacting with AO3 and when consuming the fan fiction that is posted to it every day. Moreover, authors are responsible for tagging and rating their stories appropriately, as dictated by the TOS. Readers are similarly responsible for the actions they take in consuming stories. If they decide to disregard the tags, warnings, and ratings an author has used and find themselves feeling upset by a story, it is made clear that they are responsible for bypassing the multiple warnings, and that it is the fault of neither the author nor AO3 staff. This ensures the system protects both readers and authors from giving and receiving unnecessary hate, while also protecting digital fan fiction from being suddenly removed en masse. The tags, warnings, and ratings function as key points of consent where users (whether authors, readers, or both) rely on each other in community to protect and trust each other.

CONCLUSION

In recognition for its work, in 2019 AO3 was nominated and won the Hugo Award for Best Related Work. This is a significant award for an organization that is supported only by community donations, with over seven hundred volunteers who dedicate their time and their skills for their fondness of the community and what AO3 represents to fandom as a whole. The OTW and AO3 are significant steps forward in making a safe space for fans, where fans are key players in the organization and maintenance of the space: fans are continuously improving the management of the website and its interface, reflecting the changes and desires of fandom from those who've been here for decades or those who are new. For a fan like myself, AO3 demonstrates the resilience of fandom and its ability to adapt and overcome hardships thrown its way.

The censorship of women and nonbinary people's sexualities by Strikethrough and Fanlib started a chain of dialogue among fans and instigated a desire from women, nonbinary, and queer people to have more control over the spaces they were posting their content to. AO3 is designed to be a safe space for fans and fan content that is often seen as taboo or under attack from Internet mobs like WfI or websites who prohibit certain forms of content. As De Korsnik (2016) writes, "Because a great deal of fan fiction consists of sexually explicit content written by women for women, and because female sexual expression is heavily limited by sociocultural norms, fan fiction archives are sites in which women and girls can feel that they are participating in a tradition of female writing and reading, and can experience a sense of safety in numbers" (135). The architecture and design of AO3 reflects the issues fandom experienced during Strikethrough and FanLib. Censorship poses a large threat to any fan archive. And as these spaces are largely queer- and women-dominated spaces, censorship threatens a large amount of female and queer produced and curated content. If corporations and male-dominated companies hold different values than the audience they cater to, the audience will inevitably find a new space or make a new space that values them and their interests. Preventing Internet mobs from forming and pressuring website staff to do as they say, risking both the money they receive from advertisers and the communities of authors and readers formed, is important for not only this community but other marginalized internet communities at large. AO3 puts the responsibility and the agency in the hands of its community of users to continue to trust each other, asking for and respecting consent around the material presented on the website—a model that many cis male–dominated corporations and websites might stand to learn from.

REFERENCES

Anisimowicz, Yvonne, and Lucia F. O'Sullivan. 2017. "Men's and Women's Use and Creation of Online Sexually Explicit Materials Including Fandom-Related Works." *Archives of Sexual Behavior* 46 (3): 823–33. doi.org/10.1007/s10508-016-0865-5.

Anselmo, Diana. 2018. "Gender and Queer Fan Labor on Tumblr: The Case of BBC's Sherlock." *Feminist Media Histories* 4 (1): 84–114.

Archive of Our Own. 2019. "May 2019 Newsletter, volume 135." Accessed October 23, 2019.

———. n.d. "TOS Home." Accessed October 23, 2019.

———. 2018. "Upcoming Changes to the Search & Filter Functionality." Accessed October 23, 2019.

Astolat. 2007. "An Archive of One's Own." LiveJournal. Accessed October 23, 2019.

Chin, Bertha. 2018. "It's About Who You Know: Social Capital, Hierarchies and Fandom." *A Companion to Media Fandom and Fan Studies,* edited by Paul Booth. John Wiley & Sons, Inc., 243–56.

Cronin, Lisa. 2012. *Fan Fiction Oral History Project with Rachael Sabotini.* Audio interview, 1:41:34. August 20, 2012.

Cupidsbow. 2007. "Women/Writing 1: How Fanfiction Makes Us Poor, by Cupidsbow." LiveJournal. Accessed October 23, 2019.

De Kosnik, Abigail. 2016. *Rogue Archives: Digital Cultural Memory and Media Fandom.* MIT Press.

Fanlore. n.d. "FanFiction.Net." Accessed October 23, 2019.

———. n.d. "Organization for Transformative Works." Accessed October 23, 2019.

———. n.d. "Strikethrough." Accessed October 23, 2019.

———. n.d. "Warriors for Innocence." Accessed October 23, 2019.

Fiesler, Casey, Shannon Morrison, and Amy S. Bruckman. 2016. "An Archive of Their Own: A Case Study of Feminist HCI and Values in Design." In *Proceedings of the 2016 CHI Conference on Human Factors in Computing Systems—CHI '16,* 2574–85. ACM Press. doi.org/10.1145/2858036.2858409.

Hellekson, Karen. 2018. "The Fan Experience." *A Companion to Media Fandom and Fan Studies*, edited by Paul Booth. John Wiley & Sons, 65–76.

Hills, Matt. 2012. "'Proper distance' in the Ethical Positioning of Scholar-Fandoms: Between Academics' and Fans' Moral Economies?" *Fan Culture: Theory/Practice*, edited by Katherine Larsen and Lynn Zubernis. Cambridge Scholars, 14–37.

Jenkins, Henry. 2018. "Fandom, Negotiation, and Participatory Culture." *A Companion to Media Fandom and Fan Studies*, edited by Paul Booth. John Wiley & Sons, 13–26.

———. 1992. *Textual Poachers: Television Fans & Participatory Culture*. Routledge.

Larsen, Katherine, and Lynn Zubernis. 2012. *Fan Culture: Theory/Practice*. Cambridge Scholars.

Linden, Henrik, and Sara Linden. 2017. *Fans and Fan Culture: Tourism, Consumerism and Social Media*. Palgrave Macmillan.

LiveJournal. n.d. "About LiveJournal." Accessed October 23, 2019.

Meggers, Heather J. 2012. "Discovering the Authentic Sexual Self: The Role of Fandom in the Transformation of Fans' Sexual Attitudes." *Fan Culture: Theory/Practice*, edited by Katherine Larsen and Lynn Zubernis. Cambridge Scholars, 57–80.

Romano, Aja. 2014. "For Young Women in China, Slash Fanfiction Is a Dangerous Hobby." *The Daily Dot.* March 8, 2017.

Stewardess. 2007. "Will You Rat Me Out If You Don't Like What I Write?" LiveJournal. Accessed October 23, 2019.

Web Archive. n.d. "Fandom-for-profit, or why FanLib is IMHO not part of fandom by topaz_eyes." Accessed October 23, 2019.

———. n.d. "FanFiction.Net - September 12th, 2002 - Announcement." Accessed October 23, 2019.

———. n.d. "FanLib.Com - About Us - Introduction." Accessed October 23, 2019.

NOTES

1. See "Why I Support the OTW, by Speranza, aged mumble-mumble," fanlore. org/wiki/Why_I_Support_The_OTW,_by_Speranza,_aged_mumble-mumble.

2. These projects include: Fanlore, a crowdsourced Wikipedia like website for anything and everything related to fan culture; Fanhackers, a site dedicated to increasing the accessibility of fan culture–related material to researchers and academics; Open Doors, a movement that works to save at-risk fan content from being lost due to websites shutting down; Legal Advocacy, a group that works on protecting the legal rights for fanworks to exist; and *Transformative Works and Culture*, a peer-reviewed journal that accepts submissions pertaining to fan culture.

Index

About the Editors

Michelle MacArthur is associate professor at the University of Windsor's School of Dramatic Art. Her research focuses on four main, often intersecting areas: equity in theater, theater criticism, contemporary Canadian theater, and feminism and performance. She has published in *Contemporary Theatre Review*, *Journal of Dramatic Theory and Criticism*, *Theatre Research in Canada*, *Canadian Theatre Review*, and several edited collections. She is coeditor of *Networked Feminisms: Activist Assemblies and Digital Practices* (Lexington Books, 2022) with MacDonald, Wiens, and Radzikowska, and editor of *Voices of a Generation: Three Millennial Plays* (Playwrights Canada Press, 2022).

Shana MacDonald is an associate professor in communication arts at the University of Waterloo. Her interdisciplinary research examines feminist, queer, and anti-racist media activisms within social and digital media, popular culture, cinema, and contemporary art. Dr. MacDonald co-runs the online archive Feminists Do Media (Instagram: @aesthetic.resistance). She is coeditor of *Networked Feminisms: Digital Practices and Activist Assemblies* (Lexington Books, 2022).

Milena Radzikowska has more than seventy-five coauthored publications and presentations on data visualization, HCI, and information design, including *Visual Interface Design for Digital Cultural Heritage* (Routledge Publishing, 2011) and *Design + DH* and *Prototyping Across the Disciplines: Designing Better Futures* (Intellect Books, 2021) and *Networked Feminisms: Activist Assemblies and Digital Practices* (Lexington Books, 2022). She has designed more than thirty-six interactive tools and interfaces and, in 2018, won the prestigious Design Educator of the Year Award from the Registered Graphic Designers of Canada. Dr. Radzikowska is a Full Professor in Information Design at Mount Royal University.

Brianna I. Wiens is an assistant professor in the Department of English Language and Literature at the University of Waterloo. Her interdisciplinary work leverages queer and intersectional feminist perspectives to examine the rhetorics, politics, and design of technologies, digital artifacts, and digital culture in order to explore how people use media in critical and creative ways to foster community and speak back to power. Dr. Wiens is Co-Director of Feminist Think Tank, a research-creation collective that advances work on feminist media, art, and design, out of which the digital archive Feminists Do Media is run (Instagram: @aesthetic.resistance) and the coedited collection *Networked Feminisms: Activist Assemblies and Digital Practices* (Lexington Books, 2022) was born.

About the Contributors

Sofia Baptiste is a member of Ermineskin Cree Nation, who also descends from Siksika Blackfoot and Tsuut'ina Dene Nations. Currently she is an undergrad student majoring in anthropology with a double minor in Indigenous studies and sociology. She hopes to continue on to grad school and pursue her doctorate. She continues to pursue academics with an Indigenous focus.

Morgan Bimm is a feminist media studies scholar whose research interests include integrating fan studies, popular music studies, and feminist theory, particularly as they relate to how certain cultural archives are (mis)remembered. She earned her PhD in gender, feminist and women's studies from York University, where her dissertation examined the role of women, girls, and girl culture in the mainstreaming of indie rock music through 2000s-era television, film, and internet cultures. Morgan's academic work has appeared in *Punk & Post-Punk*, *Journal of Teaching and Learning*, and *MAI: Feminism and Visual Culture*, as well as several anthologies.

Micki Burdick is a PhD Candidate at the University of Iowa studying reproductive justice, gender, women's, and sexuality studies, and communication studies. Their dissertation is a rhetorical history of the anti-choice movement in the United States through the lens of white womanhood and white supremacy. They use qualitative research methods, interviewing pro-life women as well as clinic escorts, to understand how the language of the anti-choice movement seeps into everyday attitudes and beliefs about abortion. They are also a project manager at the University of Pennsylvania in the OBGYN department.

Kristen Cochrane is a writer and researcher in the spheres of fiction and non-fiction, with work in literary, journalistic, cinematic, artistic, and performance contexts both in her home of Canada and abroad. In 2015 she received a Bachelor of Arts with High Distinction from Carleton University (major in communication studies, minor in Spanish, and an academic exchange year abroad at the University of Leeds). In 2017, she received a Master of Arts in cultural studies from Queen's University, Kingston.

Kristin Comeforo, PhD, (they/them), is an associate professor and graduate program director in the School of Communication at the University of Hartford. Committed to feminist methods, pedagogies, and praxis, Kristin applies an intersectional feminist perspective to inform the struggle against capitalism, the patriarchy, and other systems of oppression both within their classrooms and within their research. Kristin's effectiveness as an interdisciplinary teacher and scholar was recognized in 2021–2022 when they received the Donald W. Davis University Interdisciplinary Studies Award.

Francesca Dennstedt received her PhD in Hispanic studies from Washington University in St. Louis, where she also completed a certificate in women, gender, and sexuality studies. Her main areas of research are twentieth-century and contemporary Mexican cultural production with a focus on gender and queer studies. She is currently working on her book manuscript tentatively titled *Restorative Criticisms, Affective Canon* (Vanderbilt University Press) about women's cuir cultural production in Mexico. She is also a collaborator of *Hablemos Escritoras*, a podcast to promote literature written by women in Spanish.

Kelly J. Drumright (they/she.elle/ella) is a writer, artist, educator, and media-maker with a PhD in Spanish and Latin American literatures based in so-called Longmont, Colorado (Cheyenne, Ute, and Arapaho lands). They coproduce a podcast about mostly young adult (YA) fantasy called *The Library Coven*. Kelly's pedagogy is student-centered, trauma-informed, and weaves together elements from pop culture and current events. Please visit Kelly's website to find out more: https://kellyjdrumright.com/.

Ololade Faniyi is a graduate student in the American culture studies program at Bowling Green State University, Ohio. Her research interests are broadly centered on intersectionality, African feminisms, feminist data storytelling, feminist social movements, and women's political communication. Her collaborative work has been published in *Women's Studies Quarterly*, and she was chief editor of the graduate journal of African studies, *KUJUA*. A feminist activist-scholar, she has worked in Nigeria with community-driven collectives on feminist politics and anti-rape interventions. She is currently an African regional advisor of FRIDA, The Young Feminist Fund.

Neil Feinstein is an associate professor of advertising at St. John's University, a senior vincentian research fellow, and the program coordinator of the Masters in Integrated Advertising Communications. He is an award-winning advertising creative director and executive strategist and has advised some of the world's leading brands on digital marketing, integrated advertising strategy, and creative development.

Radhika Gajjala (PhD, University of Pittsburgh, 1998) is professor of media and communication (dual-appointed faculty in American Culture Studies) at Bowling Green State University. She is currently the managing editor of the Fembot Collective. Her books include: *Digital Diasporas* (2019); *Online Philanthropy in the Global North and South: Connecting, Microfinancing, and Gaming for Change* (2017), *Cyberculture and the Subaltern* (Lexington Books, 2012), and *Cyberselves: Feminist Ethnographies of South Asian Women* (Altamira, 2004). She has coedited the collections *Cyberfeminism 2.0* (2012), *Global Media Culture and Identity* (2011), *South Asian Technospaces* (2008), and *Webbing Cyberfeminist Practice* (2008). She is currently working on a coedited book on Gender and Digital Labor.

Sid Heeg is a PhD student within the faculty of environment at the University of Waterloo for Sustainability Management. They hold a BA in English, rhetoric, and professional communication and an MA in rhetoric and communication design from the University of Waterloo. Their research focuses on the spread and effect of misinformation about farmers and agricultural practices in digital spaces. In their downtime, they continue to interact with various aspects of online fandom culture, keeping an eye on current discussions and changes to how fandom communities form online.

Minna Aslama Horowitz is a docent at the University of Helsinki, a researcher at Nordic Observatory for Digital Media and Information Disorder (NORDIS), a fellow at St. John's University, New York, and an expert on advocacy and digital rights at the Central European University, Vienna. Horowitz researches platformization, public media policies, and epistemic rights and activism in the digital age.

Shaylynn Lynch Lesinski is a PhD Candidate in media studies at the University of Colorado Boulder. She is also a military veteran and mother of two. Shaylynn received her BA in radio, television, and film and her MA in critical cultural media studies at the University of North Texas. Her research areas include representations of gender in film and television, specifically depictions of the active female body onscreen and representations of birth in media. Her status as a veteran directly informs her analysis of representations of women, specifically military women, war in media, and female action heroes.

Gabrielle E. Lindstrom (she/her), Tsa'pinaki, is a member of the Kainai Nation, Blackfoot Confederacy. Dr. Lindstrom is an assistant professor in Indigenous studies with the Department of Humanities at Mount Royal University, Calgary, Alberta. Her teaching background includes instructing in topics around Indigenous studies (Canadian and International perspectives) and Indigenous research methods and ethics. Her research interests include decolonization in higher education, intercultural parallels in teaching and learning research, Indigenous lived experience of resilience, Indigenous community-based research, anti-colonial theory, and anti-racist pedagogy.

Tammy Rae Matthews (she/her) is an assistant professor in digital and sports journalism in the Jandoli School of Communication at St. Bonaventure University. Her theoretical interests address power structures in international and domestic constructions of sport and gender. She focuses on both oral histories of international and LGBTI athletes as well as historical and contemporary representations of transgender athletes in media. She believes sport has expectational power. Methodologically, she focuses on storytelling in all its forms: in the power of language, in the oral narratives based on experience, in social media and in journalism. Matthews earned her doctoral degree in media research and practice from the College of Communication at the University of Colorado Boulder. She completed her Master's of Science in public communication and technology from Colorado State University's Department of Journalism and Media Communication. Matthews received her Bachelor's of Journalism, with a magazine-editing emphasis, from the University of Missouri–Columbia's School of Journalism. Matthews, a native Chicagoan, worked in major-market print media for nearly fifteen years and was the special sections editor for the *Chicago Sun-Times* and its north suburban editions of the *Pioneer Press* for most of those years covering topics from business to the environment, from celebrations and weddings to automotive and real estate and from community engagement to holiday features. Matthews earned a certificate in Teaching English as a Foreign Language and taught English to Tibetan refugees near Dharamsala, India. She travels and plays roller derby.

Mina Momeni is an assistant professor in communication arts at the University of Waterloo and an interdisciplinary artist. She holds a PhD in communication and culture from the joint program at Toronto Metropolitan University and York University and an MFA in documentary media from Toronto Metropolitan University. Momeni's research interests lie in the intersection of digital media, bots, social media affordances, human-computer interaction, multimodal storytelling, visual culture, communication, philosophy of technology, and online activism. Momeni's artwork has been shown in international galleries across Europe, North America, and the Middle East, and uses photographs, videos, multimedia, and installation art to explore the relationship between ancient culture, symbology, monuments, and memories.

Angel Nduka-Nwosu is the creator of #SayHerNameNigeria. She is a multimedia journalist, writer and editor with bylines in *YNaija*, *Document Women*, *AMAKA Studio*, *RADR Africa*, and *Meeting of Minds* UK to name a few. Currently she works as the in-house news editor for *Document Women*.

Julie Ravary-Pilon recently completed postdoctoral research on the practices of feminist web-videographers at the CRILCQ and in partnership with the Institut de recherches et d'études féministes at UQAM. In September 2019, she began a second postdoctoral fellowship at Centre for Interdisciplinary Research on Montreal (CIRM) at McGill to complete the Station-Femmes research-action project on Montreal subway's public spaces. Her thesis, on the representation of the Motherland in Quebec cinema, was published by the University of Montreal Press in 2018 under the title *Femmes, nation et nature dans le cinéma québécois*. She was the organizer of a conference on Women and Media in Quebec at the Cinémathèque québécoise, which resulted in the collective publication *Pour des histoires audiovisuelles des femmes au Québec: diversité, divergence et confluence* (PUM, 2021). She is the codirector of the academic journal *Nouvelles vues: revue sur les pratiques, les théories et l'histoire du cinéma au Québec*.

Sierra Shade is an undergraduate student in the faculty of health, community and education at Mount Royal University and a member of the Blackfoot Confederacy from Kainai (Blood) Nation.

Keren Zaiontz is assistant professor of theatre and performance studies in the Department of Theatre and Film at the University of British Columbia. Her most formative authorial and editorial collaborations have also proven to be some of her most vital intellectual acts—acts where feminism and friendship intertwine. This includes her co-edited work with Natalie Alvarez and Claudette Lauzon, *Sustainable Tools for Precarious Times: Performance Actions in the Americas* (Palgrave Macmillan, 2019), winner of the Excellence in Editing award by the Association for Theatre in Higher Education (ATHE), and her forthcoming chapter with Ali Na, "The Political Promises of Performance Art and NFTs." Zaiontz's writing and interviews can be found in *PUBLIC*, *Theatre Journal*, *Performance Research*, *Theatre*

Research International, *Theatre Research in Canada*, and numerous international essay collections. She is author of *Theatre and Festivals* (Bloomsbury Publishing, 2018), part of the Theatre& series.

www.ingramcontent.com/pod-product-compliance
Lightning Source LLC
Chambersburg PA
CBHW031126270326
41929CB00011B/1506